AFFECT IN LITERACY TEACHING AND LEARNING

In this cutting-edge volume, scholars from around the world connect affect theory to the field of literacy studies and unpack the role and influence of this emerging area of scholarship on literacy education. Offering an introduction to affect theory and scholarship as it relates to literacy studies, contributors discuss the role of humanizing and dehumanizing influences on schooling and examine the emotional and affective dimensions at individual and communal levels. Arguing that an affective turn requires a radical rethinking of the nature of literacy, these chapters address the impact and import of emotion and affect on reading, writing and calling to action. Grounded in trailblazing research, the contributors push the boundaries of academic writing and model how theoretically-driven writing about affect must itself be moving and expressive.

Kevin M. Leander is Professor in the Department of Teaching and Learning at Vanderbilt University, USA.

Christian Ehret is Assistant Professor in the Department of Integrated Studies in Education at McGill University, Canada.

Expanding Literacies in Education

Jennifer Rowsell and Cynthia Lewis, Series Editors

For more information about this series, please visit: https://www.routledge.com/ Expanding-Literacies-in-Education/book-series/ELIE

AFFECT IN LITERACY TEACHING AND LEARNING

Pedagogies, Politics and Coming to Know

Edited by Kevin M. Leander and Christian Ehret

Routledge
Taylor & Francis Group

NEW YORK AND LONDON

First published 2019
by Routledge
52 Vanderbilt Avenue, New York, NY 10017

and by Routledge
2 Park Square, Milton Park, Abingdon, Oxon, OX14 4RN

Routledge is an imprint of the Taylor & Francis Group, an informa business

Library of Congress Cataloging-in-Publication Data
A catalog record has been requested for this book

ISBN: 978-0-8153-6771-0 (hbk)
ISBN: 978-0-8153-6772-7 (pbk)
ISBN: 978-1-351-25676-6 (ebk)

Typeset in Bembo
by Swales & Willis Ltd, Exeter, Devon, UK

To Ana Christina and Lea, two beautiful souls
who make us feel much bigger than ourselves.
Without you, what would we know about
what it is to be moved?

Kevin & Christian

CONTENTS

SERIES EDITOR INTRODUCTION

The *Expanding Literacies in Education Series* features books that highlight the changing landscape and explore new directions and theoretical tools in literacy studies as it is transforming education—including material, embodied, affective and global emphases, digital and virtual worlds and transcultural and cosmopolitan spaces. Some books in the series locate emerging literacies in practices that extend or trouble their historical uses and functions. Others cross disciplinary borders, bringing new epistemologies to bear on evolving practices that question the very foundations of literacy scholarship. Polemical and forward-looking, encompassing public and vernacular pedagogies as well as formal education, these books engage researchers, graduate students and teacher educators with new and emerging theoretical approaches to literacy practices in all of their complexities, challenges and possibilities.

In this collection, Leander and Ehret provide readers with a field-defining book on affect and literacy studies. Chapters illuminate the human and non-human nature of affect, underscoring that to be literate demands that people trace immanence across bodies, things and spaces. There are diverse voices in the book that concentrate on the dynamic, visceral dimension of affect and its relationship to communication and sense-making.

Given the lineages and histories tied to affect theory, it is humbling to be series editors for a book like this. The editors of this collection align their work with those who view affect as non-representational and pre-semiotic. Inevitably, however, the authors manage to narrate intensity into being—that is they represent intensity through their words. The book wrestles with what it means to write about charged intensity in ways that keep feeling alive in the event as it produces an ever-emerging present. The view of affect taken up in this volume challenges research methods that qualitative researchers hold dear, ourselves included—methods that draw on thick descriptions of practices in ways that inadvertently freeze events and their emotional valence. This is among the authors' most thought provoking and important contributions. It is, indeed, an honor to have this collection among our titles—expanding the breadth, depth and reach of the *Expanding Literacies in Education* series.

Jennifer Rowsell and Cynthia Lewis

References

Ahmed, S. (2004). *The cultural politics of emotion.* Edinburgh, Scotland: University of Edinburgh Press.

Ahmed, S. (2014). *Willful subjects.* Durham, NC: Duke University Press.

Ahmed, S. (2017). *Living a feminist life.* Durham, NC: Duke University Press.

Grinage, J. (2014). Reterritorializing locations of home: Examining the psychopolitical dimensions of race talk in the classroom. *Journal of Curriculum Theorizing, 30*(2), 88–102.

ABOUT THE CONTRIBUTORS

Gail Boldt is a professor in Language and Literacy Education at Penn State, in State College, PA, where she takes daily advantage of her neighborhood swimming pool. She coordinates the graduate program in Language, Culture, and Society and is the editor-in-chief of the Bank Street Occasional Paper Series. She feeds her soul through her psychotherapy practice, working with children in a community mental health center.

Cathy Burnett is Professor of Literacy and Education at Sheffield Hallam University, UK, where she researches children's technology use in educational settings. She is co-author of *New Media in the Classroom: Re-thinking Primary Literacy* (Sage, 2018) and co-editor of *Literacy, Media Technology: Past, Present and Future* (Bloomsbury, 2017) and *The Case of the iPad* (Springer, 2017). She enjoys walking in Derbyshire and Western Scotland and being alongside the more-than-human lives that share those places.

Daniella D'Amico is a PhD student at McGill University. Her research interests include social justice education and relationship building with indigenous communities. She enjoys volunteering teaching French to Syrian refugee children and is presently working with Kahnawà:ké, an indigenous community. She loves being outdoors, playing sports and cooking for those she loves.

Jaclyn Dudek is a learning designer at the University of Alabama and PhD candidate at the Pennsylvania State University. Her research focuses on exploring and designing learning environments, both physical and online. She was a guest scholar with the NEH and National Libraries project: Ancient Greeks/Modern Lives.

Elizabeth Dutro is Professor of Literacy Studies at the University of Colorado Boulder, where she studies critical, affective pedagogies in response to trauma. Recently, her work has appeared in *Journal of Literacy Research, English Education,*

Teaching and Teacher Education and *Language Arts*. You can find Elizabeth drinking coffee at any given café in her downtown Denver neighborhood, where she hopes you will want to discuss reality tv.

Jonathan Eakle (PhD, University of Georgia) is an associate professor and Chair of Curriculum and Pedagogy at The George Washington University in Washington DC, where he strolls through parks, politics, museums and other landscapes. Recent work includes the Baroque, art, and education (*Qualitative Inquiry*, 2017), research of affects around the 9/11 Memorial and a project at the Phillips Collection with human and other-than-human bodies hinged to Paul Klee.

Christian Ehret is an assistant professor at McGill University, where he investigates affective dimensions of literacy, learning and digital culture through engaged research within and beyond schools. His recent work includes the chapter, "Propositions from Affect Theory for Feeling Literacy through the Event," published in *Theoretical Models and Processes of Literacy*, 7th Edition, also published by Routledge. A new Montrealer, he enjoys exploring the city's vibrant urban art scene on long walks through its diverse neighborhoods

Ty Hollett is an assistant professor at The Pennsylvania State University. He is currently interested in learning more about what makes informal learning settings come together, cohere and sustain over time. He thinks skateboard sessions are a great example of these charged places. He has one daughter, Lillian, who just turned 18 months old, and he is trying to take in every moment that he can with her, including splashing in puddles, looking for airplanes and taking bike rides.

Ana Christina da Silva Iddings is Professor of the Practice of Education in Learning, Diversity, and Urban Studies at Vanderbilt University in Nashville, Tennessee. Her research focuses on languages, literacies and cultures with regard to immigrant and refugee students and their families and communities. She enjoys traveling to her home country, Brazil, and dancing.

Kevin M. Leander is Professor of Language, Literacy, and Culture at Vanderbilt University in Nashville, Tennessee, where his research focuses on affective, embodied engagements with literacy, dialogic and material approaches to digital media, and poststructural theory. He would like to see research and art become entangled with one another more often. Most recently, he just returned from canoeing the boundary waters, where he saw loons in the wild for the first time, as well as all the stars that the city has been hiding.

Kimberly Lenters is an associate professor at the University of Calgary where her research focuses on the material worlds of children's literacy development. Most recently, Kim's work has taken up the affordances of comedy in children's classroom literacy learning and has been published in the *Reading Teacher* (2018), and *Literacy* (2018). In her spare moments, Kim enjoys exploring Calgary's river paths and hiking in the Rocky mountains.

Erin Manning is a professor in the Faculty of Fine Arts at Concordia University (Montreal, Canada). She is also the founder of *SenseLab* (www.senselab.ca), a laboratory that explores the intersections between art practice and philosophy through the matrix of the sensing body in movement. Current art projects are focused around the concept of minor gestures in relation to colour and movement. Art exhibitions include the Sydney and Moscow Biennales, Glasshouse (New York), Vancouver Art Museum, McCord Museum (Montreal) and House of World Cultures (Berlin) and Galateca Gallery (Bucarest). Publications include *For a Pragmatics of the Useless* (Duke UP, forthcoming), *The Minor Gesture* (Duke UP, 2016), *Always More Than One: Individuation's Dance* (Duke UP, 2013), *Relationscapes: Movement, Art, Philosophy* (Cambridge, Mass.: MIT Press, 2009) and, with Brian Massumi, *Thought in the Act: Passages in the Ecology of Experience* (Minnesota UP, 2014).

Alyssa D. Niccolini completed her doctorate in English Education at Columbia University's Teachers College. Her work has been published in journals such as *English Journal, Gender & Education* and *Knowledge Cultures*. She currently lives in Germany where she is exploring the Heidelberg region and practicing words with umlauts.

Mia Perry is a senior lecturer at the University of Glasgow where she explores the role of social arts and cultural practices in formal and informal literacy education. Mia's nomadic tendencies have taken her (and her willing, well-traveled family) from Ireland to Canada to Scotland and currently, most frequently, to Africa, where she works with literacies of globality as they relate to sustainability. Her co-authored book with Carmen Medina and Karen Wohlwend, *Playful Methods: Difference, Imaginaries, and the Unexpected in Literacy Research* is forthcoming from Routledge.

Tatiana I. Sanguinette is an artist and curator who works at the Museum of Contemporary Art in Los Angeles. She earned a Bachelor of Fine Arts from The Corcoran School of the Arts and Design and a Master of Arts in Teaching with an art concentration from George Washington University. She enjoys California skies, tending gardens and riding sound waves.

Michalinos Zembylas is Professor of Educational Theory and Curriculum Studies at the Open University of Cyprus. He has written extensively on emotion and affect in relation to social justice pedagogies, intercultural and peace education, human rights education and citizenship education. He has been actively involved for many years in political and educational efforts for peace, reconciliation and reunification of his home country, Cyprus, including being appointed by the President of the Republic of Cyprus in 2016 as the Greek-Cypriot Co-Chair of the Bicommunal Technical Committee on Education.

INTRODUCTION

Christian Ehret and Kevin M. Leander

Miss Green, a heroic urban high school teacher in *The Get Down*, presents an award for the best poem of the year to Ezekiel ("Zeke") Figuero and calls Zeke out to read his poem for the class. On this last day of school, the students can't contain their bodily excitement to explode out of the building, but when Zeke is called out to read, the class becomes still and focused. Will he move? What will happen? Zeke remarks that he can't get up because his back is hurt, and there are snickers and side comments. Miss Green approaches his desk, the poem in her hand, and there is a standoff. The bell rings and the students rush out to summer.

When the film cuts back to the classroom, Miss Green is calling out Zeke personally—there is a big world out there that needs him, needs his voice and gift, and yet he hides from it. She appeals to his pride and identity. Did he really write the poem? She's not sure. So, prove it. Midstream, with obvious intensity building across his face and shoulders, Zeke starts to speak the poem without a glance at the page—not *recite* as if the poem was borrowed—but speak it out of his body, his being. The poem beats out a story of violence, trauma, struggles and strength in a rhythmic and rhyming style familiar to what would become the developing 1970's hip-hop scene in the South Bronx, where the film is set. Zeke's mother has been shot by a bullet meant for his father; Zeke calls out to "Moms" with words that move Miss Green so much that she turns her back to Zeke, hiding the intensity of her feelings. Zeke leaves the empty classroom with a firing range of intensities—anger, passion, hurt, embarrassment—his voice stuck halfway between his throat and the empty space. Miss Green is somber, stuck, her teacher authority somehow replaced in the moment with the deep sighs of another mother who loves, who is reaching somewhere she can't arrive.

Teaching, in its real and filmed versions and all the hybrid ways we mix media and life, is filled with the push-and-pull of feelings that live in bodies and are expressed through them, and is also filled with the ebb and tide of intensities in time (one moment not like another) and over time (the flow or movement of sensations and responses). Though we often try to tame teachers and students, life creeps in, and when it does, we can't predict the movements in advance, or lay out rules of what is best to do. Give Zeke the poetry award or not? Call him out? Let him be? What are the possible risks and rewards? Where is the action of the moment moving? What do we not know, and what does it mean to move toward the unknown? All of this feels somewhat too much to hold as a teacher (and student)—too much to think and too much to feel. It is surplus, we might say.

Social, Cultural and Affective Movements in Literacy Research

It is toward this surplus that we direct this volume—toward entering into felt intensities of literacy learning and teaching that are beyond our grasp and yet flood us with their importance. By "entering into" we intend not a desire to unpack or to analyze feeling so as to definitively know it, to understand it or overcome it, but rather, a desire to move with these felt intensities as a way of feeling and knowing with their movements and force in the context of literacy teaching and learning. We wish to acknowledge the surplus; we wish to tell out loud the secret that teachers seem to know—that most of what happens, on our best days, cannot be explained in rational frames. We are moved, and our students are moved, and we cannot explain just how or why.

Still, as we have begun to write, we have left out an important actor in the scene already: literacy. Literacy is not just incidental content or subject area to the interaction of Zeke and Miss Green. When Miss Green announces the annual poetry prize, there is a question hovering in the air. Who is the man or woman of words? Whose mouth, whose life has these beautiful words? Zeke's body recoils. Miss Green approaches his desk with the poem—this piece of paper with his handwriting—and a chocolate bar prize. Then, there are few words, Zeke pushing back, away from Miss Green and the words. The class is still, in the pregnant stillness of no words. Later, in the next scene, Miss Green has Zeke's words in her hand, but he has them in his mouth and shoulders and face—these are his, spoken from within, tattooed on his life. This is his story, literate yes, but personal, painful, traumatic, a complete misfit with the tamed rows of the room, non-sense. His life and story burst him from the room, leaving Miss Green holding the page. The written text of the poem, the spoken text of the poem, the words of Miss Green calling Zeke out and Zeke's refusal to speak all enter into the pushing and pulling of intensities and bodies in the spaces of the classroom, just as these words call forth spaces and places beyond the classroom—tenements, streets, gunshots.

And, across all these movements of words-as-bodies and words with bodies, literacy is also about political and ethical potentials. In these movements, words and bodies enter into relations, practices and performances that may be raced, classed or gendered in old ways that strengthen categories or new ways that extend, critique and remake social life. What if what Zeke and Miss Green are, in their relations to one another and to literacy, is not given in advance? How might we know what is on the move? And, what might be lost when we believe that their social, personal and pedagogical relations *are* in fact given in advance? This is our claim for surplus—for attending to the felt intensities of literacy learning and teaching that provide openings that may reorient us to what could be, to what should be and to shifting relations and mangled movements up close and far off.

This book is about being moved by literacy and using literacy to move. It is about understanding literacy, in practice, as evoking and compelling embodied responses that cannot be captured by rationality alone. This book is about affirming a more fully embodied and felt response to the literacies in our own lives and in the lives of those with whom we research. We follow what has been termed the "affect turn" in the humanities and social sciences and ask, what difference does it make for literacy education and literacy scholarship to feel the world, to take affective intensities seriously, to engage with the surplus and with the unspoken and powerfully unknown? At a time when education research has emphasized individual learning toward predefined outcomes (objectives or objects) within narrow epistemic domains, the affective turn has opened the field to subject–subject relations, or the role of embodied interactions, collaborations and relationships in generating and sustaining impassioned learning.

Language and literacy are among the most humane of all practices; speaking, writing, reading and imaging are the ways we tell our human stories, forge relationships and make sense of our identities as humans. However, the direction of education in language and literacy has suffered under the weight of dehumanizing influences, including the increasing regulation and commodification of compulsory schooling. Such forms of neoliberal individualism, including "measures," and "outcomes" that narrow perceptions of the purpose of education (Ladwig, 2010), have put great pressure on literacy education to lose its chiefly human and humane qualities. Children and youth, like other users of literacy, are not only concerned with decoding and producing accurate texts. Rather, they are moved by texts or not moved, and they learn in classrooms where the emotional and affective dimensions of teaching and learning may be inflated and invigorated, or left lifeless and, ultimately, inaccessible. Thus, the purpose of the affective turn in literacy education is directly related to issues of equity, functioning as a critique of narrowly defined outcomes that have intensified educational inequities (Aronson & Laughter, 2016; Baldridge, 2014).

Yet, before we turn to a more thorough discussion of affect theory, let's back up and begin at a more familiar starting place: the classroom (or rather, this classroom) and sociocultural theory, broadly conceived. Since sociocultural approaches are more familiar to the field of literacy research than are those of affect theory and related poststructural approaches, it seems a good launching point from which to sketch differences in our approach and differences that emerge from these approaches. Our method is not to replace one (earlier) theory or approach with another—to replace the old and celebrate the new—but to ask, what differences become available in this shift, in (new) ways of seeing and feeling the world opened up by affect theory? With this in mind, let's turn back to our opening scene.

Rereading Zeke: Questions from Sociocultural Perspectives

While there are many, many issues that one could raise from a sociocultural standpoint in rewinding to the scene of Zeke and Miss Green, for the sake of comparison, we will broadly sketch out three: mediation; time and development; and identity/learning. (These are the types of constructs that we have cut our own academic teeth on, as we have been engaged with sociocultural theory.) We begin with mediation, because it is perhaps the most familiar and most important construct in sociocultural thinking—to conceive of the person acting not as an isolated brain in the world, but as participating in the social mind of the world through mediated tool use. The pole vaulter with his pole, the typist with her QWERTY keyboard (Wertsch, 1985), the nondrinking alcoholics with their stories and chips (Lave & Wenger, 1991) are all familiar accounts of tool-mediated learning in central pieces of sociocultural writing that have become iconic images for literacy studies, guiding the ways in which we imagine the use of materials of all kinds (tools) and signs coming into combination in learning and development (Vygotsky, 1978). In this perspective, an earlier psychologized version of "direct" learning (stimulus–response) through the conditioning of behavior is replaced with a social perspective that prefers indirection or mediated action (Wertsch, 1998). As human subjects reach toward some outcome (the object of activity), we would focus on the tool(s) they use in this reaching and, eventually, in the mastery of this object. For Zeke, then, we might ask, "How did the poetry contest help him to develop his literacy and identity?" or "How did this particular poem and its wording mediate his relationship to Miss Green and the class community?" or, for Miss Green, we might ask, "How did Zeke's poem help her come to know Zeke and come to understand herself as a teacher of him?"

We have already suggested something of the role of time and development in thinking socioculturally (and we recognize the difficulty of treating these constructs separately, even if just for heuristic purposes). With respect to time, a sociocultural approach would generally be interested in what might be called the micro-level interaction between Zeke and Miss Green in order to understand Zeke's (or Miss Green's) learning in the moment. This learning could be then related to the longer-term process of development (learning proceeding development); a micro-level analysis might readily be related to a meso-level analysis (e.g., Zeke during the summer after school or Zeke's relationship to Miss Green over the school year) and then, finally, to a larger, macro-level stretch of time to include perhaps Zeke's entire development into a young man/rap artist and so on (Cole, 1996; Wertsch, 1985). The commitment to development and change from the sociocultural perspective also stretches over to the social world itself, so we might ask, "How do Zeke's social relations develop over time just as his sense of himself as writer changes?" Of his own development, our interest in this specific episode would want to make claims about its potential importance reaching across time: "How did the first confrontation as a poet by Miss Green in the classroom lead Zeke to engage his identity as a poet out on the streets in the year ahead?"

Finally, sociocultural theory, in various ways, posits a tight interweaving of learning and identity processes (Holland, Lachicotte, Skinner & Cain, 1998), wherein learning is sometimes itself defined as the transformation of persons (Lave & Wenger, 1991). In that sense, who Zeke is becoming (as a poet, a young man, an activist, a student) and what he is learning (poetry, social relations, his own voice) in this scene are seen as inseparable. From an identity and learning standpoint, we might also ask about what resources Zeke brings into the poetry writing from his home life to the classroom and how Miss Green recognizes and values these "funds of knowledge" (e.g., knowledge from his family, knowledge of pain, the practice of his own observations and voice at home (Gonzales et. al, 1995), in the context of classroom learning. In the connections between literacy learning and identity, from a sociocultural perspective we might ask, "How does writing and speaking this particular poem scaffold Zeke's learning about the use of poetic language for self-expression" and also, at the same time, "How does the writing of this particular poem enter into shaping the developing identity of Zeke-the-poet in his own eyes as well as in the eyes of Miss Green?"

Moving with Zeke: Questions from Affect Theory

Making a shift to affect theory in literacy studies, we hope to show, does not involve a different set of responses for the same questions, but rather asking different types of questions. These questions also invite or even compel us to adjust our relationship to the activity in question. Whereas sociocultural theory is invested in understanding the directionality of movement (toward some object, toward some future development), affect theories concern themselves with the movement itself and its qualities. Whereas socioculturalists are concerned with the betweenness of tools and language (mediation)—a theory shaped by the preposition "with"—affect theorists are concerned with energy of contact as things come together—they work the conjunction "and." At the site of this conjunction—this coming-together—are raw flows of undifferentiated energy or *intensities*. "Miss Green approaches his desk, the poem in her hand, and there is a standoff." At the movement of Miss Green to the desk, there is a coming-to-be of Miss Green-poem-Zeke energy in the room. A standoff, to be sure, but like all standoffs, held in place by intensities pushing against one another and, along with them, the potential intensities of the poem-not-yet-spoken. What are these intensities? What are the forces being moved here, in the inhale of the moments? Later, when Zeke and Miss Green are alone in the classroom, we see Zeke, speaking the words of the poem. What are the qualities of his speaking at this moment? As we draw in close, to feel alongside Miss Green, what is manifest in Zeke's speaking voice, his speaking body? What is registered on our bodies, experiencing his poem, his body, his life in words? How do we sense the movements of Miss Green's body in relation to the movements of Zeke and his poem? What is this push-and-pull of intensities involving the two of them, and also involving us as participants, drawn into the scene?

As the accumulation of actors in the description above begins to suggest, affective intensities are not merely experienced by an individual, as we often describe emotion in the vernacular, but are rather experienced in the warp and woof of movements involving multiple actors—the everyday movements of people and things approaching and pushing against one another, coming up alongside, making a dance-like turn, pulling apart. The social dance of life where movement (dislocation) produces movement (intensity) is what calls our attention as observer-sensors and researchers. The affectively charged associations among people and things in affect theory are variously described, and one such recurrent description is that of the *assemblage*, which is described by Deleuze and Guattari (1987) as a coming-together of heterogeneous materials (bodies, things, signs), held together in ways that might allow for durability but also for dividing up and reorganizing into new assemblages. The student-student-student-Zeke-Miss-Green-poem-man-of-words-last-day-of-school-doing-school assemblage comes together in the scene, and, in its heterogeneity, it has flows and vectors of energy that cannot be described in a single word and certainly not in static ways. What are these flows and vectors? What is alive in the assemblage or said otherwise? What does this particular assemblage—at this moment in time—bring to life?

The coming-together of an assemblage saturated with affective energies is suggestive of an additional dimension of affect theory that raises new questions: the idea of *emergence.* Emergence in affect theory describes a sense of time that is open and unpredictable, that is ripe with a sense of moving toward the next moment, actively unsettled. Affectively speaking, emergence describes a sense of unknowingness, a sense that next moments are not predetermined by previous ones. Emergence is the present leaning-forward, the next-next-next. The sense of time that is privileged in affect theory is not the structuring of time given by the chronologies of sociocultural theory (where the ontogenesis or development of an individual could even be related to the development of the entire species, or sociogenesis) but rather the immanence of the moment moving to the next moment. Affect theorists sense time from within time; there is no outside-of-time position for the actor or the researcher-as-actor to stand, godlike, and feel or analyze temporal units. We sense this emergence as Miss Green approaches Zeke. The few seconds are ripe with possibilities—although we know the outcome of this story because we have seen (or read) all of it, in the middle of it, there are many possible directions: Zeke could break down and read; Zeke could storm out; Miss Green could recognize the tension and back off; Miss Green could start reading the poem herself, perhaps as a taunt to him; another student could throw something; the bell could ring. What is ripe in these moments between Zeke and Miss Green and the class? What next moments are possible at the nexus of sensing the possible from within? And, how do next moments (say, the eventual standoff between Zeke and Miss Green) appear to draw on forces that repeat—familiar refrains of feeling and power—or how do they seem to open up new, unanticipated movements full of force, such as Zeke speaking his poem aloud to Miss Green without pause and without glancing at the written page? These are some of the movements provided by an attunement to emergence of the scene powered by affect theory.

In the discussion thus far we have focused primarily on human–human inter-actions and movements, while also signaling the movements and energies of nonhumans within affect theory. As informed by post-humanism, the de-privileging of the human at the center also raises different questions than does sociocultural theory or most other theories of literacy. In this episode of *The Get Down*, for instance, we might ask about not only Zeke but also his poem. In this inspiration, we might consider the poem not as a *mediator* of Zeke's identity or his relation-ships, but as some*thing* that is becoming in relationships. This idea of *becoming* in affectively charged intra-actions with other people and things is distinctive from the idea of identity. As the scene opens, we may ask, what is the unknown poem-award-Zeke-hurt-back-Miss Green becoming? Obviously, the idea of becoming is related also to the ideas of emergence and the assemblage—the ripeness of the forward-leaning present and interactions with all kinds of other actors in the scene. Yet in this case, we focus on the production of difference (as energy) through movements and associations. Perhaps the poem at the outset is a becoming-writer-recognition or a becoming-Zeke-Miss-Green-relationship, yet later, in the myriad differences produced by Zeke's bold recital of the poem, perhaps the poem is also a becoming-shot-mother as well as a becoming-Zeke-rhythm. What is the poem becoming, we ask? How is the life and energy of the poem, lived out in relation to energies all around it, not captured in a representation of the poem (e.g., the words on the page), but in its lived movements or continual becomings? These questions, importantly, push past classic English class questions of meaning. Rather, the focus for affect theorists is on the doing of becoming. What affects do these becomings have on other becomings around them? What new differences have emerged? What is the world making with our intentions and in spite of them?

Affective Movements Across Disciplines: Ontology, Representation and Ethics

Our first working title for this volume, "Where Did Life Go?," has been a refrain moving throughout the project, a moving question recurring and spur-ring us forward when we found ourselves sputtering conceptually, or struggling to locate our thinking in relation to the field. We invite readers to listen for this refrain throughout the introduction and volume, because it signals much of our own motivations for turning to affect theory. It also expresses our hope for the potential the volume opens: to recover, in literacy studies, a sense of the energy, possibility and feeling of life within the everyday ways people engage with literacy, as well as within the specialized ways we engage with research on literacy. While we are deeply concerned with texts of all sorts in literacy practices and scholarship, our experiences with texts cannot be condensed within texts themselves and the textual practices with which we come to know and express them. As academics, we traffic in representations of all sorts—including this very chapter—but our moving human experiences with these representations somehow evade us, or evaporate, or become described in ways that don't *feel moving*. "Where did life go?"

This question, and the recovery project it implies, is important in that it takes us to the very heart of our engagement with literacy. Since it evolved, over five thousand years ago, beyond pictograms and later cuneiform to communicate information about taxes and crops, literacy has never been merely about recording or transmitting information. Rather, literacy has been about being moved, being connected and finding new ways of becoming, together and apart. To recover the experiences of movement, connection and becoming is to get at the very heart of engagement with literacy—what pulls us in and what keeps us there. Affect theory provides a response to this beating pulse of literacy—the energies and qualities of our engagement with texts. Affect theorists do this work by beginning from deeply essential questions about the nature of things (ontological questions), including texts. That is, rather than beginning with texts over here and bodies of other sorts over there, affect theory asks about what is getting related or combined and when. Affect theorists' participation in the larger turn to ontology across the humanities and social sciences has enabled these insights by eschewing the constructivist assumption of an epistemological subject who is somehow separate from experience (St. Pierre, 2016). This ontological shift is important to draw us closer to moments of energy—the attractions and repulsions among bits of living material—and also to draw us into raw processes of becoming, of change. Affect theory is important because it backs us up in time to the world before it was already made, and asks, "What world could be made? Where could life go?"

With these refrains—of recovering life, of sensing life as it emerges—moving our work forward, this book takes up the affect turn in literacy scholarship, feeling out the potentials of new questions that affect theory opens. As literacy researchers, we feel confident in knowing the cultures, the collectives and the mediations in developing sociocultural questions to train our inquiry. We are far less comfortable orienting ourselves to know and express the affects that move our bodies and texture our emergent presents. We are feeling our words grasping and coming up short of the feeling. Affect theory—its movements, its ethics and its ontology—promises the theoretic tools necessary to recover this moving life of literacy that we believe postmodern critical theories have distorted or missed altogether by locating their critique in abstractions such as cultural construction and mediation alone. This is not to dismiss the salience of culture in literacy studies. Nor do we wish to ignore critiquing the disempowering effects of power. Rather, we wonder—in this volume and moving forward with the field—what comes of meeting language, culture and power in how they *matter*, through how they *feel* as fully embodied experiences that are constantly unfolding. How can we know the ways in which literacy affects our becoming different without making appeals to the *a priori* identities and unitary social structures upon which postmodern representational logic relies? How can we live in and express experiences of literacy that feel like *some*thing without making those moments into some*thing* we already knew?

Ontological premises of this nature have and are continuing to galvanize researchers across the humanities and social sciences. Their lines of inquiry have turned to affect (Gregg & Seigworth, 2010) as a loosely connecting force in vibrant conversations monikered vivaciously, for instance posthumanism (Braidotti, 2013), new materialism (Bennett, 2010), agential realism (Barad, 2007), and process philosophy (Manning & Massumi, 2014; Massumi, 2011). Authors in this volume write in moving relations with ideas that aren't always easily pinned to one of these emerging conversations. However, all the authors follow potentials generated from insights across conversations in the ontological turn (St. Pierre, 2013), illuminating in particular how the nature of literacy comes to be known differently when we become alive again to affect. By attuning to affective life and taking seriously the charges of the ontological turn, volume authors affirm affect theory's profound implications for rethinking not only how researchers come to know and express the phenomena they scrutinize, but also the ethics of how those knowing and expressing relations affect mattering bodies.

No recent writer has expressed such ethical implications as urgently as Ta-Nehisi Coates. In *Between the World and Me*, Coates (2015) shakes readers back to life from the desensitizing and politicized images and rhetoric about racialized violence that flow through the brackish waters of American media. Writing to his son, imagined as a character in the book, Coates entreats:

> There is nothing uniquely evil in these destroyers or even in this moment. The destroyers are merely men enforcing the whims of our country, correctly interpreting its heritage and legacy. It is hard to face this. But all our phrasing—race relations, racial chasms, racial justice, racial profiling, white privilege, even white supremacy—serves to obscure that racism is a visceral experience, that it dislodges brains, blocks airways, rips muscle, extracts organs, cracks bones, breaks teeth. You must never look away from this. You must always remember that the sociology, the history, the economics, the charts and graphs the regressions all land, with great violence, upon the body.
>
> *(2015, p. 10)*

For so long, representational forms of thinking and expression have dominated, especially in the social sciences, structuring knowledge from outside of moving, messy and mattering lives. These representations are made not only in and of sign systems—the charts, graphs and regressions to which Coates refers—but also about and through representational logics: binaries of subject–object, cultures–singularities, mediation–experience, Discourse–discourse (Gee, 2014). Coates reminds us how the continued dominance of such representational logics risk eliding not only the bodies and affects that defy representation, but also the visceral effects of their potential violence.

At the least, the potential violence in representational logic emanates from how representations can dehumanize and unreal—paperclips standing in for victims of the Holocaust (Magilow, 2007), for another example—as well as from what violent potentials may be enabled by underdeveloped understandings of how representations such as discourse come to affect bodies—how discourse "dislodges brains, blocks airways, rips muscle, extracts organs, cracks bones, breaks teeth." Knowing how representations such as discourse come to matter, come to mark bodies, requires a non-representational onto-epistemology that bridges the representational gap between what is and how we know it, that scrutinizes racism, for example, as a discursive–material phenomenon (Barad, 2007). Perhaps ironically then, coming to know how discursive practices are related to material phenomena, such as living, moving human bodies, requires disavowing the representational logics that place the human at the center of all reality, that place the human apart from matter. No wonder this move, this ontological turn, is often confronted with academic resistance and reticence. Apart from the panopticon of neo-Kantian and neoliberal scientism, which affect their own marks on academic bodies, non-representational knowing and expressing can feel plainly uncomfortable, even painful—just revisit Coate's quote above and feel again the intensities discursive–material expressions affect. This is hard.

Yet this move is also urgent, vital. A turn toward the ontological, toward immanence, is an ethical charge, because "if we see ourselves as always already entangled with, not separate from or superior to matter, our responsibility to being becomes urgent and constant" (St. Pierre, 2013, p. 655). Singular and everyday acts of writing, new media making and interpreting texts are all a part of the world's differential becoming, and they open to potentials with varied degrees of equity, justice and beauty *for which we are immanently responsible* in the full matter of our being. Singular and everyday acts of writing, new media making and interpreting texts all produce discourses that matter and that travel as discursive–material concepts like racism, refugee, terrorism, the environment, immigrant. These discursive–material concepts become in intra-action at multiple levels and they affect human bodies. Discursive–material concepts *matter*. They are not ways of knowing; they are knowing in the making; they are a part of matter, bodies, becoming. That number of Syrian refugees is too high; the economic impact must be more carefully (re)calculated; images of weather-war-torn tents from above; images of bodies in the distance walking and winding across the sand; videos filled more with moving blue expanses than of faces or of hands holding to rafts. These discursive–material enactments of "refugee" affect where bodies move, how (our-there) bodies feel, how "refugee" becomes toward policies, practices, the embodied futures of singular lives. Knowing and expressing these discursive–material moves as signs in a semiotic system, for instance, risks unrealing the very real lives and movements they affect. In enacting discursive-material concepts, in everyday talk, in media reports, in national policy—no matter the scale—we participate in their making, mark skin, open or inhibit movement, affect bodies. Our-there-concept can never be disentangled.

However, despite this intense charging of our present moments and the humanism it compels, ethically dubious discursive–material moves of unrealing propel much of the present social, cultural and educational atmosphere. Affect theorists have critiqued, for instance, how neoliberalisms move as discursive–material concepts and how they mark bodies:

> [N]eoliberalisms might exist as structures of feeling: dispersed qualities such as a "sense of inevitability" or an "anxiety about the state" that become part of policies, programs and projects that extend the market. If so, this gives us cause to reconsider what is meant by the phrase "actually existing" in calls to attend to "actually existing" neoliberal regimes or neoliberal states.
> *(Anderson, 2016, pp. 15–16)*

Anti-humanly charged discursive–material concepts like neoliberalism affect human bodies toward capitalistic outcomes that are not always real and certainly not in favor of the many. Yet these concepts feel like *something*, and that *something* coerces hope in imagined economic futures, the envy and excitement of celebrity for everyone just around the corner, the fear of terror emerging from every shadow and the unmanageable impulse to buy and carry weapons. As Anderson argues, these discursive–material concepts actually exist: They come to feel like *something*, and these *some*things don't always carry names—representational categories of mediating emotions—such as hope, fear, envy. They are the intensities of living that move bodies with consequence, whether those intensities become known as emotion or not.

Moving Affect Theory into Literacy Studies: Variations on a Theme of Affect and Emotion

In literacy research, a focus on affect and emotion has a relatively short history, and when they have come under examination, affect and emotion have often been associated with individual states or interpreted as socially constructed responses that can be understood through representational logic as a form of cultural mediation (e.g., Levine & Horton, 2015; Sakr, Jewitt & Price, 2016). Over the last

check

decade, however, developments in affect theory have generated new modes of inquiry and understanding that do not rely on assumptions undergirding the constructivist interpretations of emotion that currently dominate literacy studies. We highlight here distinctions between representational approaches to emotion (e.g., constructivism, cultural–historical activity theory) and non-representational approaches to affect (e.g., affect theory, process philosophy) not in judgment, but toward expanding inquiry in literacy studies toward a fuller sense of how textual engagements feel as they are becoming (affect), and before they are named with a feeling (emotion). Modes of inquiry in affect theory that follow, feeling forward, where life is going have provided insights into, for example, the emergent rhythms, atmospheres and movements of social life that exceed the theoretic reach of constructivism alone (e.g., Anderson, 2014; Stewart, 2007). From this perspective, researchers know affect through bodies' emergent capacities to move and be moved in social life, where affect is the force that compels movement (Gregg & Seigworth, 2010). Affect theory, then, has the potential to develop sociocultural perspectives by illuminating the rhythms and textures of teaching and learning, in addition to the interactions and structures that inform them (Ehret & Hollett, 2016). We feel affect theory performs such an expansion, and not a rejection.

With this expansion toward an ontology of becoming, literacy researchers may come to know how scenes of everyday activity take on singular Qualities (with a capital Q)—a living, embodied feeling of the uniqueness of every moment, ordinary or extraordinary. How do the affects of such moments animate our bodies towards new relations and potentials, connections and disjunctures, thoughts and feelings? These are the forward-looking questions that embrace the singular Qualities of moments—from inside of the moments themselves—without attempting to analyze and rationalize why they feel like they feel. Affect theory lets feeling feel. Constructivist accounts of emotion must claim emotional truths by parsing the data of lived experience bit by bit. These bits of life become building materials with which a rational mind might construct academic representations. Whether defined as an internal state or mediated action, the constructivist model assumes that emotion is "ostensibly designed to explain" (Massumi, 2016, p. 123) from outside of embodied experience, from outside of the living, breathing moment. The Quality of experience, of emotion, thereby succumbs further to an assumed, explanatory teleology: Zeke is shy in this classroom space while learning to share himself as a poet. How will this experience mediate future poetic performances within and beyond the classroom? Imagined futures are tightly tethered to the past. Opening to a different set of questions, affect theory, unconcerned with bits, refuses to parse experience, because "Qualities have intensity, not scale," not names, not representations (Massumi, 2016, p. 124). The Quality of experience, in its fullness and singularity, moves as the past meets its present mattering. Emotion is an explainable part of life; it's how we make sense, rationally, of life's intensities and try to predict where life is going. Affect is why life feels like something; it's what moves us to name emotion in the first place, and it's what moves us into where we're headed. Why would we want to describe this moment of poetry, Zeke and Miss Green if it hadn't moved us, affected us?

This volume expresses, therefore, how a non-representational theorizing of affect as indeterminate in relation to constructivist emotional categories can bear fruit for literacy studies and education. This is one of the most crucial lines of potential that the affective turn is throwing forward: a critique of emotion as a way of rationalizing and naming how bodies feel. Massumi (2002, p. 27) described this distinction between affect and emotion:

> An emotion is a subjective content, the sociolinguistic fixing of the quality of an experience which is from that point onward defined as personal. Emotion is qualified intensity, the conventional, consensual, point of insertion of intensity into semantically and semiotically formed progressions, into narrativizable action reaction circuits, into function and meaning. It is intensity owned and recognized. It is crucial therefore to theorize the difference between affect and emotion. If some have the impression that affect has waned, it is because affect is unqualified.

It's like explaining why a joke is funny: the *feeling*, the living intensities, of funniness wanes. The Quality of experience is lost. Our bodies are moved out of the moment and into reflection backwards upon action ready to be explained. This is why we, the editors, wonder where life has gone when we read representational accounts of bodies having made, read and written. The affects of literate activity wane when they are made into "semantically and semiotically formed progressions, into narrativizable action reaction circuits, into function and meaning." Toward non-representational accounts of literacies in motion, authors in this volume express becoming literate lives as relational experiences of making, reading and writing. They express the multiplicities of all this doing in more than human relations of bodies and-. . ., looking for new potentials in all those relations, and looking to affect new potentials in expressing their chapters. That's the truth that affects, not the truth that claims itself.

Where the Turn May Take Literacy Studies

The affect turn in literacy studies is clearly still nascent. While there is currently great momentum around this theory and its use for research, the task of developing a coherent and far-reaching theory of affect in literacy research, as well as a theoretically informed language for the analysis of literacy teaching and learning, remains as work to be done. We see this work, as argued previously, as of pivotal importance to the larger social and educational project of humanizing literacy learning and redressing an imbalance on text-centric frameworks and on regulatory, top-down measures. Early work in affect and literacy studies (e.g., Ehret, 2018; Ehret, Hollett, & Jocius, 2016; Leander & Boldt, 2013; Leander & Rowe,

ↆ CHECK

2006; Rowsell, 2014; Smith, 2017) and by others within and beyond literacy research (e.g., Cohen, 2006; Lemke, 2013), still functions primarily as openings and invitations to explore affective intensities that make up the Quality of life, in classrooms and beyond, and that move our bodies in unexpected ways.

Alongside chapter authors, we acknowledge that an affective orientation to literacy research and education requires a radical rethinking of the nature of literacy, as well as living and being differently as researchers and educators. However, just as we have expressed the urgent need for such reorientation, we also desire the relational difference, beauty and love our living and being differently together may affect. A constant attention to love is compelled in every pedagogic moment given an orientation to affect and immanence. Every moment is vital and profound in its potential to affect difference across multiple scales of space and time, to mark bodies and linger on the skin. As Ahmed (2006, pp. 8–9) describes:

> Orientations, then, are about the intimacy of bodies and their dwelling places [. . .] Bodies may become orientated in this responsiveness to the world around them [. . .] In turn, given the histories of such responses, which accumulate as impressions on the skin, bodies do not dwell in spaces that are exterior but rather are shaped by their dwellings and take shape by dwelling.

What might it mean to dwell in and toward love while doing literacy "teaching" and "research" (Orellana, 2016). How can our orientations to affect in shaping dwelling spaces enact love across bodies? How might our pedagogies and mentorships in using literacies (re)make discursive material concepts that move and mark bodies with more loving potentials?

Because this kind of loving is not so simple, however, affective orientations are all the more urgent for taking up in literacy research. Love can guard and inhibit change as much as it has the potential to transform. A person may contemplate: "I love my family, my country, and, although that love extends to those suffering refugees, I must think first of my family, my country." We have argued, however, how relational thinking, attuning to intensities, thinking the way in which discursive–material concepts like racism travel, opens potentials for doing love differently. We have argued how every moment, every discursive move is part of the world's differential becoming, and to feel that, to move and live in that way of being, that is love in all its transformative potential, that is the Quality of experience that makes itself known as love.

Berlant (2011, p. 690) suggested something similar in her argument that a becoming conception of love:

> would provide the courage to take the leap into a project of better relationality that would give us patience with the "without guarantees" part of love's various temporalities; a properly transformational political concept

would open spaces for really dealing with the discomfort of the radical contingency that a genuine democracy—like any attachment—would demand; a properly transformational political concept would release courage and creativity about how to make resources for living available to all objects in their thatness.

There is no guarantee that doing literacy research and education with becoming love, with better attunement to affect, would lead to this or that outcome at this or that time. There is reason to believe that an affective orientation will sometimes fail us. Loving takes courage for these reasons—because it is unpredictable and sometimes painful. But those were never reasons not to love. And those are not reasons to turn away from affect and non-representation in literacy research. Should literacy researchers come to know better the potentials love opens, across time–space, as it moves in discursive–materiality, what transformations might occur?

Becoming Love in Literacy Research: The Present Volume

This book is a desiring toward knowing and expressing more of our affective lives together, especially the affects generated in experiences of making, reading, writing and calling to action. This book is also a following of desires that springs from our reading across much of contemporary literacy research, the coded data, the codified bodies, and asking ourselves: Where did life go? How did we let so much time slip away while we stood outside of it, researchers analyzing from outside of moments we often felt so intensely *in the moment*? How can we still know so little about the affective life of making, moving and being in moments of literate activity? Moments that felt like *some*thing. *Some*thing that coding cannot make into a thing or a category, affects that our current research methods stutter to know and express. With this collection, we therefore invite literacy researchers to engage the turn to affect.

Across a yearlong graduate seminar on poststructural engagements with literacy research and multiple academic study groups and symposia, we asked ourselves and chapter authors to consider the potentials of affect theory in literacy studies through writing. We also asked ourselves and chapter authors to consider this potential beyond our academic relations: How might the affective turn transform not just literacy studies, but also our ways of thinking and living together? In her description of the radical shift in thought and being required in taking the affective turn with our academic–everyday bodies, St. Pierre (2013) argued that in the requisite ontology "thinking and living are simultaneities, and we have to think possible worlds in which we might live" (p. 655). We have asked nothing less of ourselves as bodies–editors and of chapter authors as thinker–feelers. In each chapter, authors write toward where life is going with literacy and affect: in the field, in their experiences with data and in the possible worlds that become, through their writing, the affects generated in experiences of making, reading, writing and calling to action.

We have organized the chapters into three parts that we have termed movements. The term movement intends more than, and other than, organizing themes. Rather than being centered by theme, each movement temporarily holds together energies across chapters, readings, authors and stories—emergent, uncertain assemblages. Different energies coalesced in each assemblage, unique flows and shifts were created across each assemblage, and particular forms of movement are evoked by the assemblages for their readers. We have tried to follow these energies–they moved us as readers and editors–in the course of introducing each movement within the volume.

In the first movement, "Pedagogy under the Waterline of Perceived Value," authors imagine more affective pedagogies, illustrating unique modes of inquiry into the transformative potentials of love to which we pointed earlier in this introduction. Along with chapter authors, literacy researchers must continue to investigate how pedagogic love develops in relation to the everyday institutional violence all too common in schools, and how to prepare teacher candidates to love, and to love resiliently, in the vibrant, complicated, contradictory, and mundane life of everyday life schooling. Where can we open more spaces for the feeling, loving, crying and laughing in the research and practice that seem so strangely closed to everyday affects? We continue to wonder, for example, how attuning to affect may compel the rewriting of traditional pedagogic materials. What if lessons plans were written to express potentials of human relationships around literacy learning, rather than to delineate and align technologies of learning—e.g., objectives, assessments, timeframes, etc? And what would such a view mean for rewriting current models of teacher education, attuning teacher candidates to answer the (extra)ordinary affects of teaching? As the field follows where life goes with affective turn, we cannot but imagine the possible worlds of making, reading, writing and calling to action as they may be, were they to extend from the transformative potentials of pedagogic love.

Authors in the first movement therefore consider pedagogical action in affective terms, including especially relationships between teachers and students, but also relationships between teachers, students, school contexts, objects and practices. In the context of national and international movements compressing the work of teaching and the design of teacher training to become increasingly oriented to skills, scripts and standards, authors seek to recover the moments and movements of teaching and learning as saturated with frustration, with joy, with laughter, with absurdity, with tears. Affectively charged relationships and affective atmospheres, they contend, are not merely an add on to the everyday stuff of school learning; what one learns in school is how one was moved by it through everyday affect. Authors consider the affective development of both in-service and preservice teachers, and they also contrast how children (students, kids, youth, etc.) are brought into relationships that involve embodied affect in different age ranges, across gender and across other dimensions of diversity.

In the second movement, "Uninterpretable Politics in Literacy Research and Practice," authors consider the emergence of affect in social action that confronts unequal distributions of power. Undeniably, learning is informed by socio/cultural/political pushes and pulls. Historically, scholars of social inequality have leaned on structural analyses to reveal and contest the ways these social forces reproduce systemic oppression. Yet structural analyses can amplify damages inflicted on marginalized groups and perpetuate narratives of harm and hopelessness, ignoring how people are generative in response to and in spite of structural inequality (Tuck & Yang, 2014). Engaging topics around affect and the political, authors in this movement also consider how attuning to affect might help educators and researchers engage in feeling–thinking around issues of inequality as a base for amplifying processes and possibilities for social justice. The authors ask the field to consider: How are lives affectively charged by political forces? When do nations, cities, neighborhoods and schools become spaces of inclusion and exclusion, safety and fear, expansion and contraction, generation and degradation, hope and desperation, alignment and disruption? How do these affective charges shape teachers', families' and students' experiences of learning? How can teachers, families and students leverage the political to activate literacy learning? How can literacy learning be leveraged to experiment with, claim and celebrate the potential of life-affirming engagements in the political and the power to not only be affected but to affect others with our words, actions and interactions?

In the final movement, "Affectively Charged Foldings of Literacy and Coming to Know," authors address issues of representation related to analyzing and reporting affective textures of social life. Authors consider, for example, the tensions around how the research community might understand and recreate affective truths in a time and space where rationalistic and scientific truths are given primacy, and authors problematize how academic writing can be more than a mere report of experience, expressing how writing can constitute a transformative expansion of experience itself. They imagine, desire and perform writing affectively as a mode of moving forward with experience that continually brings culture into being—for both authors and readers—through the difference-making potential of composition. In short, they provide chapters that move, push and pull us toward the breaking points of representation, toward a more deeply felt engagement with experience beyond the page. We end the book with this part desiring toward its potential to move readers, and the field, with affective writing not as a rhetorical appeal, but as a gesture toward the loving potentials of allowing life back into moments of research, teaching and writing.

References

Anderson, B. (2014). Encountering affect: Capacities, apparatuses, conditions. London, UK: Ashgate.

Anderson, B. (2016). Neoliberal affects. *Progress in Human Geography, 40*(6), 734–753.

Ahmed, S. (2006). *Queer phenomenology: Orientations, objects, others.* Durham, NC: Duke University Press.

Aronson, B. & Laughter, J. (2016). The theory and practice of culturally relevant education: A synthesis of research across content areas. *Review of Educational Research, 86*(1), 163–206.

Baldridge, B.J. (2014). Relocating the deficit reimagining black youth in neoliberal times. *American Educational Research Journal, 51*(3), 440–472.

Barad, K. (2007). Meeting the universe halfway: Quantum physics and the entanglement of matter and meaning. Durham, NC: Duke University Press.

Bennett, J. (2010). *Vibrant matter: A political ecology of things.* Durham, NC: Duke University Press.

Berlant, L. (2011). A properly political concept of love: Three approaches in ten pages. *Cultural Anthropology, 26*(4), 683–691.

Braidotti, R. (2013). *The posthuman.* Cambridge, UK: Polity Press.

Cohen, J. (2006). Social, emotional, ethical, and academic education: Creating a climate for learning, participation in democracy, and well-being. *Harvard Educational Review, 76*, 201–237.

Coates, T. (2015). *Between the world and me.* New York, NY: Spiegel & Grau.

Cole, M. (1996). *Cultural psychology: A once and future discipline.* Cambridge, MA: Harvard University Press.

Deleuze, G. & Guattari, F. (1987). *A thousand plateaus: Capitalism and schizophrenia.* (B. Massumi, Trans.). Minneapolis, MN: University of Minnesota Press.

Ehret, C. (2018). Moments of teaching and learning in a children's hospital: Affects, textures, and temporalities. *Anthropology & Education Quarterly, 49*(1), 53–71.

Ehret, C. & Hollett, T. (2016). Affective dimensions of participatory design research in informal learning environments: Placemaking, belonging, and correspondence. *Cognition and Instruction, 34*(3), 250–258.

Ehret, C., Hollett, T. & Jocius, R. (2016). The matter of new media making: An intra-action analysis of adolescents making a digital book trailer. *Journal of Literacy Research, 48*(3), 346–377.

Gee, J.P. (2014). An introduction to discourse analysis: Theory and method. New York, NY: Routledge.

Gonzales, N., Moll, L.C., Tenery, M.F., Rivera, A., Rendon, P., Gonzales, R. & Amanti, C. (1995). Funds of knowledge for teaching in Latino households. *Urban Education, 29*, 443–470.

Gregg, M. & Seigworth, G.J. (Eds.). (2010). *The affect theory reader.* Durham, NC: Duke University Press.

Holland, D., Lachicotte, W., Skinner, D. & Cain, C. (1998). *Identity and agency in cultural worlds.* Cambridge, MA: Harvard University Press.

Ladwig, J.G. (2010). Beyond academic outcomes. *Review of Research in Education, 34*, 113–141.

Lave, J. & Wenger, E. (1991). *Situated learning: Legitimate peripheral participation.* New York, NY: Cambridge University Press.

Leander, K. & Boldt, G. (2013). Rereading "A pedagogy of multiliteracies" bodies, texts, and emergence. *Journal of Literacy Research, 45*(1), 22–46.

Leander, K.M. & Rowe, D.W. (2006). Mapping literacy spaces in motion: A rhizomatic analysis of a classroom literacy performance. *Reading Research Quarterly 41*, 428–460.

Lemke, J. (2013). Thinking about feeling: Affect across literacies and lives. In O. Erstad & J. Sefton-Green (Eds.), *Identity, community, and learning lives in the digital age* (pp. 57–69). Cambridge, UK: Cambridge University Press.

Levine, S. & Horton, W. (2015). Helping high school students read like experts: Affective evaluation, salience, and literary interpretation. *Cognition and Instruction, 33*(2), 125–153.

Magilow, D.H. (2007). Counting to six million: Collecting projects and Holocaust memorialization. *Jewish Social Studies, 14*(1), 23–39.

Manning, E. & Massumi, B. (2014). *Thought in the Act: Passages in the Ecology of Experience.* Minneapolis, MN: University of Minnesota Press.

Massumi, B. (2002). *Parables for the virtual: Movement, affect, sensation.* Durham, NC: Duke University Press.

Massumi, B. (2011). Semblance and event: Activist philosophy and the occurrent arts. Cambridge, MA: MIT press.

Massumi, B. (2016). Such as it is: A short essay in extreme realism. *Body & Society, 22*(1), 115–127.

Orellana, M.F. (2016). Immigrant children in transcultural spaces: Language, learning, and love. New York, NY: Routledge.

Rowsell, J. (2014). "The mood is in the shot:" The challenge of moving-image texts to multimodality. *Talk and Text, 34*(3), 307–324.

St. Pierre, E.A. (2013). The posts continue: Becoming. *International Journal of Qualitative Studies in Education, 26*(6), 646–657.

St. Pierre, E.A. (2016). The empirical and the new empiricisms. *Cultural Studies↔Critical Methodologies, 16*(2), 111–124.

Sakr, M., Jewitt, C. & Price, S. (2016). Mobile experiences of historical place: A multimodal analysis of emotional engagement. *Journal of the Learning Sciences, 25*(1), 51–92.

Smith, A. (2017). Bare writing: Comparing multiliteracies theory and nonrepresentational theory approaches to a young writer writing. *Reading Research Quarterly, 52*(1), 125–140.

Stewart, K. (2007). *Ordinary affects.* Durham, NC: Duke University Press.

Tuck, E. & Yang, K. W. (2014). Unbecoming claims pedagogies of refusal in qualitative research. *Qualitative Inquiry, 20*(6), 811–818.

Vygotsky, L.S. (1978). *Mind in society* (M. Cole, V. John-Steiner, S. Scribner & E. Souberman, Eds.). Cambridge, MA: Harvard University Press.

Wertsch, J.V. (1985). *Vygotsky and the social formation of mind.* Cambridge, MA: Harvard University Press.

Wertsch, J.V. (1998). *Mind as action.* New York, NY: Oxford University Press.

PART I

Pedagogies

Movement 1: Pedagogy under the Waterline of Perceived Value

When we begin to describe the affective intensities of pedagogical relations, our language stutters to express the feeling of even everyday relational transformations between and among teacher–student, student–student, student–texts–and–. . . . Yet these everyday relational transformations are the qualities of pedagogical experience to which we point and say: That's what it's all about; that's when things changed; I'll never forget that. Authors in this part move beyond the ordinary work of language and attempt to express speculative propositions through which there is an explicit call upon the future to become different. Collectively, authors also move with a breadth of language in tones, styles, formats and ethos that create differences through which to feel pedagogical relations.

To question and connect, Boldt (Chapter 1) traverses her worlds as a teacher and as a psychotherapist. In play therapy with one child, "Bo," she has many, many perceptions of him and how she might reach him. Yet, nothing seems to work; nothing seems to reach across for very long. Something imperceptible is filling up all space. One day, Bo comes to therapy after trauma, and seems to have completely shut down. He silently plays in the sand table. Boldt weaves a line of thought through her narrative in her chapter—a desire to relate above all. She reflects on a proposition from a mentor: "Stay with the child. Stop trying to make interpretations." Boldt plays alongside Bo in the sand table, moving sand, trying to stay present, becoming interested after a time in shoveling, sometimes bumping into Bo, giving up on knowing but not on relating. Something moves.

The part continues with an invitation to rethink value in pedagogy. A common and important critique of contemporary education centers on our current obsession with, and standardization of, forms of assessment. Value in education in this modality creates its own economy, as Manning (Chapter 2) describes, of cycles of debt and credit, of plans, of measurement in the form of assessment. Critical reform of the assessment-driven curriculum poses its set of solutions: fewer assessments, different assessments, more authentic assessments. Yet, in what Manning terms the "undercommons" (following Harney & Moten, 2013) learning creates its own value, value that is not well perceived, perhaps not perceived at all. How do we evaluate teaching and learning in the undercommons, where "The soundscape of learning is full of inklings which reside below the threshold of actual perception?" (Manning, this volume). What does pedagogy caught up in all these inklings look like? And, in the contradictory attempt to express the ineffable, what do these inklings become?

Charlene (in Lenters, Chapter 3) lives her days in school below the waterline of perceived value, most of the time. She is labeled as seriously ADHD, she is critiqued by credit-driven fellow group members, and she returns again and again to puppy videos while her group is supposed to be working on the "oil boom" project. Lenters traces the shifting assemblages of relations between Charlene, other people, objects, practices and events in the classroom, looking, seeming to wait for an opening, a kind of differenciation with possibility across series of becomings. Some new becomings are just more striated spaces—refrains of school-as-school. The researcher and the teacher watch Charlene across time with puzzlement and even resignation. Yet, somehow, Charlene finds pedagogical possibility in the assemblage, following her deep feelings for animals, making connections to the oil boom project while being moved by puppy videos. Lenters asks of school, "Had Charlene's differenciation been recognized earlier on as more than frivolous obsession, what might have come of it?"

Across the chapters there are different terms for that-which-cannot-be-named in experience: "Thisness" or "haeccity" (Boldt), the "infrathin" (Manning), and "differenciation" (Lenters). These terms describe how the value of the pedagogical moment far exceeds measurement. This excess itself, as Manning writes, gives experience its value. Then, we might ask, what role does the work of writing the experience have? What is the role for language (and literacy) in pedagogical valuing?

These chapter authors suggest movement in the field toward rethinking expressions of pedagogies in literacy research as *speculative propositions* that have the potential to intensify future experiences of literacy teaching and learning as they unfold in present moments. Although language and signs are ordinarily propositional, speculative propositions are intentionally so, with explicit calls upon the future. Not too different from ordinary road signage reminding us to drive carefully, authors express propositional pedagogies, in a sense, whereby the affects of the pedagogical relations they present on the page may spill over to affect readers' future experiences of pedagogy, of research, of life.

Thinking alongside Whitehead's (1927–1928/1985) process philosophical perspective on the proposition, Stengers (2011, p. 416) examines how language itself is propositional:

> [I]t is the proper character of all language to give their full importance to propositions, not insofar as they have the power to cause [. . .] but in that their entertainment lures us into feeling, thinking, speaking, in short, becomes, in the most various ways, an ingredient of the experiences that will follow it.

Language thereby becomes a material actor through its capacity to affect in future experience, a capacity we might describe through its propositional efficacy.

In this conceptualization, propositions (as accounts of teaching and learning) do not state a logically derived truth that can be examined rationally, but rather they suggest, abstractly, qualities of experience that may re-emerge through feelings that change the trajectory of ongoing activity. Whitehead (1927–1928/1985) described these shifts in experience as epochal shifts, which are possible at multiple scales: For example, individual, cultural, national, etc. While the part begins with an explicit set of propositions (for radical pedagogy), we encourage the readers to read through all of this pedagogy as propositional language: propositional not because these accounts represent experience directly, but because they lure us into understanding and change, into becoming different in epochal shifts possible across scales.

Although we expect readers to imagine many more, reading these chapters again ourselves we were moved anew to consider one such shift: How might we generate an alter-economy of literacy research and pedagogy wherein new modes of expression and encounter value the excess of experience by allowing that excess to become what it could be? We feel Boldt-Bo's desire for relation because of how that desire is allowed to live through the page in a mode of research writing that resists interpreting their experiences together. This written language thereby lives beyond the page as a lure for feeling without interpretation in resonant pedagogical experiences to come. Through an alter-economy of literacy research and pedagogies we sense these pieces pushing toward values such as non-representational writing of pedagogical moments as a lure for future feeling. Our writing and living relationally produce value that cannot be interpreted and controlled by majoritarian economies that tell Charlene to focus on the oil boom, what has already been assessed as assessable. Under the waterline of a best-practices economy of education, affective currents stir.

References

Harney, S.M. & Moten, F. (2013). *The undercommons: Fugitive planning and black study.* New York, NY: Minor Compositions.

Stengers, I. (2011). *Thinking with Whitehead: A free and wild creation of concepts.* Cambridge, MA: Harvard University Press.

Whitehead, A.N. (1985). *Process and reality.* New York, NY: The Free Press. (Original work published 1927–1928).

1

AFFECTIVE FLOWS IN THE CLINIC AND THE CLASSROOM

Gail Boldt

I am a teacher and a psychotherapist. Historically speaking, I was first a teacher of third- and fourth-grade children and then of preservice teachers, and more recently, I have also become a child psychotherapist, seeing children from three to twelve years old for weekly sessions. I am writing this chapter from this both/and-ness of who I am, who I am becoming, and what I understand myself to be in relation to children. I use this chapter to bring you into the present of my work and thinking as a therapist, and as I do that, I expect to create departures in my thinking and imagination in relation to teaching. This chapter is a participant in my drive to, as Ehret and Leander suggest in the introduction, "feel the world, to take affective intensities seriously, to engage with the surplus, with the unspoken and powerfully unknown." (p. 00). My thoughts, dreams, reflections, these lines of flight, are not implications for teaching so much as they are connective tissues and resonances of affect themselves.

The intellectual and emotional struggles of becoming and being a therapist remind me in many ways of the struggles I experienced as an elementary teacher. Much of the time, I feel that I don't know what I'm doing. As both a teacher and a therapist, I fill this unknowingness with self-doubt, which I project onto the parents. I imagine their impatience and criticism. As both a therapist and a teacher, I believe that what matters includes strong relationships, coming to know the child's intrapersonal and intersubjective worlds, shared exploration and playfulness. I struggle against perceptions that the job of the teacher is to focus on the problem of what children are presumed to not know and that teaching is a rational, measurable act. Why would I be surprised that these are the same things I struggle against when therapy is conceptualized through sixteen-week treatment plans and so-called evidence-based outcomes?

When I reflect on my insecurity, I have at least the benefit of hindsight about what it feels like to become and be a teacher. Not that teaching is or should be the same thing as doing therapy, but these two occasions of being with children inevitably speak to one other, offering me unexpected ways to understand each through the other. Right now, I am most immersed—almost drowning sometimes—in the question of what it is that children might need from me and what I might need from them. It's with the help of a journal I kept during my student teaching days that I am able to remember sitting with my host teacher, crying and saying to her, "I have all of the theories in my head, but I don't know how to make them happen. There is a huge gap between what I know and what I can do." She says, "You haven't learned yet how to let the children fill that gap. You are still talking to yourself, to your own head. You aren't yet in a relationship with the children."

This question of what it might do to be in different kinds of relationship with children is perhaps the central question of psychotherapy, almost regardless of the school of thought in which one is trained. By training, by temperament and taste, the orientation through which I approach my work and that gives me a language for thinking about what happens is psychoanalysis. In this chapter, I use sketches, loosely based in my clinical practice,[1] along with descriptions of how some psychoanalytic researchers talk about what it is that matters in the therapeutic relationship. I bring these into conversation with the research of Akiko Hayashi and Joseph Tobin (2015) about how experienced Japanese teachers think about the complexities of teaching relationships. I also bring in Deleuzo-Guattarian theory, which allows different lines of flight in my thinking, and besides, it sings to me. I do this in the Deleuzo-Guattarian (1987) spirit of the and . . . and . . . and . . ., by which I mean creating an assemblage in which the individual pieces maintain their integrity but, when brought together, also create something new. In this chapter, I will perform something about how the teacher–therapist assemblage enlivens my thinking about each, and my expectation is that the reader will do the same with the experience of reading this chapter alongside her/his own experiences, thinking, imagination and desires.

I Talked and Talked

It is the early months of my practice. Dany has dumped a box of construction blocks of assorted sizes onto the floor. She is now working methodically to sort them by color, by size, by shape. She announces that this is a zoo of blocks and that people who visit the zoo expect to see the same kinds of blocks together. Dany has played this same game for the past several sessions. Each week, the sorting occupies most of our fifty minutes together. She never includes me in the sorting, never asks for my help or opinion. I'm simply there to watch. Sometimes when she finishes the sorting, if there is still time, the blocks might venture out of their area, to quarrel and physically fight with blocks in other areas. The orderliness of the zoo doesn't necessarily make it a happy place.

My mind is not such a happy place either. I don't know what I'm doing, watching her sort those blocks week after week. I don't know what it is that will help this child with the conflicts her parents have reported. I don't know what Dany wants and I don't know what she's doing. I try offering what I imagine to be an interpretation. This is, after all, psychoanalytically oriented psychotherapy.

"Your zoo reminds me of your family," I say, "with so many different people from so many different families living together in one family." This is met with silence, which I fill, in my head, with Dany's imagined response: "Gail, you are a complete idiot." Indeed.

I have elected to work with three different supervisors. In supervision, we talk over our cases with an experienced therapist who provides guidance and listens for our countertransferences or, in other words, the ways we might be enacting our own emotional issues in sessions with our clients. Until I have enough hours to earn a clinical license—something I'm working toward but that will take me many years—the state requires me to get one hour of supervision for every twenty hours of work with clients. In an average week, I choose to schedule one hour of supervision for every three hours I see clients. There are weeks when I have more supervision than clients. This speaks to the anxiety I feel about the speed of my learning.

One of my supervisors is at the clinic. She helps me with my cases and with navigating the clinic as a workplace. The second is a psychoanalytically oriented psychotherapist who lives and practices in the area, someone I have known and trusted for many years. The third is a psychoanalyst who lives a few hours from where I live. I'm on sabbatical from my university position during the first year of my practice, and I commute once a week to study with her and to spend an hour in her office discussing my cases.

In classical psychoanalysis, interpretation is the thing understood to affect change. Sigmund Freud described an unconscious that is a repository, not for repressed ideas, but for energy. In Freud's model, when an event, idea, desire or feeling occurs that is unacceptable to the ego, it must be repressed. In repression, Freud (1923/2000; 1936) argues, the idea or the thought of the thing is split from the affect; the idea is banished and the affect is pushed into the unconscious. The energy or anxiety of the affect can continue to provoke us, a thorn in the side, but as long as it is unattached to an idea, it cannot be released. Unmoored from the original meaning it held for us, the energy attaches to other ideas; the repressed returns in symptoms and behaviors that may hint at, but that also disguise the unacceptable idea. The role of interpretation is to reattach the unacceptable idea to the affect, making conscious what was formerly unknown to the client (Gabbard, 1994) so that it may be worked through and assimilated into one's conscious sense of self.

Reading the work of Melanie Klein, a central figure in the development of psychoanalytic therapy with children, I encounter interpretations, often based in the primal scene (Segal, 2012), that seemed far removed from anything I would ever think to say to a child, let alone actually say. But I do think I have to say something, and I rarely have any idea of what that might be. My psychoanalytic supervisor tells me, "Stay with the child. Stop trying to make interpretations. You're trying too hard. You need to stay in the room, with the child and with what is happening between the two of you. And even then, only say it if you feel like you have to, not just because you think you should say something." I remember my student teaching and think, "There I go again, talking to myself."

In their study of teacher development in Japanese preschools, Hayashi and Tobin (2015) take up the question of who it is that we are teaching to, or what it is that we imagine we are doing when we are with children in the role of teacher. They showed their teacher informants video Tobin filmed ten years earlier of the same informants as novice teachers. In the new interviews, informants commented that, as novice teachers, they were in too much of a hurry, their minds were too full of their own worries and goals, and as a result, they acted with too much haste and not enough composure. They commented that they were concerned with acting properly or doing it right, and consequently, they had trouble focusing on and being responsive to the child in front of them. Hayashi and Tobin report this conversation between Morita and Nogami as they watched a film of Morita in her fourth year of teaching:

Morita: I talked and talked, and kept up this kind of one-way talking, right through the origami activity, and then into lunch, talking like this, from one activity to the next, throughout the day.

Nogami: Yeah, right. It seems like you were continually focused on what *you* had to do next. Therefore, we could say that you hadn't really reached the point as a teacher that you could really *see* each child.

(2015, p. 108)

A Crisis

I have just returned from a two-week vacation to the news that, while I was out, one of my clients has suffered a terrifying trauma. When I began seeing Bo several months earlier, he was almost mute. He had spent years witnessing the violent abuse of another family member. For the first few months we were together, he moved sand around in the sand table, saying almost nothing. His lack of responsiveness to anything I said or did left me feeling frustrated, inadequate and at a loss for how to help him.

Then one session, Bo pulled out the bin containing the toy guns, ropes and handcuffs. He began to direct me in violent scenarios. For a number of months, the play was gruesome, murderous and on his part, rage-filled. At times, it was frightening for both of us. But the thing that astonished me was that as this went on, Bo's capacity to tell a lengthy, coherent narrative and to carry out an intricate conversation—albeit about the best way to dispose of mutilated bodies—was suddenly present.

So now, it is our first session after the new trauma and Bo is manic. He can't stay in the room. He runs up and down the halls. He can't stop, can't speak to me. The next week, he comes in and sits in front of the sand table and once again begins moving sand around, saying nothing. He fills containers, empties them, moves sand from one side of the table to the other. I watch, attempting to offer commentary that he seems to not hear. I try to offer interpretations; I talk about fear, anger, betrayal. Bo moves sand. I feel like a failure for not protecting him and not being able to reach him again. My feelings of being lost seem to mirror his own. This continues—me talking and talking and him mutely shoveling and shoveling—for weeks.

From Repression to Relating

In some schools of psychoanalytic thought, there has been a shift, ongoing for the past several decades, away from considering interpretation of repressed ideas as the primary mechanism of change, toward something that is more closely focused on affective flows within the relationship between therapist and client.[2] The word affect, in psychoanalytic literature, is used in many different ways. Commonly it is used as interchangeable with emotion. Because my interest in affect derives from the work of Gilles Deleuze and Felix Guattari (1987; see also Leander and Boldt, 2013), I pursue a perspective on affect as the prediscursive or unconscious affecting of the body, something that may or may not be brought to consciousness, but that is still registered in the body. This includes the ways the human body is affected by other people, objects, spaces, materials, ideas, fantasies, histories and culture. I recognize that posthuman studies do not privilege the human in the flow of affect, but as a therapist, my concern is both human experience—my clients' and my own—and how we are affected by things that exceed the human. Psychoanalysts have long considered how humans are affected in implicit and explicit, unconscious and conscious, rational and irrational ways.[3] Particularly in schools of psychoanalytic thought and practice that conceptualize therapy through a two-person model, the question of how the relationship between analyst and analysand is composed through flows of affect between them, around them and through them is central.

Writing in the 1920s, Sandor Ferenczi was the first psychoanalyst to propose a move from a one-person psychology to a two-person model. In the one-person model—Freud's model—the analysand (the preferred term for the patient or client in psychoanalysis)[4] is understood as directed by internal, biological, libidinal drives. The analyst comments on the material that is understood as already there, internal to the client as a result of inherent drives. The job of the analyst includes abstinence or, in other words, not introducing any of her/his material into the session in order that s/he could be used as a blank screen for the analysand's transferences. Ferenczi (1999/1928) introduced a two-person model, in which attending to the here and now of what was being produced between the analyst and the analysand in the specific space and time of the session was seen as the heart of therapeutic action.

The change in psychoanalytic thought from a one-person to a two-person model began to take hold with the work of Melanie Klein in the 1920s through the 1960s. Klein (1975/1935) insisted that infants seek relations with objects (the mother in Klein's work). Mitchell (1988) describes Ronald Fairbairn, writing from a British object–relations perspective, proposing that infants seek out pleasurable exchanges with caretakers, not for the sake of pleasure, but "as a vehicle for interaction with others" (p. 27). When the interactions are not pleasurable, the infant interacts even in painful ways to maintain the relationship with the important other. Fairbairn concludes that because relating is the central driving force, what a child adapts is a specific style of connection which becomes the mode or template for interacting with others throughout life (Mitchell, 1988). Considered this way, the continuation of maladaptive, painful or destructive patterns of relating, behaving and understanding are not a result of repression or pathology as an individual attribute, but rather an enactment of how the person learned to maintain vital relationships. To feel or behave differently is experienced as walking away from the possibility of human contact, the loss of ties to internalized objects (one's caregivers) which had provided, even if in painful forms, an ongoing feeling of belonging and connection (Mitchell, pp. 27–28).

So now I find myself reflecting on what it is that I expect when I offer my clients interpretations in which I try to connect their anger or sadness to the situations in which they live. My clients are rarely willing or perhaps able to reflect on the relationships they are in, perhaps because they are dependent upon their families for day-to-day connection and survival. When I think of interpretation as something that opens the door to their capacity to think critically about their situations, as one of my clients shrewdly noted, it is as if I want to kidnap them from their families. My own fantasies that I could bring them all home to live with me are not very helpful; the children love their parents and are loved in return, even if the expression of that is sometimes fraught. I must change my understanding of what it is that I can offer them through therapy and reimagine what interpretation is and what it does.

The Crisis Moves

Bo, raw from the traumatic assault he has endured, continues his silent sand work for several weeks. This session, he is once again moving sand into and out of buckets, but then something different happens. He looks up and seems to notice me. He looks at me for several seconds and then, without a word, reaches under the table, fishes out another shovel and bucket, hands them to me and then goes back to his shoveling. It is impossible to know whether he is telling me to shovel or just giving me the option, but, bored and frustrated, I begin to dig.

For the first few minutes, I barely notice what I am doing; I am preoccupied with the same anxious questions about how to help him that have characterized our sessions for weeks. But then, I become aware of myself shoveling. I become interested in shoveling. The shoveling begins to take over my consciousness, settling my frazzled mind. I begin to notice the weight of the sand, the heft of the shovel. I begin to watch the sand filling the shovel and flowing into the bucket. I feel the rhythm of my repeated movements and my breathing slows and matches it. Without thinking about it, I change the angle of the shovel, watching the sand fall, now faster, now slower. I watch how it piles up in the bucket, now smooth, now striated. I watch individual grains fall, land, then get lost. I am lost. I am floating, free.

For the next few weeks, I shovel sand with Bo. In fact, I look forward to shoveling sand with him. Now, I am again slowly filling a bucket, when I become aware of a voice, Bo's voice, trying to pull me back. I don't want to listen. His voice becomes insistent. "Gail! Gail! Why aren't you listening to me?" Speaking from what feels like a dream, I say, "When I'm playing with the sand, I don't think. It feels great." Even as I know that I have to pull my eyes from the sand, I can feel the reluctance in every part of my body. I don't want to leave the sand. I don't want to hear—or to feel—what Bo has to say. I put the shovel down and look at him. He begins to cry and says, referring to the trauma, "Why did she do that?"

Reframing Therapeutic Action

For those working from a perspective on humans as object-seeking, object relations became the model for psychoanalytic treatment. Beginning in the 1980s in the United States, Stephen Mitchell, Jessica Benjamin, Phillip Bromberg, Adrienne Harris and others[5] began developing a revised model, relational psychoanalysis. Relational psychoanalysis starts from the object relations position that the pursuit and maintenance of relationships is the central human action. From a relational view, humans are constantly emergent dynamic systems that construct and revise an internal model of the interpersonal world from the materials (experiences) available to them (Mitchell, 1988; Boston Change Process Study Group, 2010). In this model, an interpretation is one tool of therapeutic action, which can be understood as a line or moment or narrative or event that opens up the possibility for a new experience; it doesn't directly or consciously try to will the patient into a direction or perspective, critical or otherwise. Interpretation conveys information about where the analyst stands in relation to the analysand and what kinds of relatedness are possible between them (Mitchell, 1988, p. 294). I tell Bo that I have come to understand that playing in the sand frees me from thinking and that feels great. The feeling that is present for me, and perhaps conveyed to him, is deep grief along with wonder and relief that it can be, temporarily, soothed. This is an instance of interpretation, something that communicates to Bo that I understand the need to bury and to be lost. My being with Bo, holding those experiences along with him, seems to open a space for movement in which he can now dare to find his own question—"Why did she do that?" The therapeutic relationship, in being different than other relationships the client has experienced, contributes to the creation of new psychic structures that allow the client to cope more flexibly or adaptively with ongoing intersubjective difficulties and with trauma.

Philip Bromberg (2011) draws on neurocognitive studies to consider psychic movement in psychotherapy. Bromberg describes the mind as organized by multiple, shifting self-states. These self-states are, for the most part, unconsciously responsive to the relational demands of a given context. Bromberg argues that, when interacting with another, "Each partner, through his or her own way of being with the other, is affectively reacting to some part of what is taking place between them that lacks symbolic representation as an interpersonal event" (p. 70). The Boston Change Process Study Group (2010) calls this unconsciously structured mode of interacting "implicit relational knowing," referring to the patterns of expectations we have for how to initiate and maintain a relationship with another. These are patterns brought in by the client that are inevitably overlaid on the therapist, a process that is called transference. From a relational perspective, it is also inevitable that the therapist will overlay her/his implicit relational knowing, his/her countertransference, over the client, simply in the process of trying to make sense of what the client's experience is. The therapist and the client inevitably experience one another based on the relational patterns and expectations they bring into the therapy.

Relational psychoanalysts describe much of the therapeutic action that alters these internal structures as occurring outside of the conscious control or even, often, the awareness of either the analyst or the analysand. Understanding humans as dynamic, self-organizing systems, the Boston Group argues that "the mind will tend to use all the shifts and changes in the intersubjective environment to create progressively more coherent implicit relational knowledge" (p. 6). "Coherence" here suggests the mind's capacity to be more related to the unique intersubjective relationship and environment created in the therapy, which includes what the therapist contributes—as a person who is not just what the client thinks s/he is—rather than continuing to enact the patterns and expectations that were brought into the relationship by each separate from the other.

To borrow from Deleuze and Guattari (1987), therapy is understood here as an assemblage, and therefore as always taking place in the present, in the room, with the specificity of the client and the therapist involved in movements among the old and the new. The narratives brought into the session by the client are artifacts of his/her relational experiences and products of how s/he enacts these experiences. In bringing them into the session, the narratives do not function as materials from which a meaning or truth housed in the past is to be derived. Rather, to repurpose Leander and Boldt (2013, p. 36), the narratives are the materials that are shared between the client and therapist

> as living [. . .] life in the ongoing present, forming relations and connections across signs, objects, and bodies in often unexpected ways. Such activity is created and fed by an ongoing flow of affective intensities that are different from the rational control of meanings and forms.

The Boston Group (2010) write that like other complex dynamic systems, humans tend toward the achievement of greater coherence, which in human relationships is experienced as a degree of fittedness. Many, if not most, of these moments of fittedness occur as nonverbal affects, "microencounters," experienced implicitly (p. 69). We are all constantly responding to what we encounter in each new moment, what Deleuze and Guattari call "emergence" or "immanence" (1987). Movement through space and time, in that sense, creates a constantly changing field of possibility and of tension as we encounter diverging organizations. Response requires both drawing from what is already known and the capacity for creativity and improvisation. Describing how this works in therapy, the Boston Change Group writes, "In this improvisational field, all exchanges will alter the experience of the other and elaborate each person's implicit awareness of the other's available relational moves" (p. 65). The work of therapy from a relational perspective is for both therapist and client to find a new voice that is sufficiently well fitted together and yet retains enough difference that internal structures and relationship expectations are altered.

In Hayashi and Tobin's (2015) study, they discuss the understanding of Japanese teachers that "emotions need to be understood not only or primarily as intrapsychic phenomena experienced by individuals but as phenomena that are interpersonal and social" (p. 44). They cite research that shows that Japanese early childhood educators rate the development of empathy (*omoiyari*) as the most important thing children learn in preschool. Hayashi and Tobin point out that much of the knowledge of how to enact empathy is tacit and embodied. They quote Michael Polanyi (1962) to say: "There are things that we know but cannot tell" (cited in Hayashi and Tobin, p. 2). Bo offers me a shovel and a bucket, inviting me to be with him. When I accept his invitation and invest myself in doing this thing, I am newly capable of feeling what it might be like to not have to think. By immersing myself along with Bo, I offer him the comfort of being alone, in the sense of not having to answer a demand, and simultaneously being in the presence of another, so as to not have to be alone with the terror (Winnicott,[6] 1965). I am affecting Bo and he is affecting me as we work silently, side by side, close but not touching, shovels sometimes bumping as we reach for the same sand. I find myself running low on sand and he pours some out of his bucket to replenish my supply. I realize that he has stopped shoveling and is staring at the pile he has created; I stop and look too. We communicate without spoken language and, really, without much thought. We are not exactly lost in the sand, as I earlier suggested; rather, we move between being lost and being found. There is affective movement and Bo begins to speak.[7]

The outcome of relational psychoanalytic treatment is conceptualized as more flexibility and creativity in how one understands oneself, others and the social sphere, to have richer experiences of each, to find a way out of already known patterns and bring other possibilities into play (Mitchell, 1988, p. 293). To borrow again from Deleuze and Guattari (1972), if we understand relational patterns as a form of territorialization of events and relationships into already known patterns of meaning-making, relational psychoanalysis works toward deterritorializations that facilitate a capacity for movement, for a welcoming of emergence, creativity, flexibility and possibilities for both analysand and analyst that did not exist for either prior to their relationship. Adrienne Harris (2009) writes that difference is always essential in understanding psychoanalytic treatment. Writing that "minds and psyches and body/minds are best thought of as transpersonal" (n.p.), she clarifies that sameness and difference always coexist. "Difference here is as crucial as resonance. [. . .] The shared intermingling of two sensibilities will therefore always have the potential to operate as a site for movement" (n.p.). In other words, the ways we are different, that we fail to match one another, join with our fittedness in creating movement.

Hayashi and Tobin (2015) document throughout their book the ways that Japanese teachers do not mediate children's conflicts or rush in to rescue the children from frustration. The teachers report their belief that through difference and difficulties the children enact the desire to be related to others and that it is the experience of these struggles that sets the stage for the development of empathy and prosocial responses. The Japanese teachers in their study support the development of empathy through providing the children "multiple opportunities to experience social complexity and to interact to work out authentic (as opposed to teacher posed) social and emotional dilemmas with a minimum of adult mediation" (p. 46).

Several of my clients spend the first months that we work together being well behaved. They have implicit and explicit knowledge about what adults expect from them and they can only understand me through this knowledge. However, inevitably, things happen in the play that cause them to feel angry, frustrated, jealous, envious, excited or ebullient. Over time, they begin to test those feelings in their play, to try out different ways of interacting with me. For many of them, that has meant becoming aggressive toward me, calling me names, physically attacking me, accusing me of bad faith. Often, the most aggressive sessions are also ones that involve moments of intimacy and expressions of care.

I have much to learn about staying with the game. Recently, Hannah engaged me in a game of trading insults. She wrote a note to me that was full of description about my ugliness, nastiness and stupidity. In return, the note I wrote to her was full of kind language, an attempt to reassure her that she is actually a good person. Hannah read it and said, "That's nice, but that's not the game we're playing."

Haecceity

Deleuze and Guattari (1987) describe "haecceity," thisness. Haecceity cannot be understood as the qualities of a thing, its unique characteristics. Instead, haecceities are potentialities within a thing that generate the unique qualities that emerge when the thing comes into a specific field or relation with other things. They are points of tension and possibility that are unique to that thing, but that will only ever emerge if it has an encounter with something else that acts on it so as to energize this potential.

As a therapist, I experience strong feelings of inadequacy as I struggle to name, in some way I hope will be curative, the conflicts that happen in my clients' lives outside of the playroom. What happens outside the playroom is indeed part of what happens inside the playroom, but what I now understand is that my clients are bringing those events into relationship with me, with our play, our context and our time together. It is not about what has already happened; it is about the something new that happens as a result of being in a different, particular context or assemblage. The haecceity of all the elements matters, but the content or narratives that emerge are not what turns out to be really important. It is that something points to a more expansive life that might happen.

Hannah initiates the insult game and I fail to grasp what we are doing. I break the pattern. I try to tell Hannah that her attacks are not wrecking my regard for her and she tells me I have missed the point. I tell this to my supervisor and he reminds me, "You've spent two years through your constancy and acceptance showing her that you don't think she is bad. She already knows that you feel that way. Perhaps what she is looking for is reciprocity." Although she doesn't use the term "haecceity," Jessica Benjamin (2013) describes the creation of that which is neither analyst nor analysand, which is utterly unique in each analysis, and which emerges as a "reciprocal patterning based on rhythmicity, the connection based on affect resonance" (p. 16). That which is produced is not symbolized through language, although it lays the foundation for the capacity for symbolized experiences of reciprocity. Adrienne Harris (2009) describes human sociality as "deeply rhythmic and resonant ways of being together, imagining another and slowly accommodating the irreducible differences and commonalities between subjects" (n.p.).

Hannah is right; my earnest response broke the rhythm and pattern of the game we had been playing throughout the session. The request for written insults followed directly on the game that had taken up most of the session, in which Hannah moved back and forth between ordering me to play at being an angry and hateful monster and turning her into such a monster. I wrote what I did because of my anxiety that she not really think of herself as monstrous, but what I missed was her pleasure in being able to engage hatred through the relative distance and safety of our play. The trading of insults has a rhythm and the rhythm itself signals that it is and it is not a game; the rhythm signals the space of unreality that makes it possible for Hannah to try on and survive those feelings and negotiate shame.

I am trying now to let my thinking go out of focus, as it did in the sand. Freud (1912/2000) described something called "evenly suspended attention," by which he meant that the analyst should try to listen to what was being said without the kinds of preconceptions that one's theories or goals might impose over the materials. Wilfred Bion (1967) urged that analysts go into sessions "without memory or desire" (n.p.). My analytic. supervisor constantly tells me, "You have to hold your ideas about the child loosely."

Hayashi and Tobin (2015) borrow from the work of Rand Spiro and colleagues (1995) to describe their Japanese informants as teaching in an "ill-structured domain," as teaching in an environment that is not dominated by specific learning outcomes and curricular guidelines. My practice of therapy is also an ill-structured domain. In an ill-structured domain, each event involves multiple schemas, perspectives and principles, in which the pattern of events of the same type unfold and resolve in a variety of possible ways (Spiro et al., 1995). The teachers interviewed by Hayashi and Tobin describe "empty-mindedness" as characteristic of the expert teacher working in such a domain. Empty-mindedness is counter to being filled with one's own thoughts. "To be [empty-minded] means listening to what children say without judgment, preconception, or predetermined response." (p. 114).

The psychoanalyst Ken Corbett (2009, pp. 159–160) writes a description of something that happened in his work with a child that I can't stop thinking about:

> In my second consultation with him, he discovered that I could draw, and asked me to draw some mice, which I did. He colored them (six pink, one green) and cut them out. [. . .] He did not animate them, give them voice or "play" with them per se. He held them, shuffled them, and admired them. At the end of the hour, he put them under my radiator, where, as it turned out, they lived for the next two years. During his occasional visits to see me over those years, he would immediately go to the radiator, check on the mice, but never move them. He always seemed pleased to find them. [. . .] [He] said little about [the mice], and in the end, I found that I, too, said little about them. It was their security that seemed to matter the most, and once they were secured and sustained, it seemed enough.

Time and again I have pondered the power of this simple description and my attraction to it. In my imagination, I see Corbett instructing the puzzled office cleaners to leave the mice where they are. So much care goes into something so small, and such a small thing has such profound potential. The rhythms and rituals of the therapy playroom, developed between the therapist and the client, are profoundly mundane and profoundly important; the unique ways that each of my clients has for greeting me and for saying goodbye, the games, words and rituals that we repeat week after week, and the distress that can occur when I allow this to get lost or when I mishandle or disregard it. Eli says to me, "We will do this again next week" and looks at me closely. "I'll remember," I say. "No you won't," he says. "You're a liar." I say, "I try not to lie to you and I will try to remember." He is sure to check the next week and when I remember, he says nothing, but now allows me to sit just a little bit closer as we play together.

In the end, Corbett says little about the mice, but their being there and the ritual of checking matter. When I think about this through the language of education, I understand Corbett as exercising what Max van Manen (1991) describes as profound pedagogical watchfulness, profound pedagogical thoughtfulness. Van Manen describes how teachers who are capable of this kind of watchfulness see students, how the students see themselves being watched with extreme care, and how the teachers see themselves and themselves being seen, as a supreme ethical duty in teaching. The Japanese teachers in Hayashi (2015) and Tobin's study have a word for this: *mimamoru*, which means teaching by watching and waiting. *Mimamoru* means both watching to keep someone from harm and to observe and reflect on the behavior of another. It is related, Hayashi and Tobin note, to "a pedagogical approach based on waiting, patience, taking a long perspective, and watching rather than acting" (p. 21). It also involves an element of distance or, in other words, that the watchfulness is not experienced as making a demand or a judgment. Tobin and Hayashi describe, "This is the art of Japanese teaching: the art of watching without being either too little or too much present" (p. 23). For Corbett and his young client, it was the ongoing presence of the mice in the context of their relationship and not speaking about the mice that mattered. Such an approach involves children being held both in the adult's thoughtfulness and the adult's restraint.

The experience of being held goes beyond attention/distance or speech/silence. Psychoanalysts have long recognized the need to expand Freud's idea beyond what is being said—which with children is often nothing—to include the ways that the room, the toys, the time, the routine, the rituals all matter to analysands.[8] Among the rhythms, something new enters—by accident or by design—and there are shifts that are frightening or exciting, steps forward and steps backward, but always full of potential in one way or another. Japanese teachers report that knowing that their teacher is watching over them from a distance gives the children the confidence and security they need to take risks and to try to work things out on their own (Hayashi and Tobin, 1995, p. 21). And now I also begin to remember that, as a teacher, the greatest satisfaction comes from the movement between the feeling of familiar and comforting rhythms and those unexpected things that happen and give rise to creativity, improvisation and newness.

Eli tells me to remember that next week he wants to use the black paint, and I say I will remember but then I don't remember the next week and when he responds, his voice is thick with anger and hurt: "Adults are all liars—you're a liar." It sets us off in a different direction than what would have happened if I had remembered. We work with his and my own disappointment about my limitations. In some ways, whether I remember or not, the playroom, like life, is out of our control, which is what keeps the therapy in motion. Random things that happen inside or outside of the playroom, and even the car horn in the parking lot, a fly landing in the paint, a sudden sneeze, all have the potential to matter in the affective flow and in what happens next, to matter in introducing difference between what was and what might be: haeccity, the thisness of our shared time and space. Karen Barad, a posthuman philosopher and physicist, describes this as "in/determinacy:" "In/determinacy is an always already opening up-to-come. In/determinacy is the surprise, the interruption, by the stranger re-turning unannounced." (Barad, 2014, p.178, cited in Wyatt, 2015)

My clients live in a long-ago prosperous area that has now been largely abandoned to poverty. It shows in the clinic. The carpets are dirty and frayed. The toys are an odd conglomeration of McDonald's Happy Meals figures, off-brand versions of familiar products sold at the local discount store, a few expensive wooden models. The playrooms are used by several different therapists; I always reserve the same room and arrive early to try to make sure that the toys my clients have shown an interest in are there, but oftentimes they have disappeared or have been broken. Eli pulls out a game he always likes to play, only to find that in the past week, pieces have been lost. As I describe these disappointments to my supervisor, I cry in anger and frustration. I understand something of the feelings of deprivation, need and envy that my clients bring into our sessions and I feel guilty about the truth of their suspicions that there are material things that I could afford to give them but I don't. The children and I both have to be with our disappointment, sadness and anger, she tells me. This is our reality. What can we do with it?

Affective Flows in the Clinic and the Classroom

Being a therapist is not to stand outside of what is happening. When I have tried offering interpretations that take our play back to my clients' families or their lives outside the playroom, they rarely respond. A few tell me directly that I have gotten it wrong. This event—playing in the room with whatever is present—allows them to play with what has happened and what is happening and what might happen, or it allows them, as with Bo, to play with away from—though always in some kind of relation to—those things they cannot bear.

In both psychotherapy and education, there are traditions and practices in which who the people in the room are, the materials and the space, the rhythms and rituals, and the unpredictable things that happen—all those things hardly matter because what we are to become in that space is determined in advance and outside of the relationship. It can sometimes seem so rare now, so hard to hold on to a space for rhythm and movement, watchfulness and thoughtfulness, and the excitement of potential and emergence, in an era in which everything revolves around intervention and quantification of rapid results. Whether what is already understood as known is based in curriculum or in beliefs about treatment plans, the lives of the children/clients and teachers/therapists are always imagined as lived somewhere other than in the present space and time of the classroom or the clinic.

For me, being a teacher and being a therapist are coming to mean an attention to the here and now-ness. This means attending to the flow of affect and energy, as well as being alive to both the rhythms of the work and the improvisational possibilities of the moment. As both a teacher and a therapist, I am reliant upon whatever reassurance comes from having a loosely held schema of what might be happening at any given time, but an overall confidence and faith in what emerges over time. The structures of teaching—for me, the workshop structures of reading, writing and other inquiry-based work—create the canvas, the ill-structured domain—upon and against which desires and differences come into play in the forms of arguments, assertions, improvisations and creativity, and over time, the children develop enabling relations to ideas, materials, one another and me. As a therapist, I'm likewise learning to hold the frames of therapy—the space and time, the materials, my presence and the possibilities and boundaries of our relationship—as similarly providing something dependable, through and against which a complex set of relations can emerge and develop.

It is an ongoing challenge to remind myself that I am not in control of what happens in a classroom or in a clinic. I try to prepare the grounds upon which something can happen, to stay present to what happens, and to participate in it. So often we imagine that the aims of education lie somewhere else, outside the classroom and in the future, and this can be true whether we imagine the treasured outcomes of our pedagogy to be measurable skills and disciplinary content or to be critical thinking and political consciousness. As I reimagine therapy as offering the possibility of a new experience of self—one in which I cannot control or predict what will be produced for my clients or myself—I also begin to reimagine my teaching commitments. In a 2014 essay, the French social theorist and early childhood researcher Liane Mozere (2014) writes that a Deleuzo-Guattarian understanding of learning is that learning always addresses desire. She calls attention to the affective character of learning, stating that learning occurs when children are able to snatch something out of what is happening that empowers their own "forces of life" (p. 102). Learning, for Mozere, involves that which increases the power and intensity of our actions. Importantly, she points to the way the shared activities of relationships, the minor events of life shared with others, bring things to us that "read[y] us for illuminations and intensities of experience," (p. 100) creating the affective conditions of potential which ignite desire and set the unique trajectories of learning into motion for each of us (Mozere cited in Boldt, Lewis and Leander, 2015).

Sometimes as a therapist I find myself experiencing the same life-sustaining feelings that I also sometimes had as a classroom teacher. The feelings have to do with an intense sense of gratitude for how I get to experience myself in relation to the children, which has in turn to do with a kind of intense immersion in each other's worlds and the shared creation of something different that feels like it matters. It has to do with haecceity and with affect. So much of this occurs in non-symbolized forms, through flows of affect, a sudden and perhaps fleeting awareness of reciprocity and mutual recognition, moments of fittedness, a rise of excitement and momentum, a thrill of movement, a soothing comfort of rhythm and companionship.

Notes

1 To protect the privacy of my clients and their families, the clinical stories I tell herein are fictionalized. The stories do not represent any one of my clients. Names, biographical information and other details such as the words, activities used in the sessions, and details of my clients' lives and experiences have been altered. In this chapter, I do not attempt clinical case study in any form. My use of these sketches is not for the purpose of interpreting the clinical material, so these alterations do not pose a problem for the veracity of the work. While these cannot be thought of as representations of actual clients, the sketches are not unrealistic nor do they fictionalize or valorize the ways I work clinically.

2 It is important to note that there are multiple schools of psychoanalytic thought, e.g., classical, object relations, ego psychology, relational, Lacanian and others. These branches of psychoanalysis vary in the language and emphasis they give to issues including psychic structure, belief in drives, belief in what cures, and therapeutic technique. There are many psychoanalytic practitioners today for whom the practice of interpretation continues to function as their primary framework for psychotherapeutic action. This chapter is in no way intended to suggest a superiority of therapeutic style or belief nor is it intended as a linear narrative that demonstrates the "triumph" of "improving" knowledge. It is, rather, a story of how I am coming into and out of relationships with children, with myself, with therapy, theory and teaching through a language and an approach that speak to me.

3 Deleuze and Guattari's (1972) criticism of psychoanalysis is, among other things, that the concern with affect as meanings tied to already known developmental concerns (e.g., Oedipus and castration) causes psychoanalysis to function as a normalizing practice that enunciates the capitalist production of desire. However, I argue that shifts in some schools of psychoanalytic thought parallel many aspects of Guattari's psychotherapeutic practice at La Borde (see Boldt and Valente, 2016) in a concern for what the analytic relationship does rather than what it means.

4 I used "analysand" when referring to work conducted by psychoanalysts. Given that I have been strongly influenced by psychoanalysis but have not gone through psychoanalytic training in an institute, I refer to myself as a psychotherapist and the children I work with as clients. Anytime I am referring to therapeutic work more broadly, meaning applying to both psychoanalysts and psychotherapists, I use the words "therapist" and "client."

5 For more on the historic development of object relations theories, see Boldt, 2015.

6 This formulation is not what Winnicott meant when he said "the capacity to be alone in the presence of another," but I borrow his phrase for my own purposes.

7 I do not offer an analysis of the specific materiality of the sand and its impact on what happened. I recognize that from a posthuman or new materialist perspective, the sand warrants its own discussion, but beyond my description of the experience of the sand, a discussion of its materiality as part of the assemblage is more than I have space to do.

8 D.W. Winnicott is perhaps the best known (and most beloved) psychoanalyst to write about therapy as "a holding environment." See, for example, Winnicott, 1958/2014.

References

Barad, K. (2014). Diffracting diffraction: Cutting together-apart. *Parallax*, *20*(3), 168–187.

Benjamin, J. (2013, March). Intersubjectivity, thirdness, and mutual recognition. *Retrieved from:* http://icpla.edu/wp-content/uploads/2013/03/Benjamin-J.-2007-ICP-Presentation-Thirdness-present-send.pdf.

Bion, W. (1967). Notes on memory and desire. *The Psycho-analytic Forum*, *2*(3), p. 271–280.

Boldt, G. (2015). Psychoanalysis. *Oxford Bibliography of Childhood Studies*, Oxford, UK: Oxford University Press.

Boldt, G., Lewis, C. & Leander, K. (2015). Moving, feeling, desiring, teaching. *Research in the Teaching of English*, *49*(4), 430–441.

Boldt, G. & Valente, J. (2016). L'école Gulliver and La Borde: An ethnographic account of collectivist integration and institutional psychotherapy. *Curriculum Inquiry*, *46*(3), 321–341.

Boston Change Process Study Group. (2010). *Change in psychotherapy: A unifying paradigm*. New York, NY: W.W. Norton & Co.

Bromberg, P.M. (2011). *The shadow of the tsunami and the growth of the relational mind*. New York, NY: Routledge.

Corbett, K. (2009). *Boyhoods: rethinking masculinities*. New Haven, CT: Yale University Press.

Deleuze, G. & Guattari, F. (1972). *Anti-oedipus: Capitalism and schizophrenia*. (R. Hurley, M. Seem & H.R. Lane, Trans.), New York, NY: Penguin.

Deleuze, G. & Guattari, F. (1987). *A thousand plateaus: Capitalism and schizophrenia*. (B. Massumi, Trans.). Minneapolis, MN: University of Minnesota Press.

Ferenczi, S. (1999). The elasticity of psycho-analytic technique. In J. Borossa (Ed.), *Sandor Ferenczi: Selected Writings* (pp. 255–268). New York, NY: Penguin. (Original work published 1928).

Freud, S. (2000a). Recommendations for physicians practicing psychoanalysis. In J. Strachey (Ed.), *Standard edition of the complete psychological works of Sigmund Freud, Volume 12* (pp. 109–120). New York, NY: Norton. (Original work published 1912).

Freud, S. (2000b). The ego and the id. In J. Strachey (Ed). *Standard edition of the complete psychological works of Sigmund Freud, Volume 19* (pp. 19–27). New York, NY: Norton. (Original work published 1923).

Freud, S. (1936). *Inhibitions, symptoms, and anxiety*. London: Hogarth Press.

Gabbard, G. (1994). Psychodynamic Psychiatry in Clinical Practice. The DSM-IV Edition, American Psychiatric Association, 1994.

Harris, A. (2009). You must remember this. *Psychoanalytic Dialogues*, *19*(1), 2–21.

Hayashi, A. & Tobin, J. (2015). *Teaching embodied: Cultural practice in Japanese preschools*. Chicago, IL: University of Chicago Press.

Klein, M. (1975). A Contribution to the Psychogenesis of Manic-Depressive States. *International Journal of Psychoanalysis*, *16*, 145–174. (Original work published 1935).

Leander, K. & Boldt, G. (2013). Rereading "A pedagogy of multiliteracies:" Bodies, texts, and emergence. *Journal of Literacy Research*, *45*(1), 22–46.

Mitchell, S.A. (1988). *Relational concepts in psychoanalysis*. Cambridge, MA: Harvard University Press.

Mozere, L. (2014). What about learning? In M. Bloch, M.B. Swadener and G. Canella (Eds.), *Reconceptualizing early childhood care and education: Critical questions, new imaginaries and social activism*. (pp. 99–105) New York, NY: Palgreve Macmillian Press.

Segal, H. (2012). *Introduction to the work of Melanie Klein*. London, UK: Karnac Books.

Spiro, R.J., Feltovich, P.J., Jacobson, M.I. & Coulson, R.L. (1995). Cognitive flexibility, constructivism, and hypertext: Random access instruction for advanced knowledge acquisition in ill-structured domains. In L.P. Steffe & J.E. Gale (Eds.), *Constructivism in education* (pp. 85–107). Mahwah, NJ: Lawrence Erlbaum Associates.

Van Manen, M. (1991). *The tact of teaching: The meaning of pedagogical thoughtfulness*. Albany, NY: Suny Press.

Winnicott, D.W. (2014). *Through pediatrics to psychoanalysis: collected papers*. Routledge. (Original work published 1958).

Winnicott, D.W. (1965). The capacity to be alone. In D.W. Winnicott, *The maturational processes and the facilitating environment: Studies in the theory of emotional development* (pp. 29–36). New York, NY: International Universities Press, Inc.

Wyatt, J. (2015). *"Shadow bands:" Towards diffractive therapy*. Paper presented at the meeting of the International Congress of Qualitative Inquiry, Champaign, IL.

2

PROPOSITIONS FOR A RADICAL PEDAGOGY, OR HOW TO RETHINK VALUE

Erin Manning

1. Study

Let classrooms be invitations for study, not knowledge consumption. Beware of the idea that certain things "must be covered." Study, Stefano Harney and Fred Moten (2013) argue, is about creating dissonance. It's about allowing learning to continue, rather than continuously cutting learning off in the name of what we've decided, in advance of our coming together, is worthy of being called knowledge. Don't look too hard for the through-thread. Don't worry too much about drawing a line. Make learning a weave.

2. Start in the Middle

When we make study the way we enter into the pact of collective learning, we must unlearn the habit of stopping thought in order to start it again. Think of all of the times you've entered a classroom where a lively discussion is taking place only to close it down. We, teachers, tend to stage the classroom that way, marking our entrance as the start of learning. What is lost in this gesture? What is left unheard?

"Refuse to call the class to order," Harney and Moten (2013) suggest. Recognize learning's fragility. Learn to listen from the middle of the many conversations. Connect in the rhythm. Think of it as a soundscape:

> [W]hen we listen to music, we must refuse the idea that music happens only when the musician enters and picks up an instrument; music is also the anticipation of the performance and the noises of appreciation it generates and the speaking that happens through and around it, making it and loving it, being in it while listening.

> *(Halberstam, 2013, p. 9)*

The soundscape of learning is full of inklings which reside below the threshold of actual perception. Think of the site for learning as encompassing what it cannot quite articulate, and listen to what that sounds like, even if you can't quite hear it. It makes a difference. "[W]hen we refuse the call to order – the teacher picking up the book, the conductor raising his baton, the speaker asking for silence, the torturer tightening the noose—we refuse order as the distinction between noise and music, chatter and knowledge, pain and truth" (Halberstam, 2013, p. 9).

3. Think Beyond the Institution

A pedagogical process that starts in the middle has much more difficulty discerning who is doing the teaching and who is doing the learning. When this distinction is eroded, the class has always already begun. The thinking seen as a prerequisite by the institution is not what is at stake here, though it likely is being learned, by and by. The institution may provide a site, but learning cannot but exceed it. There is no way to hold learning to curriculum.

Value what is in excess of curriculum, the unknowable as heard in the interstices of the uneasy soundscape which is the ever overflowing classroom. Listen here, where value is still in the forming.

4. Beyond Value

Value at the university is measured in credits. With each credit comes a fee. For some this fee is exorbitant, leading to the vicious cycle of debt and credit. For others it is financially viable, and so debt seems kept at bay. But, one way or another, debt is at work. It haunts us, and it exceeds us, and it sustains, like the gift it is at its underside.

There is a direct relationship between credits and the value of education in the accredited academic institution. How we succeed depends on how many credits we accumulate. This accumulation makes clear demands on how learning is lived, and defined. With the accumulation of credit comes the calling to order. There is a way to learn, material to be covered, assignments to be graded. Value is squarely tied to use: part of the lesson we learn (if we succeed) is that our value coincides with our ability to be called to order.

The student in the undercommons[1] resists this call to order. But she doesn't do it in the mode of critique. Her *no* is affirmative. She is eager to learn, an eagerness that leads her elsewhere than toward the call to order, or the ordering of her credit(s). In fact, the call barely registers, she is so busy learning. This student is a bad debtor: she won't let credit run her life. She has real debt, she struggles with it, holding not one but two part-time jobs, and yet she refuses to give in. She barely hears the call of credit.

[T]he student has a habit, a bad habit. She studies. She studies but she does not learn. If she learned they could measure her progress, establish her attributes, give her credit. But the student keeps studying, keeps planning to study, keeps running to study, keeps studying a plan, keeps elaborating a debt. The student does not intend to pay.

(Harney and Moten, 2013, p. 62)

Who is this student who (un)learns, in debt, beyond credit? She is the student who reads and speaks and dreams her studies. She is the student you learn from, as long as you are willing to similarly resist the call to order. She is the one who takes a stand wherever she is and does not discriminate between degrees and shades of learning. The classroom is only one of the sites in which she invents and explores. She is the student who remains beyond interest, in a field of relation that doesn't accept the vicious cycle of debt and credit, who understands in advance that debt will always exceed the capacity for it to be repaid, who knows that learning cannot be encapsulated within a narrow understanding of interest demarcated in advance of the giving. She thinks of learning as a gift.

She knows the debt far exceeds the credit, and she is proud to be indebted to learning. She is indebted and she honors the debt. The more she learns the more indebted she is. This is a learning that refuses credit, that refuses the cycle that pretends our bases can be covered in advance. "Interest the students! The student can be calculated by her debts, can calculate her debts with her interests. She is in sight of credit, in sight of graduation, in sight of being a creditor, of being invested in education, a citizen" (Harney & Moten, 2013, p. 62).

She just isn't interested in what credit promises. She prefers the uneasy reciprocity of debt unpayable and gifts beyond return. This doesn't mean that she doesn't pay her debts. She just knows that debt and credit must not be so easily aligned, that the alignment of debt and credit discredits the gift. She doesn't want to quantify interest. She'll take the credit, but she won't work for it. She'll work despite being told what is worth and not worth knowing. She will resist the idea that learning can be captured by the interests of a discipline. She will resist discipline. "The student with credit can privatize her own university. The student can start her own NGO, invite others to identify their interests, put them on the table, join the global conversation, speak for themselves, get credit, manage debt" (Harney & Moten, 2013, p. 62). This student doesn't want a private university. In fact, privatization, as she understands it, just produces more need for credit. And so she invents other kinds of collectivities, participating in undercommons as they emerge.

5. Beyond Evaluation

She is hard to evaluate, this student who resists credit. The institution finds her slippery: She does her work, even gets the credit, but this doesn't seem to be what motivates her. She knows how to write a good paper, how to cover the necessary bases and yet when she sticks to this approach she finds herself sinking into a black hole. Something else has to be at stake, and it is this that really motivates her.

How to teach such a student who learns beyond, who learns despite evaluation? The student who feels so strongly and who follows the feeling? The student who isn't afraid of friction, who adapts not only to the question, but to what remains unarticulated but not unheard? "To work today is to be asked, more and more, to do without thinking, to feel without emotion, to move without friction, to adapt without question, to translate without pause, to desire without purpose, to connect without interruption" (Harney and Moten, 2013, p. 87).

6. Pragmatics of the Useless

A pedagogy engaged with a pragmatics of the useless invents value in the learning. It does not decide in advance what is useful. In fact, it is skeptical of the very idea that we should know in advance where learning will take us. The whole conversation about the future, about jobs and security reeks of a power politics. Isn't this the call to order? How could we possibly know what will be of value in a time yet to be invented? Even capital doesn't pretend to know this.

A pragmatics of the useless is dedicated to uselessness, to practices that have not yet been defined in accordance with value imposed from the outside. A pragmatics of the useless celebrates the fact that we do not know where a thought can take us. It delights in study for study's sake.

A pragmatics of the useless is pragmatic, in the sense that it is absolutely engaged with what is in the world right now, and speculative, in the sense that it is open to transformation by the potentializing force of where study can take us.

7. Making–Thinking

Value is often allied to what can be articulated. What of the forces in experience that are felt but remain ineffable? What of other ways of expressing that defy articulation? What of the soundscapes that move us more by their undertow than by their waves? Duchamp's concept of the infrathin touches on this ineffable undertow in experience.

The infrathin cannot be generalized across iterations of its coming to be. It is exemplary. As Duchamp writes: "One can only give examples of it" (in de Duve, 1991, p. 160). From Duchamp's handwritten notes: "The warmth of a seat (which has just been left) is infra-thin (#4)," "Subway gates—The people / who go through at the very last moment / Infra thin—(9 recto)," "Velvet trousers—/ their whistling sound (in walking) by / brushing of the 2 legs is an / infra thin separation signaled / by sound. (it is not an infra thin sound) (#9 verso)," "Difference between the contact / of water and that of / molten lead for ex, / or of cream. / with the walls of its / own container moved around the liquid. [. . .] [T]his difference between two contacts is infra thin. (#14)" (in Perloff, 2002, p. 101).

The infrathin is interested in what is backgrounded in experience, yet still makes a difference. Usually, what can actually be apprehended—the *actual* share of experience in the making—is the measure of use–value. What is not *actually* included in the occasion of experience, in the event, is considered useless. This unactualized share is not only too difficult to describe, it is unmeasurable. How could it possibly be evaluated?

Yet it is this very unmeasurability that gives experience its value. The student knows this, and this is why she learns everywhere she goes. In fact, the university is only one of many sites where she experiences the welling force of the under-commons. Sometimes she even wonders whether the undercommons doesn't have a stronger undertow away from the walls of the academic institution, but she persists because she is a lifelong learner and she loves the idea of there being a site dedicated to pedagogy. She knows, from her experience of valuing the edg-ings into experience, that there are emergent collectivities even in the most rigid of systems, and so she finds ways to keep encountering the speculative share of experience, exploring how it colours the event in its pragmatism. Like all lifelong learners, she knows about the magic of the verge.

8. New Forms of Knowledge

The verge is a new form of knowledge that's been there all along. The only reason it hasn't stood out is that it activates a kind of value that resists evaluation. We just couldn't see it, we were so busy with our evaluations. This might be to its advantage: it still has the potential for creating new forms of value, new useless ways of valuing experience in the making.

If we look up from our evaluations, we may note: thought was always trans-versal, the classroom always a site for learning at the verge. What we need is not a new classroom, not new students, but new techniques to orient perception.

To think study transversally involves a rethinking of the concept of thought itself. Thought is reoriented toward the incipiency of the event at hand, toward the *inquiry* of study, refraining from delimiting it to existing academic definitions of intellectuality. Where else does thinking happen?

We must also undo thought of its dependence on the human subject. Thought is not first in the mind. It is in the bodying. And the bodying is always in an ecology of practices. In the ecology of practices where it is not the mind that speaks, what emerges is not a subject-centered narrative, but an account of how thought moves, how it moves us and how it moves the world. A practice of collective learning is about the movement of thought, engaging thought at the immanent limit where it is still fully in the act. Learning happens through us, with us. We are bearers of thought in the sense that it is carried along. We move in this carrying, and this carrying moves us.

9. Beyond Method

A methodological approach begins to unravel if it asks what knowledge *does*. What knowledge does cannot be packaged. There is no call to order for thought in the act. Study seeps and leaks and shifts and bounces.

As study, what thought can do is begin to attend to the appetitions activated in the everyday, taking the thinking-in-the-act as rigorous on its own speculative terms. Thought now begins to coincide with the most creative definition of philosophy, philosophy that asks *how*, and *what else?* No method will ever assist philosophy in this enterprise of thinking in the act, nor will any method be an adequate mantle for the dissonance of thought's soundscape. Each thinking-in-the-act must invent its own practices for learning, its own techniques for carrying. In study, what we seek is not the homogenization of thinking-doing but the creation of conditions for encountering the operative transversality of difference at the heart of all living.

10. Research–Creation

At the SenseLab we've called this activity of thinking–doing research–creation. Research–creation, as we experiment with it, is study. We have asked: How can the rethinking of how knowledge is created in the context of artistic practice become an opening to thinking philosophy itself as a practice? How, following Gilles Deleuze, might a resituating of research–creation as *a practice that thinks* provide us with the vocabulary to take seriously the idea that "philosophical theory is itself a practice, just as much as its object?" "It is no more abstract than its object. It is a practice of concepts, and we must judge it in light of the other practices with which it interferes" (Deleuze, 1989, p. 280, translation modified).

What research–creation does is ask us to engage directly with a process which, in many cases, will not be or cannot be articulated in language. This is the paradox: that philosophy does want to find words for thought in the act. The ongoing work of the creative collaboration that is research–creation involves honoring the dissonance of the push-pull of the textures and movements of practice that refuse naming, feeling the reverberations of that which cannot quite be put into words, while activating, in writing, the infrathin that sounds as much as it says.

Research–creation does not need new methods. What it needs is a re-accounting of what writing can do in the process of thinking–doing. This involves experimenting with listening at the verge, a practice that engages with the not-yet at the heart of learning. This is radical pedagogy: the commitment to the creation of practices that foreground how learning creates its own value.

Note

1 "[T]he undercommons is not a realm where we rebel and we create critique; it is not a place where we 'take arms against a sea of troubles/and by opposing end them.' The undercommons is a space and time which is always here. Our goal—and the 'we' is always the right mode of address here—is not to end the troubles but to end the world that created those particular troubles as the ones that must be opposed" (Halberstam, 2013, p. 9).

References

De Duve, T. (1991). *The definitely unfinished Marcel Duchamp*. Cambridge, MA: MIT Press.

Deleuze, G. (1989). *Cinema 2: The time-image*. (H. Tomlinson and R. Galeta, Trans.) Minneapolis, MN: University of Minnesota Press.

Halberstam, J. (2013). The wild beyond: With and for the undercommons. In S. Harney & F. Moten (Eds.), *The undercommons: Fugitive planning & black study* (pp. 2–13). Wivenhoe/New York/Port Watson: Minor Composition

Harney, S. & Moten, F. (2013). *The undercommons: Fugitive planning & black study*. Wivenhoe, UK: Minor Compositions.

Perloff, M. (2002). *21st-Century modernism: The "new" poetics*. Oxford, UK: Wiley-Blackwell.

3

CHARLENE'S PUPPIES

Embarrassing Obsessions or Vibrant Matter Entangled in Ethical Literacies?

Kimberly Lenters

> *Charlene has been sitting quietly throughout the discussion. I ask her about the aspect of the oil boom she would like to investigate, but before Charlene can respond, Tom interjects. "No ads for puppies like you did for our newspaper!" He turns to look at me, "We all wrote articles. Except Charlene. She just wrote an ad about puppies. I don't know why . . ." Charlene and Tom go on to exchange heated words with each other, Charlene defending herself with a statement of her love for puppies and Tom providing the final word, "It was dumb." Tom turns to me and, with a friendly, yet knowing smile, attempts to fill me in: "She's obsessed with puppies!" Charlene, now smiling, nods enthusiastically.*

In the puppy incident to which Tom refers, Charlene and Tom had been grouped with two other classmates for a project that preceded the multiliteracies project discussed in this chapter. Along with other small groups in the class, they had been assigned a town in the province and they were to design a newspaper, set in a time period of their choosing, which would provide a history of the town through articles, editorials, letters and want ads. While Charlene's contribution of a piece that advertised puppies for sale fell in line with the genre of writing she was to employ, the inclusion of puppies in a social studies project was another matter, as far as Tom was concerned. Charlene carried this passionate attachment to puppies forward into the next group project thereby provided a fascinating example of the kinds of learning produced when a child, working within the striated space of a school multiliteracies project, finds a space of affective intensity that sets her off on an unexpected and important learning trajectory.

This volume takes up the matter of movement in literacy—what it means to be moved by literacy and to use literacy to move. As suggested in the vignette above, and those to come, the affective intensities of Charlene's "obsession" with puppies, her interactions with puppy videos, and her passion for animals in general, were not without controversy. Produced by the intra-action between people, objects and events in the arena of Charlene's group project, this affect pushes at the boundaries of what is typically allowed in school. It also prompts uncomfortable questions about what is to be done with a child who breaches school literacy learning norms and what may ensue when that break goes unchecked. In this chapter, I ask a broad question about how purpose *and* pleasure may work together in a form of learning instruction that builds authentic and caring human relationships—literacy practices that erase the pleasure–purpose divide evident in some earlier expressions of new literacies (Skerrett, 2016). How does Charlene's erasure of the pleasure–purpose divide demonstrate the kinds of literate becomings made possible when a student pursues a differenciated path (Deleuze, 1968/1994) in a literacy learning assemblage? In the introduction to this volume, Ehret and Leander ask: "What difference does it make for literacy education and literacy scholarship to feel the world, again, to take affective intensities seriously, to engage with the surplus and with the unspoken and powerfully unknown?" (p. 00). It is my hope that this chapter, by attending to the affective intensities of one child, whose work was so readily considered surplus, will lead to an understanding of her participation in the learning assemblage as one that made possible an ethical encounter with a contested topic.

Affect and Differenciation as Ethical Encounters with Literacy

Viewing the participants in the oil boom group—Charlene, Tom, Hyo, Penny, the teachers, me (to name a few)—as an assemblage at work and play with the material and non-material—objects, practices, events—provides a framework for viewing Charlene, her puppies and her literacy learning in an alternate light. Bennett (2010) focuses our attention on the agency of non-human participants in assemblages with the term, *vibrant matter*. For Charlene, puppy videos and puppies themselves were vibrant indeed—bright, pulsating with energy—and in their vibrancy, enticing and irresistible. Puppies, puppy videos and Charlene's enchantment with them also provide an excellent forum for exploring the force of affect (Ellsworth, 2005) in one child's experience with schooled literacies. Charlene's work in the multiliteracies project, when viewed from cognitive developmental perspectives, would suggest a child who is experiencing concerning delays in her literacy development—a child in need of remediation. However, when an assemblage perspective, with its onto-epistemological approach, shapes the data collection, analysis and interpretation, new possibilities emerge. Charlene's potential as a child learning to assert her voice—amidst the micropolitics of interaction concerning a larger, politically charged topic—comes into view.

Onto-epistemology—a term coined by feminist scholar, Karen Barad (2007), whose work is informed by Deleuzo-Guattarian philosophy—confronts the tendency to view ways of being and ways of knowing as separate processes. An onto-epistemological understanding of learning brings the two together, viewing learning as something that is produced when the body and mind—the bodymind—come into relation with other entities (Semetsky, 2013). For this onto-epistemological exploration of Charlene's learning, three tenets of Deleuzo-Guattarian philosophy inform and infuse the approach I take: the observation that social worlds are constituted by assemblage of the human and non-human; their central philosophical question; and the concept of differenciation (Deleuze, 1968/1994; Deleuze & Guattari, 1987/2004).

Assemblages

Assemblages are temporal, forming for a particular purpose (*territorializing*) and continually re-forming (*deterritorializing*) as circumstances, purposes and interests change. *Territorialized assemblages* tend to produce territorial motifs—for example, the sets of rules and procedures they generate—as a means of consolidating themselves and providing predictability (DeLanda, 2006). Territorialized spaces may also be thought of as striated spaces. Assemblage theory recognizes territorialization or striation as a persistent and inevitable social tendency. However, while practices, procedures, policies and rules may offer stability, the territorialization they bring also rigidifies the assemblage's function (DeLanda, 2006).

Deleuze argues that the main question of philosophy is not "What is it?" (a question of being) but rather, "What can it become?" (Holland, 2013). A being and the assemblages in which it dwells are never static but continually becoming, emerging, and an individual's identity, likewise, is continually emerging. In Deleuzo-Guattarian philosophy, identity is not located in essential properties of an entity. Rather, identity is that which is produced through relationship with another entity (or other entities)—it is constituted by the ever-shifting set of relations in the ever-emerging assemblage of which it is a part. This understanding of identity, a differential ontology, holds that difference is not an observable relation between two entities but rather it is difference that constitutes an entity (Cisney, n.d.).

Affect and Differenciation

For this exploration of the assemblage of which Charlene and her puppies were a part, I utilize the concept of *differenciation* (Deleuze, 1968/1994) to suggest an alternative approach to thinking about learning. For Deleuze, difference is the process of continually becoming different—differenciation—and understanding difference is about inquiring into *how* things become different and how they will *continue* to do so as time and assemblages shift. Classrooms typically take up difference in two ways—with intolerance to deviation from what is considered 'the norm' or with pre-planned, teacher-designed differentiated instruction. However, even with the equity sought through differentiated instruction, as Davies argues, policies connected to neoliberal managerialism predestine classroom learning assemblages to be end-product driven, a situation that heightens "individualism and competition *against* the other" (Davies, 2009, p. 17). In this competitive environment, difference becomes an alienating force. With its design orientation, multiliteracies easily becomes an end-product driven form of pedagogy and, as we will see, in Charlene's case, a different-than-expected end product in the multiliteracies project indeed served to alienate her from at least one of her group mates.

Drawing on Deleuzian concepts of difference and differenciation, highly territorialized classroom spaces—over-coded, striated and product-driven spaces—may be tempered by shifting the pedagogical focus from differentiation to differenciation (Davies, 2009). When educators come to view learning as differenciation, as children becoming something other through intra-action in learning assemblages, new possibilities for building the capacities of students become available. One of the driving forces of differenciation is affect. As participants in learning assemblages move in and out of relation with each other, affect is produced. Affect, a form of knowing, first begins as unconscious and visceral knowing and often informs our immediate, practical actions (Gregg & Seigworth, 2010; Semetsky, 2013). "It precedes the articulations of language and thought. It is felt in the body before it is overladen with meaning" (Gannon, 2009, p. 74). Affect is, according to Ahmed (2010), "what sticks or what sustains or preserves the connection between ideas, values and objects" (p. 29). The stickiness of affect is "what gets named, remembered, embodied, and performed, serving as a catalyst in the ways we learn to become and move through the world" (Thiel, 2015, p. 40). Or, as Kathleen Stewart (2010) puts it, these "pre-personal intensities lodge in bodies. Events, relations and impacts accumulate as the capacities to affect and be affected" (p. 339). Jane Bennett (2001) frames this intensity of affect as enchantment. As she puts it, "To be enchanted is to be struck and shaken by the extraordinary that lives amid the familiar and the everyday" (p. 4).

Enchantment with the extraordinariness of the everyday, the stickiness of affect and the visceral intensity associated with it, fuels the act of differenciation. In literacy learning, consideration of affect provides a means for exploring the other than conscious forces—physical, emotional and cognitive intensities and enchantments—within an individual's learning assemblage that work to support, motivate and inspire differenciated literate engagements. In Charlene's case, considering the force of affect provides a means for seeing the possibilities that opened up through her enchantment with seemingly frivolous vibrant matter in the multiliteracies project.

Multiliteracies, Pleasure, Enchantment and Ethics

In her work with youth multiliterate engagements with music, in transnational contexts in and out of school, Allison Skerrett (2016) identifies a "pleasure–purpose divide." Skerrett argues that the pleasure-driven literacies of two youths that found their way into school in her study, while most often met with resistance by the educators in the youths' classrooms, embodied the goal-driven and sophisticated literacy work sought after by their teachers. However, because of their belief in a distinction between pleasure and purpose in literacy practices, their teachers were not positioned to recognize the value of these self-sponsored, embodied, imaginative and affective literacy practices. The pleasure–purpose divide then resulted in missed opportunities to build upon robust and sustainable bridges for literacy learning. These observations are akin to Ann Dyson's (2003) work in the area of children's pop culture literacies, so often unwelcome in the primary school writing classroom, and her argument for more permeable boundaries between school and out-of-school literacy practices. Both Skerrett and Dyson build a strong case for understanding and working with the literacies that bring pleasure to children and youth—the vibrant matter that evokes intense affective responses.

Such an approach runs counter to multiliteracies pedagogy in other ways, as well. As originally put forward, multiliteracies pedagogy encourages students to distance themselves from the topic they are studying, in order to engage with it objectively (New London Group, 1996). However, for many of the students in Charlene's classroom, the opposite came to be true—it was through coming closer to the imagined lives of those they were studying that the students were able to take a critical stance (see Lenters, 2016). Suzanne Gannon (2009) makes the case for an "ethics of responsibility materialized in pedagogical encounters" (p. 74). She argues that in encounters involving topics in which they are emotionally invested, students, teachers and the focus of their inquiry, are brought into an "affective and ethical relationality" (p. 74). Drawing on Deleuze, Levinas and Diprose, Gannon views these ethico-aesthetic encounters as "sensitive to socio-historical contexts and materiality" and "contingent on a vulnerability to the other in an embodied encounter" (p. 74). Also linking ethics to affect, Bennett (2001) argues that moments of enchantment and "the affective forces of those moments might be deployed to propel ethical generosity" (p. 3).

In the case of Charlene and her puppies, we see an openly expressed vulnerability to the other through her enchantment with puppies and an opening to an ethical encounter in the classroom multiliteracies project. I will put forward an argument for considering her transgression of the pleasure–purpose divide by bringing her "puppies" to school as more than childish obsession, but rather as an enchanted practice of differenciation. This differenciation allowed Charlene to engage critically in the fourth grade multiliteracies project in ways that illustrate an ethical generosity missing from the work of others in her class.

Charlene, Her Classmates and the Multiliteracies Project

Charlene's fourth grade class of fifty students was taught by a team of three teachers in a school that had been collectively pursuing design-based learning for approximately three years. The teachers and students were engaged in a multiliteracies project that involved an inquiry into the history of the province through identification and exploration of major events. In small groups, the fourth-grade class was investigating the fur trade, early settlers to the province, the founding of the province, the building of the railway, local effects of World Wars I and II, the Calgary Stampede, the work of the Famous Five, natural disasters, the Spanish influenza epidemic and the oil boom. Each group formulated inquiry questions and researched one of the events using online media (websites, videos, digitized museum artifacts), field trips and classroom social studies textbooks. This information would then inform the design of fictional artefacts—e.g., newspaper articles, letters, diary entries, poems, recipes, wanted posters, maps and photos—depicting social aspects of life at the time of that event. Following multiliteracies pedagogical framework of situated practice, overt instruction, critical framing and transformed practice (New London Group, 1996), or as they later came to be framed, experiencing, conceptualizing, analyzing and applying (Cope & Kalantzis, 2009), the final production for the unit was to be a digital scrapbook in which each group would have a double-page spread to gather and display their individual and collected work.

The teachers had formed the groups based upon who they felt worked well together. Charlene's group—Charlene, Penny, Hyo and Tom—had chosen to inquire into the oil boom, although some of the group members may have chosen the topic for reasons other than an interest in the growth of the oil industry in the province. Charlene, as a child identified with severe attention deficit with hyperactivity disorder (ADHD), was placed in this group because the teachers felt the other group members would be tolerant of her difficulties with sustained focus on tasks involving reading and writing. Charlene's teachers had been unsurprised by her puppies for sale ad in the previous project, with one of them commenting she was just pleased Charlene had contributed something to the group's newspaper.

Mapping the Participants in the Shifting Assemblage

In the parts that follow, I lay out salient moments in the unfolding learning assemblage, in the form of vignettes, as they unfolded over approximately four months. The vignettes reflect the shifting assemblage of people, objects, practices and events in the fourth-grade classroom, drawing upon field notes written during four months of daily classroom observation, a focus group interview with Charlene's group, and written, visual and embodied texts produced by Charlene and her group. For the analysis, I followed the three steps for an actor–network-theory (ANT) rhizoanalysis, as outlined by Latour (2005): map the assemblage (i.e., follow the participants); examine the assemblage; and address political relevance. Following Latour and incorporating Deleuze's concept of differenciation, by mapping the participants in Charlene's assemblage as they presented themselves over time, I was able to make connections amongst them. In making those connections, it then became possible to ask how things became different in Charlene's learning (differenciation), how they might continue to differenciate. Throughout these accounts, it will be evident that even I, as a researcher committed to differenciated pathways for children's literacy learning, could not see what was unfolding. It was Charlene's tenacity and the affective intensity of her love for puppies and animals in general, in addition to a certain amount of benign neglect on the part of the teachers, which allowed Charlene's ethical stance to emerge.

Beginning at the End: Pumpjacks, Trucks and Refineries

I begin at the end of my time in Charlene's classroom—the culmination of my mapping of Charlene's learning assemblage. In this vignette, I have just conducted an exit focus group with the oil boom group. Charlene had just provided an elaboration on a story she wrote for the class scrapbook. In its written form, the story seemed to have little connection to the class project—her explanation of it seemed only to confirm her group mates' sense that Charlene had contributed little to the class project. It also raised my concern for her other-ness in this assemblage to a state of alarm.

> *I've come to the point in the focus group where I realize the oil boom group is getting restless. Some of their classmates have come into the computer lab with one of the teachers. Tom has just asked if the group could stay in the lab to play computer games until recess. Penny is telling a couple of students who are approaching our corner of the room that we are doing an interview, when suddenly, Charlene announces that she has something to say. Briskly, confidence evident in her voice, she states, "I know what pumpjacks bring up. Oil and . . . two things: water and oil, because both of them come out mixed in the water. And it goes into a water tank and the oil goes into an oil tank and big trucks take them. . . . Well, they get separated and big trucks take the oil to places to put it into the gas tanks for the cars, and then the water goes to taps. . . . Or it gets cleaned out and then it gets sent into taps." I respond, "Isn't that interesting. I didn't know that water was part of the process. So that's when they're pumping it out of the ground?" And Charlene punctuates the exchange with, "Yeah, jackpumps. That's what jackpumps do."*

I begin with this final moment of saliency for me as a researcher intra-acting in Charlene's assemblage as a means of illustrating my own complicated affect produced by her differenciated learning trajectory. Charlene took me by complete surprise with this explanation of pumpjacks and the oil refining process. Later, as I looked back at the photos constructed for a group photo shoot depicting their understanding of important moments in the oil boom, I realized what Charlene was doing in the background of one the photos. In the photo, her peers are enacting the exchange of money and prestige associated with the oil industry, while Charlene is using her body and playground equipment to demonstrate the activity of workers on an oil rig.

Charlene's elaboration of the work of pumpjacks, in addition to her enactment in the photo, clearly illustrate that her time during the multiliteracies project was not only spent feeling the plight of the animals she loved. Yet, as the next few vignettes that take up the story from the chronological beginning illustrate, I did not see this happening. It seems that I, too, had been caught up in an enchantment of a different sort—one that kept me from feeling anything more than concern for Charlene—that prevented me from seeing where her intra-action with the puppies was taking her.

Puppies, Oil Spills and the Price of a Barrel of Crude

Having missed my daily visits to the classroom the two previous days, I am now catching up with the oil boom group on what they've been up to. Seated around a large piece of paper on which they have drawn a cluster map showing their inquiry questions, I quickly scan their work. They have asked: "What is the oil boom?" "How did it happen?" "Was the oil boom bad for our earth, our plants and our wildlife?" "What was the oil boom used for?" "Where did the oil boom take place?" Underneath their questions they have made a list of concepts they feel are connected to the oil boom. This work sits on the left-hand side of the paper. On the other side, the writing appears to be that of an adult. There is a + sign, with $$ written underneath, followed by "Richest Province in Canada." Beside this is written, "Oil can run out—then what?" with an arrow joining the question to the students' question regarding the oil boom's effect on the earth, plants and wildlife. I ask about it. Penny tells me that it's the teacher's writing and these are the things the teacher would also like them to think about.

The students had been asked to engage in a familiar task: brainstorm the kinds of things they would like to investigate in relation to their topic and create a mind map or thought cloud on chart paper to record those ideas. They were then to begin looking through classroom resources for key words and concepts that might be useful in their inquiry and list those on the chart paper. Charlene's group chose to map the questions they had about the oil boom. Most of the questions seem to reflect a factual level of inquiry. However, one of the questions, "Was the oil boom bad for our earth, our plants and our wildlife?" reflects an awareness of the potential hazards of oil extraction for the natural and human environment. Set within the space of an inquiry-based classroom and the linear path of a multiliteracies project, the kind of work done by the children as they began their inquiry captures a moment in which they were able to freely include their ideas and set a course for themselves to begin their inquiry.

When one of the teachers later sat with them to discuss the work they had done, it appears she felt the group's plans were not expansive enough. In the recording of their initial brainstorming, the students had not included the economic effects of oil on the province. Her additions of "Richest province in Canada" and "Oil can run out—then what?" added new lines of inquiry they in all likelihood had not discussed. Through this intervention, the teacher not only established possible new learning trajectories for the group, but also, because of her role as the authority figure in the assemblage, added a new layer of striation to it. By adding an economic angle to the inquiry and not assisting the students to add depth to their own questions, it could be argued that the economic aspect of the oil boom was privileged.

Approximately one week after the formulation of their inquiry questions, I sat with the four members of the oil boom group again. In the following, I return to the opening vignette with further detail. The discussion reveals the confusion some, perhaps all, of the group members had regarding what an oil boom is. It also marks my first awareness of Charlene's affinity for puppies.

> I am sitting with the oil boom group and I have just asked them how the research is going and how they have decided to proceed with this stage of the project. Penny tells me she is interested in workers who left home to work in the oil fields in the oil boom and that she is looking for information on that. Hyo, with his limited English, then tells me he doesn't understand what an oil boom is. With the rest of the group listening in, I spend a couple minutes explaining the term to him, trying to focus on the idea that there actually have been several boom periods for the oil industry in Alberta. I am so intent on working out how to explain this that I hardly notice the expression on Tom's face. Finally, he bursts out with, "Oh, I thought the oil boom was a giant explosion!" We all chuckle at this. I move on to ask Tom what he is thinking about in relation to the project. He tells me that he wants to know more about the people who became rich from the oil boom—I can't tell whether or not his plan has been altered by his new less explosive understanding of oil boom. Charlene has been sitting quietly throughout the discussion. I ask her about the aspect of the oil boom she would like to investigate, but before Charlene can respond, Tom interjects. "No ads for puppies like you did for our newspaper!" He turns to look at me, "We all wrote articles. Except Charlene. She just wrote an ad about puppies. I don't know why . . ." Charlene and Tom go on to exchange heated words with each other, Charlene defending herself with a statement of her love for puppies and Tom providing the final word, "It was dumb." Tom turns to me and, with a friendly, yet knowing smile, attempts to fill me in: "She's obsessed with puppies!" Charlene, also smiling, nods enthusiastically.

While Tom and Penny appeared to have followed inquiry paths related to the production of oil, and Hyo sought clarification, which ultimately assisted both him and Tom, Charlene did not reveal her plans for the inquiry. Time to speak with Charlene was curtailed as the group was called to another activity. It was interesting in this moment, however, that while Charlene was initially quite upset by Tom's disapproval of her puppy ad in the previous project, her response to being pronounced "obsessed with puppies" was one of agreement or acknowledgement. For Charlene, it appeared that "obsessed" was not pejorative but rather a logical descriptor of her love.

In the next vignette, which maps a space temporally located a few days after the first puppy reference, Charlene and her group are conducting research online.

> *Half of the class has been given thirty minutes to work in the school's small computer lab. When their time is over, the other half of the class will come in. Some of the groups are seated together and quietly chat about the media they are accessing in relation to their group's topic. The foursome known as the oil boom group is—mostly—seated together. Tom, Hyo and Penny sit side by side, while Charlene sits several seats away. On her screen, tiny, fluffy puppies can be seen tumbling over one another, as their mother observes in the background. Tom stands up and strolls over to Charlene's monitor and stays to watch with her. The sound is muted, presumably, to avoid unwanted attention from the teacher supervising the research period. It seems to me that Charlene has done this before. When I join the pair, Charlene glances up, cheerfully announcing, "Puppy videos!" And then in apparent acknowledgement that this is not how the period is supposed to be spent, adds, "I can't help myself – I just love puppies."*

This was a scenario that repeated itself over the four months I spent in Charlene's classroom—during the introductory unit (in which the group researched the history of a particular town) and during the multiliteracies project itself. At times, seating of human bodies in the assemblage would shift and she could be found beside her group mates but, regardless of seating arrangement, Charlene was frequently on YouTube either watching or searching intently for puppy videos.

Charlene's activities are, no doubt, familiar to most classroom teachers who allow students to access the Internet for research. Her activities are, in all likelihood, those most educators would categorize as off-task, unfocused and time-wasting. I, too, was inclined to feel this way. Because Charlene was classified as a student with severe ADHD, Charlene's teachers were continually sensitive to her struggles to maintain focus. When I inquired early on about the video watching, Ms. Allard acknowledged the activity with an air of resignation. As I watched Charlene deviate from the expected learning path, I worried. Where was her extreme departure from the planned learning assemblage going to take Charlene? Clearly it was a space of affective intensity for her—puppy videos on YouTube, with their cute and cuddly tumbling balls of vibrant, fluffy fur, seemed to enchant Charlene, pulling her into their online assemblage, eliciting an intensity of focus that I didn't often see with her. But how could intra-acting with puppy videos on YouTube, this extreme differenciation, ever help her to learn more about the province of Alberta or most other school topics, for that matter? At that moment in time, Charlene seemed to me to be caught up in an affectively charged space foreshadowing an uncertainty trajectory.

Ethical Encounters in a Literacy Learning Assemblage

This final vignette maps the penultimate moment of saliency in my observation of Charlene's unfolding learning assemblage (and takes us back to the entry place of this section). I had entered the focus group exit interview, illustrated below, with hesitancy. Knowing what Charlene had contributed to the digital scrapbook and Tom's reactions to the previous puppy ad, I anticipated another outburst on his part and worried about Charlene's vulnerability.

> The multiliteracies project is winding up. The digital scrapbook has come together nicely, and I'm now sitting in the computer lab clustered in front of a screen with the oil boom group with the intention of conducting an informal focus group interview. With Charlene in control of the mouse, we flip through the digital pages of the scrapbook, enjoying the productions of the other groups. When we get to the two-page oil boom spread, I ask the four group members to tell me about the artifacts they designed as contributions to the group's page. Penny tells me about the letter from an oilfield worker to his family that she composed. Hyo tells me about the map of the first big oil discoveries and his diagram depicting objects associated with oil production. Tom explains that he has written a newspaper article about a man who became wealthy as a result of finding oil. He then directs my attention to two photos, produced by the group for a photo shoot they planned and executed, pointing out the exchange of money in both. In one of the photos, Charlene sits beside Hyo and Tom, a rancher observing the transaction of two businessmen. In the other, she is in the background, applying something that looks like a lever to a larger vertical pipe.
>
> Up until now, other than the occasional tussle with Tom for control of the mouse, Charlene has remained silent. I turn the conversation to her work. She has written a story for the scrapbook and the title reads, "Animals vs Oil Spills." After some hesitation, Charlene begins to tell me about it, "It's about the animals that lost their home in one of the oil spills in 1944." I ask her to elaborate and she adds, "A few of them lost their lives. A few of them ran off because they were scared of the oil spills, because they were listening to the man talking, because they were all in the pasture. After they were done, the people were going to go out and bring them into the barn and they disappeared. And then they died."

As she talks about her story, Charlene's voice conveys sadness and her description is followed by silence in the group. I ask her what she hoped people would feel when they read her story and she says quietly, "I didn't really write what I just said but I wanted to." I respond by asking what she hoped people would learn from her and Tom jumps in before Charlene can reply, "It was supposed to be a poster." I try to ignore Tom, silently willing Charlene to do so, as well. I ask again about what she hoped people would take away from her story, and Charlene responds, "Not to let their animals run away." "Were you worried about the effects of the oil on the animals? Is that one of the things you were thinking about?" I ask. As I am speaking, Charlene takes a deep breath and begins to draw her small frame up. Suddenly and explosively she proclaims, "I love animals!" Again, silence in the group. I ask if she has any other ideas she would like to share before we move on. As she is shaking her head and saying, "No," Tom, in an adult-like voice, chastises, "Charlene! You just embarrassed us." Charlene giggles and adopting a meek tone, says, "Sorry." Still giggling, she adds, "I like animals. I just had to get that whole animal thing over with."

Drawing on her love for animals and story as a genre, Charlene composed "Animals vs Oil Spills" for the digital scrapbook. The story begins with some background: "This is a story about the farm animals and pets that got lost in one of the oil spills in 1944." Without this opening line, it is difficult to see the full connection between her title and oil spills in the rest of her story as it is written (see Figure 3.1). However, her explanation makes the connection clear,

ANIMALS VS OIL SPILL'S

This is a story about the farm animals and pets that got lost in one of the oil spills in 1944.

Once upon a time there liv to farmer's and there name's were one was Madsen and the other was Alex. They where so happy untilled someone came to there front door and knocked on the door. Hello said Madsen then suddenly she jumped back oh hello there she said I didn't see you there. Oh hi Madsen. Madsen. Yes Madsen said there is an oil spill it is going to be coming strait here right away. Do you have a husband? Asked the man. Way yes I do Madsen replied Good. So then tell him. So she did tell her husband And so now their farm is saved.

THE END

FIGURE 3.1

"It's about the animals that lost their home in one of the oil spills in 1944. . . .
A few of them lost their lives. A few of them ran off because they were scared
of the oil spills."

Considering the affect generated by the intra-action between some of the
participants in Charlene's learning assemblage—Tom, Tom's newspaper article,
the materials Charlene viewed as she researched the oil boom topic, the teacher's
amendments to the group's inquiry questions, and the tangential relationship the
three teachers had to Charlene's writing—provides a route for understanding the
ethical orientation of her work. Tom's reactions to Charlene and his response to
her explanation indicate that he was not clear on the connection between her
story and the group's scrapbook page on the oil boom. As she addressed the gap
between what she wanted to write and what she had actually recorded, Charlene's
proclamation of love for animals, like the earlier declaration of her love for puppies, was laden with affect. Her outburst, "I love animals!" provides an indication
of the deep empathy and concern that motivated her work. Charlene, having
come into association with a recount of an oil spill and animal death through her
research, was moved—upset by the plight of animals for which humans had not
taken responsibility. The intensity of her affective response became the catalyst
for a story to prompt her readers to think of their animals during times of envi-
ronmental disaster.

Charlene's work did not fit with the poster she had contracted with the
teachers to produce, but because of past difficulty with finishing assignments,
Charlene's teachers did not challenge her final written production. Her story,
an object produced along the way in her differenciated learning trajectory,
however, did become that which provoked Tom's affective responses. It was
a flash point in the collision between Charlene's differenciated learning trajectory and the trajectory Tom followed, which incidentally adhered more
closely to the guidelines set out by the teachers. Tom's work followed the
economic line of inquiry. He constructed a newspaper article on the rags to
riches story of a landowner who discovered oil on his property in the 1940s.
For Tom, the economic angle introduced by the teacher appeared to provide
a helpful disruption, which, once he understood that the term "oil boom" did
not refer to an explosion, set him off on a trajectory of learning, that operated
within the teachers' circumscribed purposes and imaginings.

Tom's comments to Charlene, "It was supposed to be a poster" and "Charlene!
You just embarrassed us," indicate their colliding learning trajectories in the
assemblage. Not only do his comments demonstrate his understanding of what
was supposed to be done in the project, they also convey a sense that Charlene's
story and motivation for writing it were a poor reflection on the group as a
whole. Tom was highly invested in having his group produce a page for the
scrapbook that he felt his teachers and perhaps, I, the literacy researcher, would
find acceptable—a page with artifacts that conformed to what he thought his
teachers and I would like to see.

While not in any way wanting to dismiss the work done by the other members of the oil boom group, I do want to suggest that Charlene was the only member of her group whose work ultimately took a critical position—a stance in keeping with the aims of multiliteracies pedagogy. Charlene was the only member of her group to pursue the one critical question they originally posed: "Was the oil boom bad for our earth, our plants and our wildlife?" Her differenciated puppy path, while originally seeming to carry her off in a direction far from the group's topic, may very well have positioned her to follow a critical line of inquiry and take a political stance.

Differenciation as Transformative Ethical Literacies

In this chapter, I have asked how Charlene's erasure of the pleasure–purpose divide (Skerrett, 2015) and the affective intensities associated with that move, demonstrate the kinds of literate becomings made possible when a student pursues a differenciated path in a literacy learning assemblage. I've attempted to show the way one child's breach of protocol in the pursuit of vibrancies typically considered too frivolous for the classroom—that is, obsession with cute puppy videos—set her off on an important ethico-aesthetic learning trajectory. In hindsight, this learning trajectory proved to be purposive and resplendent with culturally significant wisdom and knowledge missing in some of her peers' work.

Charlene's transformative work has much to teach us about the children's development as ethical citizens. As she interacted with the topic of the oil boom in her home province and associated phenomena for which she was passionate, visceral responses germinated within Charlene's body and her learning assemblage. It was this affective response that made and preserved the connection between ideas, values and objects (Ahmed, 2010), enabling Charlene to launch on an ethics-infused learning trajectory. Love for puppies, specifically, and animals, in general, uniquely poised Charlene to grasp one aspect of the downside of oil production and from that place of deep knowledge, craft a response. Charlene's ethico-aesthetic encounters with the effects of oil spills on living beings demonstrate an "ethics of responsibility materialized in pedagogical encounters," her experiences "contingent on a vulnerability to the other" (Gannon, 2009, p. 74). The strength and durability of Charlene's affective responses and her ontological willingness to be vulnerable with her group as she spoke about her work embodies the stance of a child well located to engage her world with an ethic of care and responsibility for the other.

Pedagogically, Charlene's case demonstrates the potential for embodied transformation when students are given space to be enchanted, to experience and to experiment, to become. In Charlene's case, these were nurtured by the general parameters of the multiliteracies project and the personal intensities of love for animals from which she doggedly worked. That it would go this way was not necessarily a fait accompli. Her attraction to puppies may well have continued to hold her in a striated space, stuck in a continuous loop of clandestine video watching and little more. However, the assemblage of sanctioned classroom activities, how she was imagined in her classroom and her enchantment with animals all came together to produce a deeply meaningful learning space. While her teachers stood back to a certain degree, pleased that she was doing any work at all, Charlene's experimentation, her differenciation from her group, can be seen as a coagulation of affect in one who is "embedded and invested in particular sorts of identities" (Gannon, 2009, p. 71). Just as Charlene was heavily invested in her passion for the welfare of animals, the coagulation of difference is not without difficulty in her assemblage, as seen in its bumping up against Tom's investment in his "smart kid" identity. However, this serves to remind us of Davies' contention that "ethico-aesthetic connections do not take place in neutral space" (2009, p. 29), they are always fostered in relation to the Other. The question remains then: Had Charlene's differenciation been recognized earlier on as more than frivolous obsession, what might have come of it? What new capacities might have been unleashed within the Oil Boom group? Following Bennett (2001), how might the power of the contemporary world to enchant have been cultivated to encourage all members of Charlene's group to engage with the topic at an ethical level?

I end this part with a series of questions evoked by my interaction with Charlene and her puppies. I do so in the hope that differenciated paths to learning might come to be considered productive pathways in children's literacy learning.

> How might educators support children's affective responses as ethico-aesthetic encounters capable of leading them to take political stances on issues of concern? How does one know where that differenciation is going, if it is going to be "productive?" What might happen were we as educators and researchers to let go of our "obsession" with control? Are things such as puppy videos frivolous distractions to learning? What would have happened had the whole class started their research for the multiliteracies project in the same manner as Charlene? Did Charlene know from the start where her fascination with puppy videos would lead her?
>
> How might the picture have changed had the pedagogical space valued differenciation, rather than viewing it as a deviation simply to be tolerated in a child labeled with attention deficit? Would the deep ethical roots and a strong connection to one of the lines of inquiry her group had originally set out to examine be seen? How might Charlene have benefitted from opportunities to give voice to her love for animals and the connection their welfare has to the way humans interact with the material world? Might the story she "didn't really write" have made it to the page and might her ethical expression of care have been seen as something other than an embarrassment?

Beginnings

Charlene's differenciated learning trajectory breathes life into our understandings of a learning approach informed by an ethico-aesthetic pedagogy of becoming. Where Charlene's learning will go from this point in time is as uncertain now as it was from the moment I first worried about what it might mean for her to give in to her apparent obsession with puppies. However, by following Charlene's differenciation over the four months, it is evident that allowing her to pursue her own differenciated learning trajectory, nurtured by her affective intensities, within the supportive structure of the pedagogies that bounded the project, produced multiple encounters with the oil boom within Charlene. She came away with not only factual knowledge of the oil extraction and refining process, but also a deep understanding of oil as a contested and complicated commodity. Given what she came to know and be through differenciation, it seems Charlene is well positioned to make the most of ethical encounters with contested topics. Children such as Charlene are present throughout the educational milieu. By taking an alternative look at the matter that matters to them and the way they intra-act with it, educators can open new avenues of potential for ethical literacies—for those children, for their peers, and by extension, for society in general.

References

Ahmed, S. (2010). Happy objects. In M. Gregg, & G.J. Seigworth, (Eds.). *The affect theory reader* (pp. 29–51) .Durham, NC: Duke University Press.

Barad, K. (2007). *Meeting the universe halfway: Quantum physics and the entanglement of matter and meaning.* Durham, NC: Duke University Press.

Bennett, J. (2001). *The enchantment of modern life: Attachments, crossings, and ethics.* Princeton, NJ: Princeton University Press.

Bennett, J. (2010). *Vibrant matter: A political economy of things.* Durham, NC: Duke University Press.

Cisney, V.W. (n.d.). Differential ontology. In *Internet encyclopedia of philosophy: A peer-reviewed academic resource.* Retrieved from: http://www.iep.utm.edu/diff-ont/

Cope, B. & Kalantzis, M. (2009). "Multiliteracies:" New literacies, new learning. *Pedagogies: An international journal, 4*(3), 164–195.

Davies, B. (2009). Difference and differenciation. In B. Davies & S. Gannon (Eds.) *Pedagogical encounters* (pp. 17–30). New York, NY: Peter Lang.

Deleuze, G. (1994). *Difference and repetition* (P. Patton, Trans.). New York, NY: Columbia University Press. (Original work published 1968).

Deleuze, G. & Guattari, F. (2004). *A thousand plateaus: Capitalism and schizophrenia* (B. Massumi, Trans.). Minneapolis, MN: University of Minnesota Press. (Original work published 1985).

DeLanda, M. (2006). *A new philosophy of society: Assemblage theory and social complexity.* London, UK: A&C Black.

Dyson, A.H. (2003). "Welcome to the jam:" Popular culture, school literacy, and the making of childhoods. *Harvard Educational Review, 73*(3), 328–361.

Ellsworth, E. (2005). *Places of learning: Media architecture pedagogy*. New York, NY: Routledge.

Gannon, S. (2009). Difference as ethical encounter In B. Davies & S. Gannon (Eds.) *Pedagogical encounters* (pp. 69–88). New York, NY: Peter Lang.

Gregg, M. & Seigworth, G.J. (Eds.). (2010). *The affect theory reader*. Durham, NC: Duke University Press.

Holland, E. (2013). *Deleuze and Gurattari's a thousand plateaus*. New York, NY: Bloomsbury.

Latour, B. (2005). *Reassembling the social: An introduction to actor-network-theory*. Oxford, UK: Oxford University Press.

Lenters, K. (2016). Telling "a story of somebody" through digital scrapbooking: A fourth grade multiliteracies project takes an affective turn. *Literacy Research and Instruction*, *55*(3), 262–283.

New London Group. (1996). A pedagogy of multiliteracies. *Harvard Educational Review*, *66*, 60–92

Semetsky, I. (2013). Learning with bodymind: Constructing the cartographies of the unthought. In D. Masny (Ed.), *Cartographies of becoming in education: A Deleuze-Guattari perspective* (pp. 77–91). Rotterdam, Netherlands: Sense.

Skerrett, A. (2016). Attending to pleasure and purpose in multiliteracies instructional practices: Insights from transnational youths. *Journal of Adolescent and Adult Literacy*, *60*(2), 115–120.

Stewart, K. (2010). Afterward: Worlding refrains. In M. Gregg & G.J. Seigworth (Eds.), *The affect theory reader* (pp. 349–354). Durham, NC: Duke University Press.

Thiel, J. (2015). "Bumblebee's in trouble!" Embodied literacies during imaginative superhero play. *Language Arts*, *93*(1), 38–49.

PART II

Politics

Movement 2: Uninterpretable Politics in Literacy Research and Practice

A goal we share across these movement introductions has been not to interpret chapters but to experiment from them. This goal is especially relevant to a part on politics, literacy and affect given the relationship between poststructural theories of affect and what has recently been termed "minor inquiry" by process philosophers (e.g., Manning, 2016) and methodologists (e.g., Mazzei, 2017). Minor inquiry begins with a concept rather than a method (Lenz Taguchi & St. Pierre, 2017), producing a different image of "method" through which inquiry proceeds by thinking with theory "in the act" (Manning & Massumi, 2014), in the middle of experiences in the field. Ingold (2017, p. 37) describes such inquiries of thinking–feeling concepts through the experience of research as a process of education in the minor key:

> Thus we could say of an education that leads out, through exposure rather than indoctrination, that it is conducted in the minor key. The musical analogy is apt, for the difference between major and minor modes is precisely that while the major is confident, assertive and affirmative, the minor is anxious, unsettling and inquisitive.

Minor modes of inquiry disrupt the stultifying oppression of sameness that confident, assertive, and scientist qualitative methods take into experiences of empirical inquiry, or lay over such experiences in post hoc analysis. Minor inquiry is education *in* and *to* experience that "does not begin with the subject, or method, or the desire to give an account" (Mazzei, 2017, p. 676), but rather with the anxious desire to unsettle majoritarian tendencies to (re)produce order and sameness from within existing structures.

Because we refuse interpretation while not limiting ourselves to an anti-interpretive stance, our experimentation with ideas arising from our experiences reading these chapters is a political act. For instance, in their experimental reading of Kafka, Deleuze and Guatarri (1986) explore moments across Kafka's work that express "states of desire independent of all interpretation" (p. 16). For Deleuze and Guatarri, the states of desire expressed through the lives of Kafka's fictional characters are inseparable from the political milieu in which Kafka, a Jewish author in early 20th-century Prague, wrote: "this is the way that Kafka defines the impass which bars Prague's Jews from writing and which makes their literature an impossibility: the impossibility of not writing, the impossibility of writing in German, the impossibility of writing otherwise" (p. 16). Kafka's literature is minor because it arises from the collective anxiety of its milieu, unsettling and inquisitive in disrupting the major tendencies that sought to control through the production of such anxiety. Kafka's minor literature was a reorienting of collective feeling and intensities toward the production of difference.

Kafka's experimental difference production through language and written expression is uninterpretable through the major tendencies that sought to control it: the individualism of early German Romanticism and the nationalism and industrialization of early 20th-century Europe. Similarly, we wish to affirm an alternative to majoritarian modes of doing politics in literacy research and education during an era in which majoritarian tendencies are overdetermining research and practice, generating dehumanizing anxieties through outcomes, measures and best practices. We therefore introduce these chapters through experimental readings, wherein we looked for moments that expressed alternatives to research and practice that would be uninterpretable through the systems and structures of education in which chapter authors' work is situated, for example, the forced closing of a museum school, and the after-affects of the Arizona ethic studies ban. We read in the minor key, imagining potentials for an uninterpretable politics in literacy research and education when moments from the chapters forced us to stop and think about such potentials.

Alongside these moments, we imagine alternatives to research and practice that cannot be codified and thereby easily controlled by power because they refuse to work within systems of power. Experimentation is the antidote to interpretation, to the now majoritarian modes of critique that identify modes of power but still operate within its systems, that deconstruct without affirming minoritarian pathways outside power's current modus operandi. We imagine, alongside chapter authors, how minoritarian modes of inquiry may lead to an uninterpretable politics in literacy research and practice, and we do so moved by the intensities of uninterpretable moments from these chapters that forced us to imagine potentials to reorient literacy research and practice to new modes of minor inquiry that disrupt and unsettle.

Dutro brings us to such a moment at the very start of her chapter, letting Lara, a second grader, "undo" readers with the story of her uncle's deportation. Lara's story sets a proposition for the chapter, a proposition not of fact or meaning (Manning, this volume), but of quality; this quality of story produces unnamable feelings that compel our acting and becoming differently (Ehret, in press), even as we read the chapter. Lara's story-proposition opens readers to the possibilities for reading and talking together that undo, or deterritorialize, the majoritarian politics of school curricula and the forced necessity of meaning-making as unit of analysis or pedagogical focus in literacy research and practice, respectively. There is no major meaning in Lara and Dutro's opening. Only a minor quality compelling desiring toward difference.

Though focused on methodology, Mazzei's (2017) take on Deleuze & Guatarri's (1986) notion of deterritorialization applies to the practice of uninterpretable literacy pedagogies that Lara and Dutro illustrate: "Deterritorialization [. . .] is the process of uncoding habitual relations, experiences and ordinary usages of language to separate the constructs of a major language that orients dogmatic thought and thereby method in a specific manner" (p. 678). Later in the chapter, Malina and five of her second-grade classmates read *Amber is Brave, Essie is Smart* during their "Lunch Bunch" group led by their teacher, Megan, and focusing on testifying to themes of poverty, loss, peace and race and racism. The shared quality of experience the reading group develops outside the normative politics of school curriculum is crucial to the minoritarian pathway it develops for leading reading groups differently and for dislodging "habitual relations, experiences and ordinary usages of language" for the researcher watching video data of the group later: "But sitting there, knowing aspects of the children's lives and losses they had shared with me over time, the charge of that text–lives encounter was a palpable body memory, then and now." Deterritorialized pedagogies produced "data" that themselves become uninterpretable through conventional humanist research methods.

Perhaps this is one reason why Eakle and Sanguinette co-write alongside each others' experience of love and the materialities involved in the closing of the Rockemellon School of the Arts and Design. The collective experience of the school closing was relationally produced, experienced—and ultimately narrated in their chapter—across multiple times, spaces, people and things that together form "the subject" of the school's closing. As Deleuze and Guattari (1986) describe: "There isn't a subject; *there are only collective assemblages of enunciation*" (p. 18, emphasis in original). There is no one voice for the love-laden experience of loss, but rather a whole quality of experience expressed through the collective assemblage of voices. Refusing to reduce experience to a single, speaking subject, the authors maintain collective power against power, a political maneuver essential to movements not only in making it difficult for power to locate the movement's source in order to stifle it, but also in affecting *the sense* of a movement that keeps it alive and acting: A national feeling of hope through an election; the intensities of anger, hurt and passion that actualizes in a #marchforourlives. The feeling and marching forward is not in any one body, text, image or post, but in a collective enunciation of a whole becoming different through a shared quality of experience. This is the closing of the museum school and the uninterpretable politics of collective action propelled by collectively produced desire. Where does power aim a hammer strike? What meaning can the academic place on the sheer totality of embodied, atmospheric experience? What single voice can say it all?

And yet, even as it participates through collective enunciations, a single voice alone is also immediately political in that "every individual matter is immediately plugged into the political," making the individual "even more necessary, indispensable, magnified microscopically" (Deleuze, Guattari & Brinkley, 1983, p. 16). In their two chapters, Niccolini, and da Silva and Leander, magnify microscopically the movement between individual experience and collective enunciation. Doing so, they both express the political immediacy through which minor pathways to change make themselves known to political bodies but uninterpretable through majoritarian tendencies. Niccolini describes how the politically immediacy of a policy subject, the Arizona state ethic studies ban, HB 2281, injected itself into her dissertation research on contemporary school book bannings. Following this minor pathway beyond her immediate dissertation project, the subject moved Niccolini through fieldwork in Tuscon, replete with experiences from which she presents a chapter resonate with the "affective imprint of objects, conditions, histories and bodies in Arizona." Niccolini compels inquiry as an emergent political act forced into being through the affects of policy, and as an political affect of bringing individual voices of "objects, conditions, histories and bodies" into collective enunciation toward change.

Also from Tuscon, da Silva Iddings and Leander focus on the "interval" between subjects through which place is constantly remade toward a home for immigrant families who themselves remake the larger place of Tuscon, Arizona and North America through minoratarian practices. They argue that researching alongside these families and coming to know their practices of cultural production requires moving away from a practice of merely recording data, as participant observers, and into the position of "feeling alongside." Feeling through the intervals of placemaking and "data" collection is therefore both a political act against majoritarian conceptions of method, and an act of feeling the political immediacy of a place becoming difference across scales: from one family's home, to the immigrant communities of Tucson, to the minor movements of a nation becoming different. These movements remain uninterpretable through the majoritarian tendencies of conventional humanist methods, just as they are part of a larger movement toward change as literacy researchers and educators practice in the minor key, eliding the institutional languages of power that have no words to describe or contain their potentials for changing the world.

References

Deleuze, G., Guattari, F. & Brinkley, R. (1983). What is a minor literature? *Mississippi Review, 11*(3), 13–33.

Deleuze, G. & Guatarri, F. (1986). *Kafka: Toward a minor literature*. Minneapolis, MN: University of Minnesota Press.

Ehret, C. (in press). Propositions from affect theory for feeling literacy through the event. In D.E. Alvermann, N.J. Unrau, M. Saylors (Eds.), *Theoretical models and processes of literacy* (7th Edition). New York, NY: Routledge.

Ingold, T. (2017). *Anthropology and/as education*. New York, NY: Routledge.

Lenz Taguchi, H.L., & St. Pierre, E.A. (2017). Using concept as method in educational and social science inquiry. *Qualitative Inquiry, 23*(9), 643–648.

Manning, E., & Massumi, B. (2014). *Thought in the act: Passages in the ecology of experience*. Minneapolis, MN: University of Minnesota Press.

Manning, E. (2016). *The minor gesture*. Durham, NC: Duke University Press.

Mazzei, L.A. (2017). Following the contour of concepts toward a minor inquiry. *Qualitative Inquiry, 23*(9), 675–685.

4

VISCERAL LITERACIES, POLITICAL INTENSITIES

Affect as Critical Potential in Literacy Research and Practice

Elizabeth Dutro

The Sad Story

I need to tell you something I heard my uncle say something to my dad
I thought that it was going to be something good but it was not so good
news. He said I'm going to work the whole weekend in a far place. Then
on monday after he went with his whole company to eat they were waiting
for the food. Then the police came wiow wiow he got out of his car and
said who has identification! But my uncle didn't have one so he and four
people had to go to jail!! But then the police left him in mexico. Now my
aunty is leaving to mexico because my uncle is in mexico. It is not the same
thing with out them because they always used to come visit us and when it
was christmas he would bring lots of presents and he would say to do some
tomales and we would do some different food called bunellos! [ends with a
picture of uncle behind bars frowning]

Lara, Second Grader

We are undone by each other. And if we're not, we're missing something.
Judith Butler

Can you smell the beloved uncle's absent Christmas tamales? Are your ears still
ringing from that siren's scream? Lara's story of her uncle's deportation is sensational, in the true meaning of that word. It is full up with senses, steeped in the
visceral, saturated, we might say, with affect. Loss is the absent presence of the
beloved uncle and aunt, absence that will surely change the taste of those tamales.
Longing is the wish for the usual present-bearing, familiar figure at the door at
Christmas. The threat of immigration policy and the fear and dread caused by the

authoritarianism of the system is in the drawing of the sad-faced figure behind bars she includes with her story. What is the taste, the smell, the sound, the *feeling* of violent immigration policy?

I start with the senses and the feelings they evoke because they point to the slipperiness of affect in the ways scholars across disciplines are drawing it into their work. As a theoretical term, a lens, affect is a wonder in its both/and: not at all meaning what it means in everyday usage and still very much evocative of that everyday meaning. Realizing affect's critical potential, I will posit, requires detangling affect from feeling, while acknowledging that part of the analytic power of affect is that affect and feeling are entwined. Indeed, affect, as conceptualized by many taking it up, asks us to reckon with emotion and what that word means (too much) and can hold (not enough). Thus, Lara's story, as an example of an affectively charged account of the lived political in and through school literacies, poses important questions about what affect *does* in literacy classrooms in relation to particular bodies and the stories they tell and that are told about them.

How might we think about affect and its critical potential to make more tangibly available the visceral stakes of the political in classrooms? Affect—as theory, as metaphor, as conceptual pot to steep in—offers compelling potential for considering the political and personal stakes of lives lived and shared in classrooms. At the same time, as a critical project, affect requires navigating some productive paradoxes. For instance, affect invites us to consider experiences that elude language's imposition of structure even as the inevitability of language that pre-exists the affective moment *imposes* structure. In another layer, critical lenses demand that the stakes of structures of power—the systems and institutions that perpetuate injustice—must always be viewed as suffusing any and all encounters; however, some affect scholars seem to suggest that affective encounters elude those structures. As a literacy researcher who has centrally identified as a critical scholar, I am interested in what is importantly and productively complex in the embrace of the affective turn for literacy educator-scholars who wish to view their work as part of the larger project of the pursuit of justice. In my work with children and teachers, I am finding that it is precisely in those seeming contradictions that affect's critical potential lies. To explore that potential here, I first discuss some of the shared and disparate landscapes of critical perspectives and affect theory. I then turn to explorations of how the contact zones between affect and the critical might move us (in both senses of the word) toward a collection of what I will call critical–affective practices in literacy classrooms that are graspable and actionable. Although I do separate those moves into sections, it will be clear that they are mutually informing, interdependent practices. First, I discuss the potential of affect as opportunity to "slow the quick jump" (Stewart, 2007) to certainty, to un-name categories, and to un-know well-worn tales that reiterate what we may think we understand—about culpability, advocacy, control, longing, loss, connection, distance, blame, fear and the visceral presence of the political in classrooms. Second, I turn to a critical–affective practice of conceptualizing and actualizing process *as* the goal of striving toward justice in the day-to-day of classrooms (and the simultaneous letting go of the fantasies of final, reachable achievement of those goals). Third, I explore how affect theory facilitates a never-ceasing critical practice and process of entangling and disentangling from Others. As critical–affective practice, this involves contending with the desires and imperatives of both "awayness" (Ahmed, 2010) and proximity when differently positioned bodies and stakes converge in schools. In the illustrations I share from a second grade classroom, I particularly focus on the presence of life stories in literacy classrooms, those narratives explicitly present in the literacy practices of curriculum and instruction and interaction and those implicitly always circulating through the bodies present in classrooms.

Affect as Critical Potential

In starting with Lara's story as an instance of a child's rendering of the political through school literacies, let's see the artful way she infuses her story with the intensities of affect—the sonic punctuations of the sudden and callous raid, the losses made tangible through vivid images, the way she makes the political visceral in ways that demands response. She deftly does what poets and storytellers so wish to do—building immediate investment, a sense of urgency, of anticipation, of what might be coming next. The political content follows her pull of her reader into intimacy, starting with words reserved for trusted friends, something she overheard in adult conversation, a sense that this was not meant for her ears. In this way, she prefigures her empathetic listener.

It is worth dwelling for a bit on empathy, as one word to call the feeling response to Lara's story. Empathy is evoked because of felt connection, right? That feeling in reading her story surely is about my own uncles at childhood Christmases, because they are just that kind of uncle she describes. No doubt the feeling is your own holiday food, whatever it may be, that when you smell or taste it is the scent and flavor of the people in that house with you. Or, it may very well be that the feeling comes from your own sense that this is what others have in their lives that you've read about always, seen on screens, and so wish you had. You know from your depths the longing she captures for what you do not have or do not have any longer. What would you call those feelings evoked? If you were to describe them, to yourself, to others, what names would you reach for? Nostalgia, wistfulness, sadness? And then, because this, for Lara, was so damn preventable, was so unjustly imposed on her and her family: anger, outrage, frustration? Oh, but let's not lose sight of those other feelings Lara's story would evoke in some readers, decidedly not outrage and frustration at what happened to her family. Those sensations that also get quickly turned into those named emotions are aimed at her uncle for having the gall to cross that border in the first place. We might say, "Hear this story and turn away, listen even with half an ear to this child's account and *still* hold to your xenophobic, deportation rhetoric? Well, then, face your own moral decrepitude." But, all the way around, in putting response into language we find intensities of feeling.

Affect's critical potential is caught up in productive puzzles. For educator-scholars in literacy, those complexities connect to important conundrums of school literacies. For one, literacy classrooms are spaces steeped in narratives—prompted, foreclosed, carried, subsumed, invited, read, interpreted, misinterpreted. Yet, the presence of high-stakes, bottom-line, surveillance-steeped policies can create the illusion of classrooms stripped of narrative. Further, invitations to children to make their experiences count in school literacies are crucial; yet, proffered wantonly, such invitations may be as dangerous as their absence. This is because life narratives, when shared, invite the risk of overidentification, on the one hand, and disidentification on the other. Surrounding all of this is the presence of feelings in the day-to-day, moment-to-moment of classrooms—feelings ascribed, described, fueling, deflating, connecting, alienating. Those expectations of feeling something, and the stakes of response, are tangibly present and politically charged when the personal is invited into the literacy classroom and children take up the call.

The contact zone of critical and affect theories is also a conundrum-rich space. I sometimes feel my critical antenna spark to attention in some sentence or paragraph or observation in an essay or book by colleagues engaging with affect. Sometimes in reading a scholar engaging with affect I whiff a suggestion of bracketing sensation from the also present lurk of structure. For instance, at one point in her book *Ordinary Affects*, Stewart (2007, p. 4) writes:

> Models of thinking that slide over the live surface of difference at work in the ordinary to bottom-line arguments about "bigger" structures and underlying causes obscure the ways in which a reeling present is composed out of heterogeneous and incoherent singularities.

I don't want to overstate that observation, as in much of affect theory (in ways I point to in what follows), I clearly see or tangibly sense the critical goal as never far from view. Stewart offers the metaphor I include in my title in the section that follows this one, a metaphor that captures well one of the critical–affective pedagogical moves for which I argue as powerful practice in literacy classrooms. Nevertheless, I do want to take that prick of discomfort as a suggestion, a challenge to be vigilant about keeping power in the frame. Otherwise, affect could be misconstrued as permission to live in the emotions we have already named rather than space to undo that naming. No doubt we can, as Stewart implores, slip into rather than elide those affectively alive surfaces, for, as Ehret and Leander write in the introduction to this volume, "the intensities of living [. . .] move bodies with consequence, whether those intensities become known as emotion or not" (p. 00).

However, part of what should animate the affective moment is absorbing the stakes of those bigger structures in which it is inseparably enmeshed. Those stakes are part of the incoherence and incomprehensibility of the affective encounter. As I explore in what follows, all of these conundrums, and so many more, require critical immersion in complex intangibles, rather than critical tunneling through toward clarity. Furthermore, in yet another productive paradox, those intangibles in the contact zones of critical and affect lenses suggest meaningful, tangible moves (or non-moves) critically oriented literacy educators can enact in classrooms. I turn to those moves in the sections that follow.

"Slowing the Quick Jump:" Critical Potential through Elusiveness

Scholars taking up affect have posited ideas of how the affective can support such submersion in the elusiveness I described above. Cultural studies scholar, Brian Massumi, for instance, emphasizes the importance of the relationship between structure—those things we perceive as containable and comprehensible—and aspects of what we experience that lie beyond our comprehension of what we're encountering. In an interview (Zournazi, 2003), Massumi described affect as "simply a body movement looked at from the point of view of its potential—its capacity to come to be, or better, *to come to do*" (p. 6). In this way, affect can be seen to represent aspects of experience prior to be-ness or do-ness, before a moment's capacity is constrained by the preformed categories and names that make much of the world understandable and accessible to us. Massumi (2002) argues that in "actually existing, structured things live in and through that which escapes them," suggesting that those experiences we think we understand and are so wont to categorize hold meaning only through all of the elusive, slippery aspects of experiences that evade our attempts to contain them.

Other scholars immersed in affect as social theory also describe this key idea of the affective as something that lies outside of and slips away from language's drive toward comprehensibility. Ehret and Hollett (2014) describe "affective atmospheres produced between bodies" and provide the example of elation in sports stadiums that "is felt by spectators and athletes alike, who are both producing and reproducing the feeling" (p. 433). They emphasize the layers of understanding and crucial questions offered through attention to the affective atmospheres that permeate bodies, objects, time and space as children and youth navigate composition processes in classrooms. Such analytical attention actively resists the certainty of more common preconstructed frames for analyzing those processes. Affect, in this way, functions to "slow the quick jump to representational thinking and evaluative critique long enough to find ways of approaching the complex and uncertain objects that fascinate because they literally hit us or exert a pull on us" (Stewart, 2007, p. 4).

Indeed, to take up affect is to consider the idea of potential and what it offers. Leander & Boldt (2013) describe the recurring idea of potential in affect theory as "energy, excitement, an assemblage of emerging possibility that is founded in movement, affect and desire, that in turn produces both more of the same along with the inevitability of something new" (p. 37). We may often think of potential as positive. Living up to our potential, seeing potential in something or someone—those are good things. Potential is so often tinged with promise. Potential, though, is there for harm, danger, pain, rejection, exclusion, failure— as many negative words as we might conjure. As Kathleen Stewart (2007) describes, "ordinary affects are immanent, obtuse, and erratic, in contrast to the "obvious meaning" of semantic message and symbolic signification" (p. 2). The questions affect poses, she posits, are "not what they might mean in an order of representations," but, rather, "where they might go and what potential modes of knowing, relating, and attending to things are already somehow present in them in a state of potentiality and resonance" (location 32). Such is the critical power of the concept of potential, because in affective encounters both "more of the same" and "the inevitability of something new" encompass all of those potentials for consequence when the structures of meaning assert themselves, as they will.

To take up one of Stewart's (2007) questions, then, in response to classrooms, where might affective enounters go? In Lara's story, there may be relating and resonance in just the ways I described above. There is potential for fueling empathy, advocacy and political commitment toward justice, and the potential for pity, antipathy and political commitment toward injustice. Yet, in the not-yet-named space of such an encounter lies, in these theories, a suspended pre-meaning space where the direction it goes is not yet determined and, thus, open to rerouting. It is not unlike making a turn my phone's navigation has not foreseen and hearing Siri's voice, the tangible evidence that another route is available and I am taking it, perhaps through no conscious decision at all. I have described this previously as a pedagogy of incomprehensibility that is full of critical potential in its invitation to not know, in its offering of a pause to reframe, unknow and re-know, to understand more by drenching in the impossibility of understanding (Dutro, 2013; Dutro & Cartun, 2016). Not yet comprehended sensations in encounters with each other—understandings suspended even for instants, or even as suspension of disbelief that such hovering outside of signification were possible—can offer a space to question the meanings that assert themselves so quickly and persistently and can position children so harmfully.

The promise of the affective encounter as location for that pause before naming, that slowing of the quick jump to certainty that prompts us to question, is why, for Massumi (2002), affect is a source of (if not a synonym for) hope. He explained, "In my own work I use the concept of 'affect' as a way of talking about that margin of manoeuvrability, the 'where we might be able to go and what we might be able to do' in every present situation. I guess 'affect' is the word I use for 'hope'" (p. 3). As that not-yet-categorized space that eludes naming, affect "gestures not toward the clarity of answers but toward the texture of knowing" (Stewart, 2007, p. 129). Since the un-comprehended is always in process of being encountered, it can represent the potential for movement to "try and see" rather than the possible paralysis that comes from "projecting success or failure" (Massumi, 2002, p. 3).

In the critical potential of affect for life in classrooms, this moment of pre-naming within encounters with one another is significant and importantly graspable and actionable in work in classrooms. Few adults who enter classrooms wish to pull ready-made labels and stick them to children. Yet stick they do, those labels, to some children much more than others, all the time, persistently, and consequentially. Affect offers a way to think about how those sensations we feel and sense in others can reveal the human constructed-ness of the names we've given them and how those names are sorting children into who and what counts as valued and valuable in schools. In my teaching, I relate this particular critical potential of affect to stories of going to an amusement park, like Disneyland, where I got to go pretty often as a kid from a middle class Southern California family. If you're like me, you are taken in by the constructed reality of such places. But, then, sometimes, you see pretty clearly that it's not real—you see one of the workers repainting a "rock"; or you realize the music is coming from a speaker masquerading as a tree. In this analogy, I hope to convey to new teachers how affect points to the visceral aspects of school literacies and that space where language fails us can open up questions of the categories we create. The intensities of encountering each other's stories in literacy classrooms erupt into feelings that, in turn, quickly move to sorting themselves into hovering categories. If we can see the value in this pausing on the brink of comprehension affect offers, then it is crucial to understand the stakes in that movement from the wriggle room of incomprehension toward the fixation of knowing.

Let's get specific about what prefigured narratives are being interrupted: within language in schools and policy, the pervasive "us" (white, economically more privileged adults) versus "them" (children and families of color, working class families, those facing poverty, immigrant families of color, and families whose first language is historically and perpetually devalued); hierarchical, individualized narratives of success and promise; disciplinary policies that target and criminalize even the youngest of children. Attending to affect can interrupt the prefigured narrative by those with privilege (e.g., from race, class, gender, sexual preference) concerning why "they" may deserve what they get, reap what "they" sow; how all of it is surely simply chickens coming home to roost. Challenging very sticky, preprinted tags for children or their behaviors requires posing questions that muddle the labels as soon as we find them there, on the tip of our tongue. What does resistance mean? What does recalcitrance mean? What does disengaged mean? What does bored mean? What does quiet mean? Who do those names stick to? And, just as important: Who gets the pity? Who gets the empathy? Why and how do some get blamed and others get the benefit of the doubt? We must always be knocking our fists on "rocks" to see if they are hollow.

"Only the Ladder is Real:" Process as the Critical Goal

Affect's critical potential is also found in its embrace of process *as* the goal of resistance to ongoing, entrenched oppression. In Massumi's (2002, p. 3) words:

> [O]ne of the reasons [affect is] such an important concept for me is because it explains why focusing on the next experimental step rather than the big utopian picture isn't really settling for less. It's not exactly going for more, either. It's more like being right where you are—more *intensely*.

Such embrace of process *as* the goal of the critical project resonates with many metaphors we might find in scholars' and activists' writing, as well as media texts. In Deleuze & Guattari's (1987) proliferation of metaphors in *A Thousand Plateaus*, one they use on this particular point is that of ants. "You can never get rid of ants," they write, "because they form an animal rhizome that can rebound time and again after most of it has been destroyed" (p. 9). Ants are always building forward, not looking back with frustration and exasperated sighs at the collapsed tunnel walls caused by some human or animal tread above—just digging, building, constructing and reconstructing. This focus on process as goal is there too in Anzaldua's (1983) reminder, "Voyager there are no bridges. We build them as we walk" (p. vi.). And, one night, while watching *Game of Thrones*, I find another metaphor on just this point I return to again and again, when Baelish, reprehensible as he is, says, "Only the ladder is real. The climb is all there is." (Yes, I did turn it into a meme). Affect here, then, is the reminder that action lies in each step, even when it feels no progress is being made—the imperfectly placed foot, hastily laid plank, crumbling passage wall and all.

What does it offer to be "right where you are—more intensely" in classrooms? For one, it interrupts the constant narrative surrounding public schools of reaching, striving, and, much of the time—particularly for schools serving children who are not wealthy and/or white—perpetually failing to reach what has been deemed adequate. As Deleuze & Guattari (1987) write, "The various forms of education or 'normalization' imposed upon an individual consist in making him or her change points of subjectification, always moving towards a higher, nobler one in closer conformity with the supposed ideal" (p. 129). So, in this way, focus on process is another tangible move for us as literacy teachers. Simply, but importantly, process *as* the goal allows for consistent interruption of metanarratives of utopian ends and the imposing threat of failure to get there. Similarly, it supports interruption of the smaller, more micronarratives in the day-to-day of life together in classrooms. Of course, those stories are also inseparable from the larger ones, but the affective space for maneuvering, the urgent reminder offered by affect to be intensely present, is attached here to the particular bodies gathered in that contained space. Those larger narratives in which those specific, day-to-day converging bodies are caught up, gather children's and teachers' bodies into larger groups and categories. Both are consequential, and, in the relationship between them, the stakes could not be higher.

In a writing unit on small moments, Malina wrote:

> My Dad was in jail. I was sad and mad because my Dad is always being a bad Dad and I do not like it. I wish he was not a bad person. Then I would be proud of him. But I am not proud of him. I am angry at my bad dad. That is why my mom does not let us see our dad. The End.

Her father, who had not been a physical presence in her life for at least a few years, is a central presence in her writing. When drafting a poem about love, she writes, "Love is true. Love is here. I love my Dad. I love my Mom. I love my family." When writing a list of facts about herself, "I have one Dad" is there right after where she was born, when she was born, and that she has two sisters. Her father's incarceration is also a theme echoing throughout her writing that year. In another entry in her writer's notebook, she writes that her mom loves her so much "she can brake out of a sell [cell]." If her mother was in prison, no bars could keep her from her daughter.

There are plenty of important ways to approach the critical task of analyzing the social forces in which Malina's narrative is a part. Her storied experience is inseparable from the crisis of over-incarceration, criminalization and murder by police of African-American men and boys. It cannot be detangled from the never adequate and increasingly evaporating social safety nets for single-parent families trying to make it on one low-wage job. Children, as literacy researchers have emphasized, are cosmopolitan intellectuals (Campano & Ghiso, 2011), sophisticated social theorists (Jones, 2012), and bring epistemic privilege that is chronically undervalued (Dutro, 2010). Children living in oppressive systems have insights that are unavailable to adults who are economically, racially and/or linguistically privileged and those insights are not often in view in the policies, curriculum and instruction children encounter in schools.

However, affect offers something important for critical projects in its dual offerings of, for one, that suspended space of not yet knowing or naming and, for another, insistence that each unfolding moment matters to revolution. This space to see classrooms as accumulating moments matters also because, well, I am undone by my time with Malina, on and off the page. That sense certainly must be connected to how she responded with such perfectly heartful matter-of-factness to my mention of my own family experience with incarceration (more on that later). But it's not just that overlap of (very different) experiences. I am also set afloat by her insights, ideas, artful turns of phrase. I want to crawl into her sentence "Writing is what lets me know about what I don't do and what I did do" and curl up for a while. It is the presence of the absence that floors and delights me. It is that very specific insight that in chronicling the large and small moments of life, whether on the page or in memory, we can also read for the companion narrative, always there, of what we did not do, who we did not know, all the things we did not happen to see, hear, taste, smell, sense. I had noticed many things in Malina's interviews before and, surely, this sentence was tagged, along with many other children's insights, in the categories of "children's perspectives on writing," "feelings about writing". However, right now, with Malina's voice in my head, I am halted and consumed by this nugget of brilliance that I get to have and hold for the rest of my life. I am in it before it gets subsumed into a larger category (even though it already is part of that category).

What is the revolutionary potential in lingering in one child's single sentence spoken in response to a question about how she feels about writing in school? In being awash in the senses of encountering a child's images of the vivid, vivacious presence of absence? In pursuit of justice, classrooms are spaces of everyday revolution. Our critical traditions and mentors all emphasize this, from W.E.B. DuBois to Paolo Freire, Maxine Greene to Gloria Ladson-Billings. Affect layers into this conversation in its attention to the pulsations of the always-unfolding moments that make up those every-days. Recognizing the potential of being more intensely affected by proliferating moments with children in classrooms allows for absorption of who is targeted and in what ways, who experiences those losses and how they are imposed, and how and why a reasonable person would respond in just the way children respond to their positioning by forces outside of their control. Moment to moment, affect's offer of a pause before naming, the feeling of what is fleetingly beyond categorizing, *is* revolutionary. It is just that "seeping edge" Massumi (2002) describes of what cannot and should not be contained that insists on renaming and reframing. Feeling the crack in the structures, no matter how thread-thin, insists on resistance.

However, we also feel the moments we let slip by, when we slipped up, when, as Malina says, we realize what we didn't do. I can let my feet dangle in the moments during a school day or a class when I felt *there*, intensely—when I noticed a child in a classroom or a student in my own courses, really noticed; when I took an action or said that thing that felt like advocacy. I can dive head first, though, in what (to borrow Malina's words) I don't do—the looking back at the collapsed walls of missed opportunities; the always-lurking question of whether I have dismantled the bridges I so want to build. The novice teachers in my literacy methods courses, barely out of high school themselves, immersed as we are with children in our school-located course, are often pitching from euphoria of connection and relationship with children, the glow of moments they sense as success, to the certainty of their own inadequacy, their failure to be the teacher of their dreams. Focusing on process over progress, though, pushes back on the intensities of despair that threaten to derail the best of critical intentions, particularly for those who have the luxuries of retreat to privilege. We cling together to our image of the ladder disappearing into the clouds, no top in sight to berate us at our lack of progress, but many rungs to take, one at a time.

Viewing the critical pursuit of justice as a moment-to-moment process is a hopeful movement toward sustainable engagement and away from despair of the relentless climb that has no summit. Deleuze and Guattari (1987, p. 177) capture the hope in viewing the critical pursuit of justice as an ever-unfolding, moment to moment, never accomplished process:

> Will this all be in vain because suffering is eternal and revolutions do not survive their victory? But the success of a revolution resides only in itself, precisely in the vibrations, clinches, and openings it gave to men and women at the moment of its making and that composes in itself a monument that is always in the process of becoming, like those tumuli to which each new traveler adds a stone.

Some of those stones are each lingering on a child, being enveloped in the senses of those encounters, the hopeful sense of next moments of striving to be the ally and advocate that child deserves.

Tangling and Detangling: The Knotty Lures of Identification and Extrication

The lure of feeling in response to others' stories is both unavoidable and crucial *and* necessitates cautions and interrogations. Emotion without the not-yet-labeled and maneuvering space of affect I have discussed above is seductive and can draw us to assumptions of both dissolve and division. I am reeled into feeling when immersed in children's stories. Being hooked into compassion and resonance and hope and dejection and recognition and alienation and love and guilt cannot but build fantasies of both what it all means (life) and what it all means to and for me. Berlant (2011) reminds us that "whatever accounts of attachment to normative fantasy we make need a more complicated notion of object choice and of what it means to desire to have a cluster of affects and feelings in lieu of having a world" (p. 1). Her words help me consider how, in the literacies and lives shared in classrooms, a desire to feel and feel deeply, to gather and cling to sensations in encounters with others, is desir*able*, even as it is dangerous. It is not and cannot be one or the other. Yearning for connection is dangerous and resisting connection is dire.

This is what I have described as a pedagogy of testimony and critical witness in classrooms (Dutro & Zenkov, 2008, Dutro, 2008, 2011; Dutro & Bien, 2014). Critical witness, as its own set of tangible pedagogical moves, involves the simultaneous deep embrace of the shared vulnerability of human experience and arms-length distance to analyze how and why people are positioned very differently in and through those experiences. The shared experience of being human is, in Radstone's (2007) words, "grounded in the space between witness and testifier within which that which cannot be known can begin to be witnessed" (p. 20). That is the space of unknowing that can be tapped for a productive paradox: knowing each other better in our comprehension of what we cannot know of another's experience. As a conscious pedagogical strategy, simultaneous tangling and detangling with stories is crucial, as privilege and normativity often get subsumed and made invisible by stories, particularly narratives of difficult, painful experiences. Butler (2004) points to how realizations of shared fragility can destabilize our self-narratives. What shared human experiences, such as grief, display, she writes:

> is the thrall in which our relations with others hold us, in ways that we cannot always recount or explain, in ways that often interrupt the self-conscious account of ourselves we might try to provide, in ways that call into question the very notion of ourselves as autonomous and in control.
>
> *(2004, p. 23)*

Literacy classrooms, as story-filled spaces, are risky places that require conscious efforts to make visible the differential role and consequences of challenges. "The hegemonic," as Berlant (2011) writes, "is, after all, not merely domination dressed more becomingly—it is a metastructure of consent" (p. 185). Affect offers a metaphorical space for the both/and presence of domination and critical resistance and advocacy embedded in life narratives lived, invited and responded to in literacy classrooms. Literacies that viscerally connect and move us can both make it impossible to detangle ourselves from others (an essential move) and promise a brief pre-articulate pocket of felt recognition that tidy and alluring metanarratives are *not* inevitable and can be countered (also a crucial move). The affective, in this way, offers an underscore to the critical emphasis on the twin traps of overidentification and disidentification.

Butler (2004, p. 23) captures a sense of the ubiquity and frailty of the ever-present, writing "I:"

> I might try to tell a story here about what I am feeling, but it would have to be a story in which the very "I" who seeks to tell the story is stopped in the midst of the telling; the very "I" is called into question by its relation to speechlessness, but does nevertheless clutter my speech with signs of its undoing.

Whether narrating experiences that matter to me, or responding to others' narratives that pierce me in my tender spots, "I" is always present, even as it crumbles in the inadequacy of language to convey its visceral memories, senses of things past or what's incomprehensible in the connections and disconnections felt with another.

Here, then, a tangible critical–affective move may be found in the metaphor of the always ongoing process of being entangled and disentangled from the stories lived and shared in the day-to-day of encounters in literacy classrooms. We cannot, nor should we try, to encounter children's stories with the expectation that we can and must avoid their snare. Rather, I posit, the disentangling of the I and you must be done within the visceral encounter of sensational moments with others and their narratives. If we have not gotten close enough to even risk the reach of the vine around an ankle we will have nothing at all from which to detangle. We'd best be wrapped in others so that even with the shallowest breath, the smallest gesture, we feel the snug push and pull of their presence. Surely detangling is best a mindful process, each spring-green, curling shoot needing to be gently grasped and unwound from wrist, throat, chest; the last coil requiring stepping carefully out of its comforting embrace; stepping back, then, just far and long enough to see and appreciate that story's pain, its beauty, its distinctiveness, its stakes that may not be your stakes. What is left is the feeling, the lingering imprint that encounter has left on limbs, even as we are always already entangled in the multiplying encounters that precede and follow it. Each of those impressions shifts the way we move in the world. But, in the space of the visceral, within the intensity of its grip, lies the knowledge, once and for all, that another's story is not me. At the same time, it cannot be dismissed as "theirs" either, as it deeply implicates its witnesses.

In this dimension of critical–affective pedagogy, we have to contend, though, with questions of whose lives and stories we are most likely to hear and respond to with vulnerability and empathy. Affect scholar Sara Ahmed (2010) writes compellingly about the relationship between *what* we like and what we *are* like. In her words, "We come to have our likes, which may even come to establish what we are like. To have our likes," she continues, "means certain things are gathered around us. Those things we do not like we move away from" (p. 32). She describes our "likes" and our related moves toward "awayness" as constituting our "bodily horizons." Those things we nurture as dear to us and those things that cause us discomfort or distaste, those things are inclusive or not of others, increase or not our likelihood of intersecting and interacting with others, make more or less possible our opportunity to see others (or walk by, unseeing, or not walk by at all). So, in this way, the idea of "awayness" is stark in the context of children. Of course, what we keep at bay and what we pull in (not consciously, but because it just feels right) does not just apply to physical proximity, though it does raise questions about literal proximity. But, the stories we tell ourselves about what surrounds us also construct a sense of awayness, a sense of what is *not* me. Ahmed's discussion of bodily horizons is a compelling illustration of how binary terms must be raised and function to make a felt point; in defining what is part of my horizon, I have to contend with what and who is, then, painted outside of the canvas, not there between the place where I stand and as far as my eyes can see.

It is not that a "we" is impossible to fathom, or should not be exactly what must be the hoped-for texture underfoot on every rung of the ladder. We can will ourselves to acknowledge (and value) the intractable "I" while commanding ourselves to realize its capacity to lose its grip to the possibility of "we." Connection and collectivity *must* be the elusive hope. Seeking to disrupt oppression or exclusion is, to draw on Stewart's (2007) words, "an experiment that starts with sheer intensity and then tries to find routes into a 'we' that is not yet there but maybe could be" (p. 116). Perhaps this idea can be most tangible through encounters with experiences that are unfathomable, yet somehow recognizable, and wriggle free from attempts to contain them in the language we reach for (though we keep reaching; we can't help ourselves) and that reaches for us (e.g., the language of school literacies that we most certainly can't escape in the spaces of schooling). Such encounters happen all the time in classrooms where storied lives rise and swirl like steam from the hottest shower, like smoke from a kitchen fire, to fill every nook and cranny.

Classroom Moments as Critical–Affective Potential

In the quotation from Judith Butler that I paired with Lara's story at the opening of this chapter Butler's words are statements: "We *are* undone by each other. If we're not we *are* missing something" (emphasis added). I read these statements as imperatives in how we best consider and absorb the extraordinariness of the everyday encounters with one another in lives lived together in the (all at once) intimate and alienating spaces and systems of schools. However, in the context of considering critical–affective pedagogies and practices, in the way I have described them, Butler's words also prompt a question: What does it mean to be undone by each other *and* know with certainty that we are missing something? To briefly consider this question, in light of the practices I've explored above, in all of their both/and-ness of the concrete and the ephemeral, I turn to a couple of moments of interaction from a second-grade classroom.

One spring day, Malina and five of her second-grade classmates were reading *Amber is Brave, Essie is Smart* as part of their Lunch Bunch literature discussion group with their teacher, Megan. Megan formed the group as part of a children's literature project she needed to complete for a graduate course taught by one of my colleagues at the university. The project asked teachers to plan and enact an experience with literature that the teacher would define as socially and culturally relevant for students. Megan chose to focus on themes of poverty, loss, peace and race and racism and we decided to fold it into our ongoing inquiry into pedagogies of testimony and critical witness in her classroom. I was there for Lunch Bunch that day, on the fringes of the group, listening, but also ensuring that the audio and video would be clear. I didn't want to miss anything.

In the book, which is written as a series of poems, someone asks the sisters, Amber and Essie, "Where is your dad?" This is "The question that always made Amber cry." This is how readers first learn that the father is absent, but they don't yet know why. Although it is soon revealed that the father is in jail after being convicted of check fraud, at the point when the cause of absence is not yet known, it is just father loss, in all its forms, that fills the space. As the speculations began about why the father might be gone and where he might be, I felt the presence of this particular absence and how I knew it connected to some of the children's experiences.

Abran said, "I think their dad passed away and they can't forget about it and they keep talking and it makes them cry. They think about all the fun times she had with her dad and now he's gone."

Wren followed with her own prediction, saying, "I think I know too. I think their dad was really mean to them and sometimes they think about what it would be like to have a dad who would be really nice and they ask their mom for another dad and she probably says yes, but she can't find a dad who is nice."

I had to pause here, close my eyes, and feel the puddling dissolve before life can continue, as it already had. Words will fail, so it is ok that you can't feel this moment's import as you read. But, you have to know that Abran's own father had died two years earlier. His writing and talking about his father across second grade was full of those fun times they had together and the punctuated suddenness of "now he's gone." And, Wren's father? He had died when she was an infant and he was a wistful, literally angelic presence in her writing. As Wren shared with me that year in conversations and in her writing, her mother had brought a few different boyfriends into the home over time. None of them, she told me, were nice.

That day, the pause for puddling into that moment is indeed the metaphoric knowing that something crucial has happened, has seeped from what can be consciously absorbed. Moments are by definition quick in their passing. Others had predictions too and the children all wanted to discover why that father was gone before it was time to take trays back to the cafeteria. Megan affirmed the children's ideas and continued to read, stopping after the poem that held the reveal: The father was in prison. My eyes went straight to Malina. Her eyes widened as she sat up straighter and bounced a little in her chair. She immediately looked over and caught my eye, giving me a small smile. We shared a nod of recognition as Megan closed the book, thanked the children, and told them she's so glad they would get to continue tomorrow.

The next day, as soon as all had settled at the kidney-shaped table and opened their cardboard cartons of milk, Malina volunteered to summarize what the group had read and discussed the day before.

Malina:	We met Essie and Amber and the part we stopped at was they were remembering that their dad went to jail because he wrote a fake check. And, she [pointing to Elizabeth] has a connection. She remembered her brother did that too.
Megan:	She does. Did she share that with you?
Malina:	Uh huh.

Megan:	Wow. That's a powerful connection. Thank you for sharing, Ms. Elizabeth.
Elizabeth:	So, I had shared my connection that my brother also went to jail.
Megan:	Do you want to share that with us, with the whole group?
Elizabeth:	Sure. Because in small moments [a recent writing unit in the classroom], Malina had a small moment and I was connecting that my brother went to jail. He was in . . . He's been out of jail for two years and he was in jail for a long time. So, we were remembering the moment when we heard that people in our lives were going to jail and it's a connection to this book too.
Megan:	Thanks for remembering that.
Sherri:	I remember my connection that, um, Otis in Winn Dixie went to jail just like the dad.
Javier:	I have a connection too. [he says this as Sherri begins to talk. She initially gets the floor]
Javier:	[louder] I have a connection too, cause my dad was in jail.
Megan:	He was. But, he's home now, isn't he? And that was an idea that you said, Javier—that you could have, you could write a small moment about it.
Javier:	[nods].

I can freeze the video right at the moment on that first day when the poem line lands and Malina suddenly seems to sit higher in her chair, eyes about to turn to mine, and again the moment a day later when Javier gets his words in edgewise and his face reflects whatever would be the opposite of trepidation. But sitting there, knowing aspects of the children's lives and losses they had shared with me over time, the charge of that text–lives encounter was a palpable body memory, then and now. I feel a spark of recognition pass between us in Malina's immediate glance my way. I'm in that moment intensely with her, with Javier, because I sense the charge, impossible to adequately capture in words, of some bit of life shared by others on and off a page. Can we feel the slow motion suspension that moment offers to not rush through, scurry past? Recognize it for the hard-won ecstasy it represents in the rich potential of school literacies? Something has happened that knocks you a little sideways. Can I sense it as the fragile gift it is, so easily shattered by dismissal, discomfort, pity, fear, the press of curricular expectations? Can I follow Megan's lead and invite it to be present and to return, in a conversation, a squeeze of a shoulder, a look that tries to convey an appreciation for what that just meant for *you?* Yet, it is also an invitation for experience to be present as a small moment in a personal narrative, a reading response, a persuasive paragraph, a poem, a point of departure for a research report—in whatever form the day and the curriculum offers at any given point.

What does affect offer in these classroom moments? For one, affect as pedagogical lens requires recognizing these moments as extraordinary, as instances of the affectively charged air that all are always breathing in classrooms, whether consciously realized or not in the unfolding of a day. In this way, those Lunch Bunch scenes are illustrations of the "ordinary affect" Stewart (2007, p. 128) describes as:

> a surging, a rubbing, a connection of some kind that has impact. It's transpersonal or prepersonal—not about one person's feelings becoming another's but about bodies literally affecting one another and generating intensities: human bodies, discursive bodies, bodies of thought, bodies of water.

The father/brother -missing, -longing, -dreaming, -wariness in the children's and my response to *Amber and Essie* certainly resonates with the necessary shift Leander and Boldt (2013) describe as the need to consider literacy "activity as not projected toward some textual end point, but as living its life in the ongoing present" (p. 27). At the same time, though, this interaction cannot be extricated from its presence in school, its very *being* as part of school literacies. In Lunch Bunch, all of us in that space used the language and patterns of school literacies to engage with all that was sparked by a shared text—expressing predictions, connections, phrasing responses as fully formed sentences. In Megan's classroom, the children's use of "I have a connection" consistently appeared as one of the tangible manifestations of Megan's pedagogical commitment to sanctioning and supporting all aspects of children's experiences as resources for school literacies, but, of course, pulsations of recognition defy capture in that language, any language, and come unmarked, unsignaled. Those sensations, whether or not acknowledged, are both completely a part of the language and patterns of a textual end point and completely apart from such destinations.

To return to the conundrums discussed earlier, literacy classrooms are full with the mutual intrusions and invitations of the institution and the exclusionary systems on which it is built *and* the ongoing presents of lives. Children and teachers are immersed in the language of school literacies by virtue of entering classrooms, a language of text and space that cannot help but give signals of what is valued as a means to understand, to comprehend, to connect and that, perhaps, offers currency for navigating the systems that create and sustain it. Nonetheless, of course, school literacies cannot be extricated from the curling ribbons of recognition wrapping some of us up with each other and poems of fathers, loss and incarceration. If they are sensed as of a piece, then every encounter holds affective intensities of proximal lives and distal consequences.

In this way, visioning critical–affective pedagogies and practices is not extracurricular nor extra-revolutionary. Every day, the identifications, resonances and empathies matter, for at least the reason that "The victory of a revolution is immanent and consists in the new bonds it installs between people" (Deleuze & Guattari, p. 177). Bonds, though, as the vital affective sensation of connection to another, are also always suspect in systems permeated by power. Let's hope that you can grant me my surge of connection with Malina; let it take you too to a place where you've felt a wave of recognition with someone, like the whiff of Grandpa Klein's Thanksgiving stuffing as Lara's uncle's tamales enter her house. Let's also hope, though, that you raise a skeptical eyebrow that holds me accountable for keeping power and privilege and my own culpability in view. Because that is what affect with/in the critical seems to offer, a way to sense and reject creeping dichotomies between "'bigger' structures and underlying causes" of difference and the bonds of the "reeling present" of shared humanity (Stewart, p. 4).

In the children's experiences I have shared, a tangible sense of the stakes—the vulnerability in how their stories could be used against them, the oppressive systems punctuating their experiences—have to be part of the intensities of the affective encounter. The sensations that turn to connection, empathy and advocacy (as one potential) or antipathy, pity or resentment (as another) are wired to a very different sense of what those stakes are. So, when questions creep up as I read affect–centered scholarship about where and how power is (or does not seem to be) infused in discussions and analysis, I want to listen. Those questions can serve as a challenge to be vigilant about keeping power in the frame. Otherwise, affect could be misconstrued as permission to live and love and sense in the feelings we have already named, rather than space to undo that naming.

I cannot help but identify, resonate and feel when encountering children's stories. I cannot help but wrestle the affective moment into language that imposes structure. For those reasons, affect's critical potential can only be realized if the systemic and systematic oppressions of social and institutional structures are always in view. For some, of course, life *is* that view. For others, who, like me, benefit from white supremacist, class and gender-biased and hetero-centric systems, it has to be a conscious and continual scan of the horizon. That means doubling-down on insisting that new teachers are mentored into frameworks for analyzing power and provided with analyses of how current crises (of the continued institutional sanction of the murder of African-Americans, the criminalization of border crossing, the fearmongering against Muslims, the backlashes against hard-fought LGBTQ rights, to name but a very few) are one more segment of the tentacle unfurling of history. It is necessary, then, to *always* link affect with the critical, but, given what affect offers, we might also insist that the critical also always be attentive to affect.

The practices I have explored here offer ways to envision metaphor as tangible critical–affective pedagogy. I can sense and use the pause offered in the visceral moment to "slow the quick jump" to naming, linger on the hope of accumulating moments to hush the taunts of mythical summits, feel the hug of recognition and the peeling away of appropriation in encounters with others' stories. Within the mundane catastrophes (Forter, 2007) and benign ecstasies that everyday surround and occur in classrooms, I'd better be destroyed, joyed and buoyed to action by it all.

References

Ahmed, S. (2010). Happy objects. In M. Gregg & G. Seigworth, *The affect theory reader* (pp. 29–51). Durham, NC: Duke University Press.

Anzaldua, G. (1983). Foreword. In G. Anzaldua & C. Moraga (Eds.), *This bridge called my back: Writings by radical women of color.* New York, NY: Kitchen Table: Women of Color Press.

Berlant, L.G. (2011). *Cruel optimism.* Durham, NC: Duke University Press.

Butler, J. (2004). *Precarious life: The powers of mourning and violence.* New York, NY: Verso Books.

Campano, G. & Ghiso, M. (2011). Immigrant students as cosmopolitan intellectuals. In S. Wolf, K. Coats, P. Enciso & K. Jenkins (Eds.), *Handbook of research on children's and young adult literature.* New York, NY: Routledge.

Deleuze, G. & Guattari, F. (1987). *A thousand plateaus: Capitalism and schizophrenia.* Minneapolis, MN: University of Minnesota Press.

Dutro, E. (2008). "That's why I was crying on this book:" Trauma as Testimony in Responses to Literature. *Changing English, 15*(4), 423–434.

Dutro, E. (2010). What "hard times" means: Mandated curricula, class-privileged assumptions, and the lives of poor children. *Research in the Teaching of English, 44*(3), 255–291.

Dutro, E. (2011). Writing wounded: Trauma, testimony, and critical witness in literacy classrooms. *English Education, 43*(2), 193–211.

Dutro, E. (2013). Towards a pedagogy of the incomprehensible: Trauma and the imperative of critical witness in literacy classrooms. *Pedagogies: An International Journal, 8*(4), 301–315.

Dutro, E. & Bien, A.C. (2014). Listening to the speaking wound: A trauma studies perspective on student positioning in schools. *American Educational Research Journal, 51*(1), 7–35.

Dutro, E. & Cartun, A. (2016). Cut to the core practices: Toward visceral disruptions of binaries in PRACTICE-based teacher education. *Teaching and Teacher Education, 58*, 119–128.

Dutro, E. & Zenkov, K. (2008). Urban students testifying to their own stories: Talking back to deficit perspectives. In *57th yearbook of the National Reading Conference* (pp. 172–218). Oak Creek, WI: National Reading Conference, Inc.

Ehret, C. & Hollett, T. (2014). Embodied composition in real virtualities: Adolescents' literacy practices and felt experiences moving with digital, mobile devices in school. *Research in the Teaching of English, 48*, 428–436.

Forter, G. (2007). Freud, Faulkner, Caruth: Trauma and the politics of literary form. *Narrative, 15*(3), 259–285.

Jones, S. (2012). Making sense of injustices in a classed world: working-poor girls' discursive practices and critical literacies. *Pedagogies: An International Journal, 7*, 16–31.

Leander, K. & Boldt, G. (2013). Rereading "A pedagogy of multiliteracies:" Bodies, texts, and emergence. *Journal of Literacy Research, 45*, 22–46.

Massumi, B. (2002). *Parables for the virtual: Movement, affect, sensation.* Durham, NC: Duke University Press.

Radstone, S. (2007). Trauma theory: Contexts, politics, ethics. *Paragraph, 30*(1), 9–29.

Stewart, K. (2007). *Ordinary affects.* Durham, NC: Duke University Press.

Zournazi, M. (2003), "Navigating movements: An interview with Brian Massumi." Retrieved from http://www.theport.tv/wp/pdf/pdf1.pdf

5

ASSEMBLING DESIRE, LOVE AND AFFECT IN AN ART MUSEUM SCHOOL

Jonathan Eakle and Tatiana I. Sanguinette

The work at hand is an assemblage comprised of art, desire and love—the latter about its "dreams of wide open space" and strange circulating, affective flows (Deleuze & Guattari, 1972/2000, p. 120)—that passed in and around an emblematic art museum school. This assemblage is deliberately and expressly cut from desire and the productive traversals between content (e.g., of institutions and other bodies) and forms of expression (Buchanan 2015; Deleuze & Guattari, 1980/1987; Phillips, 2006), particularly those involving art, whose principal aim is to produce affects and sensations (Deleuze, 1981/2002; Deleuze & Guattari, 1991/1994). Moving through following lines are matters of power, race, belonging, loss, identity, flows of capital and so on, rippling with intensities.

In the middle of this assemblage is a love event, a fantasy comprised of enacted, passionate literacies tenuously anchored in space and time in order to follow the "detours" that desire can take (c.f., Berlant, 2012, p. 77). These desiring literacies go well beyond engagements with printed texts on paper or electronic screens, although there are bits of such printed bodies ticking through the assemblage. Rather, the literacies below travel along in multimodal ways, of sorts, from The New London Group (1996) and beyond (e.g., Eakle, 2007, 2015, 2017; Leander & Boldt, 2013; Leander & Rowe, 2006) to a connective reading and writing of the world and affects (in other words, this is the stuff of moving "rhizome" books and not those of steady state institutions, Deleuze & Guattari, 1980/1987).

Moreover, this love event and related matters, like other events, "has no present. It rather retreats and advances in two directions at once, being the perpetual object of a double question: What is going to happen? What has just happened?" (Deleuze, 1990/2004, p. 63). Vibrating in this middle territory of event are fluid oscillations of affect, intensities and sensations, and, to one side of this middle space, are accumulations of time, historical debris, that funneled toward something like a lightning strike or a slash of a knife, Hitchcock-like, coming out of nowhere, flung from a "what has just happened," as follows . . .

Historical Debris of Institutions, Art and Humans: What Just Happened?

The Golden Age of Rockemellon

Our story begins rather dryly by turning to a great archival wall of past history, to a most romantic 19th-century period when the Rockemellon School of the Arts and Design (a pseudonym) was established by its wealthy namesake as a fusion of an extraordinary art museum and education institution. It was one of the first such institutions in the United States, located in a grandiose Beaux-Arts-style building near the center of political power in Washington DC, and chartered by the federal government. Over decades, presidents, kings, military generals and other dignitaries walked Rockemellon's labyrinths and vast galleries, and the art collection eventually grew to house an extensive multibillion dollar art collection from which its students and teachers could learn and draw inspiration in the most humanist and progressive of ways.

> [Note: We, like Braidotti (2013) put our cards on the table before inching further; we "are none too fond of Humanism, or of the idea of the human which it implicitly upholds," laced with racial, economic and gender superiority, and so forth (p. 16). Instead, we come and write from a space that only glances back to that master model in relation to the art museum school, aware of those, such as Spivak, Kristeva, Deleuze and Foucault, who successfully dismantled humanism, and also knowing full well, that "Vitruvian Man rises over and over from his ashes" (p. 29), slasher-horror-movie-like, visible through recent United States political movements and national elections. In short, like other authors of the present volume, we have little interest in retrieving Humanism from the rubble of history—borrowing from the opening pages of this volume: it's not where we want life to return or go.]

For more than a century, Rockemellon was a much-loved focus of the local arts and humanities community's activities, and it hosted workshops and traveling art shows of international stature. Along the way, it wore on its sleeves and monumental banners great masterpieces of the romanticized era of its origin and the accompanying United States Westward Expansion and acquisitions of territory. These art museum school banners carried themes of the killing of the last buffaloes on vast prairies, railroads penetrating landscapes and narratives of a grand, dreamy painting of a mountain vista named for, and sold to, Rockemellon himself, for a king's ransom.

As with many leading centers of the arts and humanities, the museum school matured through the decades and consistent with late modern attitudes, it thrived on pushing against political, social and creative boundaries, while it promoted civil rights, social justice and equality through liberation pedagogies; Rockemellon often did so by producing mammoth art shows with intensities, sensations and affects.

Rockemellon's Slow Death and Wake

Progressive and independent as it seemed during these late modern years, Rockemellon was dependent on, in fact, wedded to outside institutional and wealthy donor support. The extent of that bond to institutions and private donors, particularly their capital, became clear in the late 20th century when it announced plans to display a high profile, controversial exhibit containing passionate homoerotic bodies, sometimes in chains and leather, and with various corporal penetrations. The mere mention of the themes and content of this planned show stirred intense affects along Washington corridors that radiated outward to the larger public. In the end, Rockemellon folded from the pressures of rightwing congressional and other conservative bodies, and abruptly killed the show.

Partly because of the fallout from this high-profile folding to conservative politics—and the affective ripples it caused in the liberal arts community—alongside high art-conservation costs, massive building disrepair, rumors of mismanagement and so on and so forth—the art museum school began to bleed red ink, leading to, as one of its former directors claimed: "a desperate situation," similar to those of other visionary art endeavors of the late 20th century (e.g., The Barnes Foundation; see Anderson, 2013; Rosenblum, 2010). Over more recent years, multiple efforts to keep the original Rockemellon vision of a progressive art museum school intact crumbled.

The historical debris of the past, fueled with sad passions (Spinoza, 1677/2003) and anxious, depressive public affects (c.f., Berlant, 2011; Cvetkovich, 2012), and years of litigation and legal wrangling to solve its fiscal troubles, led to Rockemellon's final dissolution as an independent art organization. The dissolution brought about grief-ridden affects circulating among local patrons, students and faculty, which were made palpable by a public mock funeral service held for Rockemellon complete with coffin, hearse, tombstones and tearful, mourning-clad participants who included well-known artists, city politicians and museum sponsors. On Rockemellon's closing day, stunned members of the art community were frozen motionless in the colossal marble atrium space of the museum, not knowing which way to go, until being nudged outward to the streets by tearful museum security personnel. A museum institution had been put to rest alongside the corpses of its humanist dreams and desires.

Yet, during the Rockemellon dissolution, wake and closure, there were inklings of its resurrection: announcements were made that its multibillion dollar art collection, although divorced from the school, would be accessioned by another major national museum down the powerful corridors of Washington, a few hundred yards away, and its school of art would be reimagined under major research university oversight and remain in its grand architecture. Pulsing through all of these circumstances were powerful literacies enacted among diverse bodies that were comprised of legal texts, priceless art and other material bodies, human and otherwise, that caused radiations of affects, after affects, and intense, rippling movements.

There were also months of denial by members of the old Rockemellon school as they desperately tried to hold on to its glorious, rotting, humanist body (and their related jobs, ideals, programs of study, etc.). A most crushing final moment for them arrived a few months after the legal die described above had been cast: a heavy wooden gangplank suddenly appeared jutting out of the grand Rockemellon portal, which is guarded by two large bronze lions. And, save for a few deeply entrenched architectural elements of the museum's Beaux-Arts structure, the entire vibrant art collection was hauled away. It was during this heart-sinking institutional transfer of art and other transitions of bodies that an art arrangement (installation) expressly about love, unfurled subsequently, was conceived and designed for display in a Rockemellon gallery.

The histories and notions presented in the preceding lines of this present chapter section about vibrant human and nonhuman matters, spaces, legal actions and other debris have been established as part of an archival wall, museum-like, presently put to ink and public display, and became some of the bricks from which we, the authors, with pilfering, swarming barbarian movements spreading out, sought to use Deleuze (1970/1988), and others, to hunt down the capacity of these parts (i.e., desiring machine appendages), as well as actions and ideas of a larger body, to affect and be affected (c.f., Massumi, 2015). Our movements were powered by the editors of the present volume's calls for experimental affective contributions about literacies and their question of "where did life go?" which appeared when Rockemellon's demise had just happened.

Now, months later, Rockemellon's romantic, humanist vision is clearly dead, its body gutted of its content, last rites administered, much like the theories and institutions established by the old guards of education suggested in the opening pages of the present book. Throbbing in the background of these wakes of "what had just happened" at Rockemellon, and suspended amidst past debris and possible future, is a second question pertaining to events: what is going to happen?

Traversing Posthuman Bodies

Assemblage Grounds: In and out of Rockemellon and Different Bodies

Our assemblage of love, affect, art and wide-open literacies now crawls out from the old Rockemellon ruins and drifts to material areas and processes from which the present affective project was launched. Important to distinguishing the parts that follow is that *assemblage* can refer to different, sometimes related, ideas (Buchanan, 2015; Phillips, 2006). In art circles, assemblage is commonly known as three-dimensional pieces comprised of found objects (e.g., Joseph Cornell's art boxes/arrangements stuffed with diverse materials, scraps taken from everywhere—junkyards, sidewalks, dime stores, etc., Solomon, 1997/2015). These forms of "art arrangement" (Phillips, 2006, p. 109) can be mashups of human and other-than-human bodies (Nichols, 2016), such as will be shown below in a Rockemellon exhibition about love. However, our approach to this chapter is not by arrangement, but by way of assemblage (*agencement*, Deleuze & Guattari, 1980/1987; also see Eakle, 2017), a deliberate process expressly hinged to desire and productive traversals between content (e.g., histories, institutional structures, etc.) and forms of expression, both of which move in and out of love, affect and desire with serial connections.

Moving along with these ideas, as our chapter project advanced, we wafted through humanist, anti-human and posthuman ideas (e.g., Braidotti, 2013; St. Pierre, 2016), and landed on shifting names and pseudonyms and Deleuze and Guattari's (1980/1987) question of why we authors would even want to use our names (as chiseled way up above, below the title, like epitaphs on tombstones, and other old, worn printed text cut into museum facades and separated from life and its movements), in a collective assemblage, and lighted upon:

> Out of habit, purely out of habit [. . .] Also because it's nice to talk like everybody else, to say the sun rises, when everybody knows it's only a manner of speaking. To reach, not the point where one no longer says I, but the point where it is no longer of any importance whether one says I. We are no longer ourselves [. . .] We have been aided, inspired, multiplied.
> *(Deleuze & Guattari, 1980/1987, p. 3)*

That is to say, we (the authors) are bits and pulses of a larger collective body that in part is uncovered in the referential quotes, notes and actions passionately ripped from various historical debris marked above and below in archive fever (Derrida, 1996). This larger body is comprised of nonhuman and human bodies and their organs that scream out for "realms of the asignifying, asubjective, and faceless [. . .] *this requires all the resources of art, and art of the highest kind*" (emphasis added, Deleuze & Guattari, 1980/1987, p. 187). Yet, to convey facelessness under institutional constraints (e.g., social science publication in an organ-ized field such as literacy education) requires "small supplies of significance and sub-jectification" (Deleuze & Guattari, 1980/1987, p. 160).

As such, and with institutional ilk and "small supplies," we could say that author one is a white male research professor and artist and became temporary director of Rockemellon's art education program shortly after the dissolution agreement noted above. We could say that author two, at the time of our com-position, is an African-American female graduate student in the final year of art education study. Regarding this institutional *one-two*, we could also say, reflective of the Rockemellon institutional transition and its mournful wake, and as Deleuze (1992) points out, that we share the sense that "everyone knows that these [kinds of humanist] institutions are finished [. . .] It's only a matter of administering their last rites and of keeping people employed until the installation of the new forces knocking at the door" (p. 4); but, we did not say any of that.

Or, riding a razor's edge between forms of content and forms of expres-sion pertaining to assemblage (Deleuze & Guattari, 1980/1987) we could ask, like the frozen, mourning Rockemellon faculty and students laid out above or like Alice (in Wonderland), "which way, which way?" (sliding along Deleuze's (1990/2004) logic of sense and postulates of linguistics (Deleuze & Guattari, 1980/1987)). And, perhaps, we mused, we should safely jump on a smooth and even walkway trampled by first persons or stroll into a Do-it-Together collec-tive comprised of individuals (e.g., Maizels, 2014), hold our noses, and simply acknowledge the constraints of the times and social scientific domains that we occupy. After all, literacies education, social research and the whole body of life is rather like:

> walking as controlled falling [. . .] [which conveys] the sense that freedom, or the ability to move forward and to transition through life, isn't neces-sarily about escaping from constraints. There are always constraints. When we walk we're dealing with the constraint of gravity. There's also the con-straint of balance, and a need for equilibrium, you have to let yourself almost go into a fall [in our case at hand, perhaps a falling into love], then you *cut* it off and regain balance. You move forward by playing with the constraints . . .
>
> *(Massumi, 2015, p. 12)*

Which way, which way? Is the question of our event (and times) and in it we decided to turn our backs to the great wall comprised of individual, humanist, independent first-person bodies—the past—and, at least for a while, pivot toward affective intensities (in any case, in the end, art aims to produce affects) and jump on Deleuze and Guattari's witch's line, whereon notions of individuals dissolve, multiply, crossover and are hurled at great, interlocking and powerful signifying walls (c.f., Barthes, 2001; Deleuze & Guattari, 1980/1987; Foucault, 1997).

In this vein, the chosen experimental plan(e) and trajectory of what follows is pitched to other bodies, second persons. That is to say: *you* become part of the present assemblage because *you* were always a part of it. Subsequently, with blurring moves among bodies, the second person becomes professor, becomes artist, becomes audience, becomes student and perhaps becomes other vibrant bodies, such as swinging chandeliers. And, in the end, you might ask "What is it like to be a bat?" (Nagel, 1974); or as did Alice: "Do cats eat bats [. . .] do bats eat cats?" (Carroll, 1865/2005); and, you might ponder, as did we while moving along, that even "my own inner experience is inaccessible to me," as Shaviro writes (2010, p. 26). In sum, if you choose to continue, *you* are glued and entangled in a middle space, an event of folding and unfolding assemblage that teeters on an arrangement about love exhibited at the old Rockemellon as it was dying.

Affect and Movement around a Show of Love

You pass along the corridors of power and through the Rockemellon grand threshold that once bore a purged inscription "Dedicated to Art," carrying along a research notebook, fantasy, a whistle and a tune. The threshold itself is fantasy-like with great bronze lions, hints of gold, human guards and Greek goddesses alive in veins of marble. Sparkling from an upper room, slivers of painted gems wink down, and a romantic love poem of color and "light that sets birds to dreaming in the trees" (Verlaine, 1869) vibrates through your body. You think utopian bodies in series: Dewey, Marx, Barnes and of de Stihl, Bauhaus and the Black Mountain progressive arts experiment (Duberman, 1972), and of buzzing parts of student and faculty bodies merged with nonhuman bodies, vibrant matter (Bennett, 2010; 2015), rare earth paint, silver nitrite gurgling down drainpipes and hanging on images, chipped porcelains and so on and so forth, in lovely creative art processes unfolded in sticky, happy affects (Ahmed, 2010).

You think with joyous extension and of Spinoza (1677/2003) as you gaze up at a loving embrace of two nude figures with undulating flesh, Baroque-like, which are ever so slightly frozen in luminous marble and intensely alive. You approach and make stealth contact, rubbing, touching, as human guardian eyes roll away. You likewise turn and vibrations of other nude bodies and Rockemellon ghosts, Mapplethorpe's bareback men and erect penises, point to an obscured event that, during those years before, had led to crushing affects, of anxieties, shame and to political controversies in the museum (Ellenzweig, 1992). Hovering above us all is a triangular monument to Freud and all that's attached to him, that oedipal thing.

A tired, worn love plot glides past: you, the researcher, the lover, "hungers to have her object right where she can love it" (Berlant, 2012, p. 25), which is a grim plot hatched by a "mirage of the ego that gives you an [artist] 'I' and a name to protect you from being overwhelmed by the stimuli you encounter [in this art museum school space], and/or of a social order, which teaches you to renounce your desire's excess and ambivalence" (p. 52). [Note: "We are now focusing on the space of desire in a field of scenes, tableaux, episodes, and events" p. 75.]

You face a great white wall of interlocking signifiers (Deleuze & Guattari, 1980/1987) and turn to the right and toward a museum colonnade where, among other bodies (pillars of stone and art, conference tables, sheets of plaster bearing little Greek bodies, conference tables and chairs, etc.), there rests a dark, wispy graduate student who you know, wedged among yet other bodies, real and otherwise, conjured by additional sorcerers or muses: "'The Woman thou shalt never know!' the impossible ideal, not of love, but of artistic passion, pursued by hearts from youth to age, always in vain!" (Hearn as cited by Bisland, 1906, p. 114). There hums the drone of desiring production not to fill a void, but to leap a crevice toward the future, to desperately make something, to capture sensations as enduring as a museum, as Cézanne might say.

Cast in vain winds, compasses whirling, you both crisscross in mutual event. You talk of love's passions and its archives, of art and affect and the possibilities of facing these sensuous diverse bodies and these actual archival and concrete walls, including those of faint memories and even fainter hearts, and art arrangements you had put together at Rockemellon that are now dismantled but ever present and of drawing blood, flesh and nerve from it all. And, then, you turn to the side and to another space comprised of endless vibrating pools of desire, by devising (mapping) a plan(e) (or, as Deleuze, 1988/1993, might put it, "cartography-art," p. 66) to traverse these two independent dimensions of forms, content and expression, in an assemblage driven by desire (*agencement*, Deleuze & Guattari, 1980/1987) to provoke a "what will happen?" kind of space.

Grounds of a Love Chapter

You know that each year at Rockemellon, a major year-end art show is put together to promote the "brilliance and promise" of its graduating students, as school administrators and other official mouths describe it. This year an exhibition of over 100 working art parts is hooked up and put into motion as rumors circulate that it would be the last one like it ever to be held, due to the art museum dissolution contracts. Paradoxically, in the suspended state of the question "what is going to happen" (to faculty jobs, current students' programs of study, etc.) the student exhibition is called "Next." Despite depressing affective waves radiating throughout the school from the removal of its art collection and the sad passions and fears of impending job losses, and so on, the show goes on and you are pulled along and into the theatrical flow.

Opening night and you watch as a general public passes between the two cold, metal-coated lions and through Rockemellon's broken portal, with its 4000-pound-bronze-coated-oak doors swaying on weak hinges, for the first time since the multibillion dollar art collection has been shuttled away. On marble floors and among Doric columns are traces of transition: a cool, smooth enclave that once held a stone Artemisia, goddess of nature, is empty, lonely; and, at the top of a towering staircase where weeks before held *Immortal Love* (sensuous, undulating rock made bare flesh in rapture; French, 1923) now stands an overweight and hollow male torso, headless, cast by a student in clay. You sigh.

Turning and gliding across the Rockemellon's grand atrium and heading due north is "Dasein," a student art arrangement, which is a half-open and half-closed off temporary room comprised of two walls. Hammered to one wall is a mounted trophy head of a blue-white man with horns, and there is a floor of crunchy dead leaves and a canopy of lifeless branches. Being here and there is a near, but "not yet" space; and, shuddering, in the end, and on stage, is death that "*stands before us—something impending*" (Heidegger, 1927/1962, pp. 293–94). Next, impending, in a state of suspension, you wonder if the blue-white devil is a jab to those bringing down the old Rockemellon romantic vision and its ghosts.

To Dasein's side a university provost taps a microphone and speaks to an audience of walls, leaves, branches, hollow clay torsos, potential donors, artists, students, faculty and other bodies about Rockemellon changes, university visions and new beginnings. Nearby, plaster crumbles and falls from a ceiling, gallery lights flicker and sirens blast from a White House motorcade. Bodies disperse and rove to and fro and into a labyrinth of monumental galleries; one spits out digital waves and whirs, and still another is of wide open spaces dripping from murals, light and nature. Turning bodies and corners, you think of serial love and love's repetitions, as light is eaten up by an odd, dark exhibition room where a veiled plaster form hovers over a laid out coffin; dead Syrian names looping on audiotape are called out and recorded ambulance sirens radiate through barred museum windows and meld to the blasting ones in the outside streets.

Spinning by Syria and closer into the heart of the museum, bodies crash into a barrier: a padlocked door with a slit opening to a Versailles-like room that leaks crystal chandeliers and gold gilded oak loved and rescued earlier from a grand French hotel by a rich industrialist. Barely absent is a headless African "Girl on a Globe," Victorian clad, Dutch wax fabric wavering on warmed slick earth (Shonibare, 2011), that was evacuated days before, with other bodies of art, to the national museum nearby. Behind the door is another barricade: a metal cage that is scarcely visible; and before it is a uniformed guard with walkie-talkie crackles. Beyond the cage, an escape on musical refrain—throbbing with strings and hung with love (hear The National, 2010). Serial love repetition, again . . . Tingling, stuttering, a tear hangs, drops and flows through to the other side of the gilded wall and into *Love, Chapter One* (Figure 5.1).

Love, Chapter One

Again, and repeating from above: "each love is serial [. . .] once again, 'beyond' lies the ultimate, at the point where the assemblage changes, where the assemblage of love is superseded by an artistic assemblage" (Deleuze & Guattari, 1980/1987,

FIGURE 5.1 *Love, Chapter One* [art arrangement]. T. I. Sanguinette, 2015

pp. 438–439). Before "beyond," and with steps back and forward, like an geographer measuring scales, distances and spaces, you approach your *Love, Chapter One*, a Rockemellon art arrangement, and see that it is part of a broader machine-like assemblage fueled by desire. Your image of it centers on your somewhat ordered, clean, white, yes white, full bed, which holds your body's imprint [and, in it the traces of a previously self-identified "queer black woman artist" who, years earlier, had arrived at Rockemellon, what you came to perceive as a mostly white elite art school, carrying with you the desire for a smashing career in art, to be immersed in and produce art, to place your art on public display in magnificent halls and galleries, and to achieve respect and acceptance at Rockemellon and beyond; all is desiring production . . .].

Stepping back and yet again forward, and on to an exhibition classroom stage, you quiver as you present the germinal ideas of the art arrangement, *Love, Chapter One*, for critique by other Rockemellon art students and their faculty; your clean, white bed sketches are compared with a notorious art arrangement (Emin, 2016) that is comprised of pill packets, used condoms and "her own bed in all its embarrassing glory. Empty booze bottles, fag butts, [urine and menstrual-flow] stained sheets, worn panties, the bloody aftermath of a nervous breakdown" (Saatchi Gallery, 2016, n. p.) tossed together by a renegade artist. Although *Love, Chapter One* puts to public stage similar intimacies and confessions, you know that it is about other textures: a lovemaking place, a nest, a harbor, a safe space where among other things, books, cards, letters and dreams are read with love, in love, and by love. You think these and their complexities are literacies of highest order.

In a still further forward time and space, abandoned to an underground corner is a clean, white bed you borrow from a landlord's basement storage and haul through the city to Rockemellon. Along the way, it vibrates with you in fits and starts, with whirring pickup engines and DC potholes as waves fill your body and reach for crescendo. Down and into a similar cavern, a small Rockemellon studio, you put the bed to temporary rest; you paint a chair white, label it off limits in a literacies of limit, to be included in the impending museum show. Before its placement, in a wave of troubled rage He, bursting strong white male, appears and crushes your chair to little pieces. His blows leave behind a hole wider than a church door.

Trembling in the wake of this happening and its after affects and to be present, to fill the holey space, you take the wooden pieces and cobble together another art piece about pain and longing as a companion to your love chapter art, to hurl this violence out and away from your loving bodies. A mirror is procured that is precisely like the one from your mother's house, and takes its place alongside the bed in your art studio.

To another side and passing the mother mirror, underfoot pieces of art scatter as you, research book clasped between throbbing breast and hand, measure and survey the student art around you, the bed and the narrow spaces that it occupies. You trip by pieces; you teeter on the constraint of balance, almost fall, *cut* it off and regain balance (c.f., Massumi, 2015). Thoughts rush forward as you recollect Kafka's cramped writing spaces and Deleuze and Guattari in 1975—a becoming year for you—and muse with Marcelina who told you about these cramped spaces in the Illinois springtime (Piotrowski, 2016); you exhale and retrace impossible ideals, "not of love, but of artistic passion, pursued by hearts from youth to age, always in vain" (Hearn, as cited by Bisland, 1906, p. 114), the intensities that fueled and filled the years in between, and the bodies, human and otherwise, through which desire flowed.

You think of earlier days and a "24X24 inch piece of flat wood on which was applied white gesso and hand-sanded to create a smooth painting space" . . . and a "dark background," from which a grid "completely covered with lines of variable inflection" (i.e., Baroque folds (Deleuze, 1988/1993, p. 27)) which is produced with "lines and measurable speeds, [that] constitutes an *assemblage*" (p. 4) (Eakle, 2017). You pass 'round Rockemellon corners among affect and capacities of bodies to be affected and are absorbed by silver metal captured and escaping from flat, even emulsions, draining toward one of the school's abysmal black, wormy holes. Left behind and tentatively fixed, by hypo and on photographic compositional planes, shiny particles pick up slivers of luminosity as they drip out of the dark room and into public view. You want to linger on this non-human edge of light and dark.

To another side, before the mother mirror you stand and cut a single curl of hair from that small, soft spot between nape of neck and the back of your head. A solitary lock is laid to table, and you think: "oh, Black women and their hair . . ." You want it to look a certain way. You don't want it to be dead straight.

You don't want it to be this thick, coarse texture. You want it to be like it could belong to anyone. Add water to make it softer, straighter. Pressing and smoothing it out. Aesthetically perceived, it needs to be altered and authored. You don't want it to be part of something that does not want you. You want to be part of what is here in this art school. Desiring to belong. This lock was a part of you. A remnant you will offer up to be judged. To be respected. You say it is about respect. Belonging. And balance. Love is each.

You think about affect, sensations and passing through thresholds of intensities, the slings and arrows of shocking romances; and, *Don Juan's Reckless Daughter* (Mitchell, 1977). "Walking [and the] constraint of balance, and a need for equilibrium, you have to let yourself almost go into a fall, then you *cut* it off and regain balance. You move forward by playing with the constraints." (Massumi, 2015, p. 12). You fall in love sometimes and sometimes fall back up and out. Desire hums along as you stagger to balance.

Turning in dark silhouette you shed tears. You didn't want to become that . . . You are not proud of the choice and that dreadful cut. You don't want to let loose your dark roots. You shiver, sink and sigh. You don't like these feelings. Refracted in the mirror is a menacing white table, your lock of smoothed hair and a lamp that bends over in wavelets of light; and, the hair, the lamp, the mirror, the bed and other fragments are gathered together and made ready to move into public view as art, because in the end:

> We always make love with worlds [. . .] [which are opened up] to masses and large aggregates.
>
> *(Deleuze & Guattari, 1972/2000, p. 295)*

Turning Down a Bed to Love

In the half light of next early morning and with birds that have long passed their dreaming in trees, the collected pieces in your studio open toward the art arrangement; the bed, with other moving body parts, is hauled upstairs to Rockemellon's Gallery 43. The table finds its place to the left, with circling rose quartz, the lock of hair you cut, written words between covers, a vase, red tulips and a long-kept wrinkled letter upon which "I'm sorry" is scrawled over and over and over and over again, as if forever, and on verso: "The last thing I ever wanted to do is hurt . . ." As you make the bed and hang the mirror, it catches your gaze and reverberates with the long serializations of your loves. A tape recorder is tested with anonymous voices, friends, family and strangers, bodies flowing together, murmuring what love is:

> Love is connection; love is magic; love is freedom; love is laughter; the color pink, and also purple . . . in the ocean and throughout our bodies; in the edge of our fingertips; love is consistency even when that means consistently

> inconsistent; love is this moment . . . love is in words, the arrangement, the feelings, the sentences and sentience . . . love is a line and a boundless plane, love is also the boundlessness; love is in the music, the songs that never get old and the moments they take you to; love is tingles . . .

Sheets are tucked, pillows positioned and the quilted white spread is furled to gallery and smoothed out. A book tumbles from a shelf as almost afterthought; it's *All About Love* (hooks, 2000). You try to find that special page in it; you thought it was marked, you read it during that lovely time; it has a black woman's voice; you want to make it your own as you read with love, in love and all about love.

The white cotton sheets are unfolded to one side and you take the daring leap, a lover's leap, to sleep in the gallery at the heart of a museum. You have to experience it, and to make it a safe place; you drift in and out of the book of love as fellow art students pass around the gallery preparing exhibit spaces as you nod. The foot of the bed, your foot, reaches out to a sculptor who works wet clay across the room with no intention, only in process, as moist earth passes around fingers, breathing, forming, reforming, intuitively rising and collapsing as people come and go and meld with clay. You flutter, close your eyes and dream a lovely forgotten dream.

Morning rise and rose quartz pebbles circle round bed, smooth, body-warmed sheets, and on the sleeping white spread, your book is laid to rest among other corpses of literacies and love past: a cache of printed notes, stacks of postcards from here and there, west of sun and east of moon, snapshots, filled journals, writing instruments and coupling flowers brought together in strange dialogue. In a distant atrium space, a provost taps a microphone and talks about visions and campaigns of capital. Flows. Syrian sirens pass around corners only to be drowned by the anonymous voices of recorded love looping through the spaces of your Gallery 43:

> Love is an immeasurable higher consciousness and manipulates the flow of the current reality and merges vibrations that are taken as lessons and live as memories. [Chuckles] Love, love, love is an ancient reality, ultimately a spirit in itself; love is an experience I had in first grade when my teacher . . . allowed us to take our shoes off and play in the mud; love is being at home; Corinthians, love is patient, love is kind; love is choosing . . .

As the recorded voices circle along, and other bodies crowd around, you leave Gallery 43 for a break from love. Resting, turning and returning, you are jarred by a scattering of your rose quartz pebbles, once beaming with love, neatly circled and by a violent reshuffling of your bed texts. Kneeling, the stone circuit around the bed is remade; rising, the bed texts are not as easily re-placed. Restacked to the top of a pile of cards is a *Head of a Moor* (Regnault, 1870, Figure 5.2), a painting of a dark, powerful romantic man who you had loved and hidden, secured below, among other postcards and paper. "He was your treasured love, kept safe in the shadows."

FIGURE 5.2 *Head of a Moor.* [oil on canvas] H. Regnault, 1870

You look up at the mirror. You wonder why someone had penetrated your love, stirred and exposed your Moor; you tremble in affective excess; you knew that bodies move and change; you are open to that; and, after all, you are making art about love and sometimes love is messed up. Yet, a wave of feeling enters your gut, a little jab rises, as you wonder if the Moor had been forced to the surface of your neat arrangement to remind you that you are a Black woman and in a world of the other. Suddenly, children rush across the gallery to your bed, jumble on it; toss its sheets, laughing. You smile as vibrations gather of new beds and loves to be made, ideas to sleep on, to take in, dream and let go.

What is Going to Happen, Yet to Come

This episode skipped along material planes to explore what assemblage (*agencement*) and desire might do around love and art, constraints and creative release. It experiments with affects by toggling back and forth among body parts, art productions and exhibits of debris, and by transforming materials and processes with an aim to leap into, and to put on public display, flows of desire, love, affect and sensations. The skipping was intended to create varying speeds as it passes through different spaces of changes, identities and collectivities, and in order to put a few things out on a line, to air laundry and to toss other things to the wind and into wide open spaces. On one side of your assemblage is a crushing tide of what had just happened in the wake of an art museum school's demise where diverse people merged to one, a second person, and assembled a literacies book project about love, desire, affect and art.

What had just happened in the art museum school echoes the slow, lingering death of the wider human project of years gone by and the vain attempts to keep its corpses alive. Many of you reading the present volume, teachers, other educators and scholars, might find and lament similar death throes of arts and humanities in comparable education institutions, such as public schools where children are marked by numbers (e.g., class sizes, end-of-year test scores), fill state-of-the-art data rows and columns comprised of colors, disabilities, languages and so forth, and are stuck to old literacies in crumbling books of knowledge that separate schooling from life. In other sections of the current book, there are calls to move beyond such dehumanizing practices, or return to the human past. Yet, the human, of individualized Western, white male stature, and his ruins of war and acquisition vibrating with anger, pity, cruelty, shame and guilt—sad passions—and his longing for power over others and nature is unworthy of resuscitation, and you turn your back.

Instead, and standing on a plane with historical, human debris, you hum in a state of perception and with a longing to not recover, but leap beyond the human and the anti-human, into posthuman territory (Braidotti, 2013). On your horizon is a flight away from individualism and its greed, hurtful things and accompanying affects. Perhaps feeling a bit like a chicken scratching at a hard, cold ground, through the present chapter, you attempted a slight undertaking in this direction, falling forward, trying to find balance, swallowed by second person mergers as you assembled desire, love and affect through the happenings of an art museum school.

One of the moving pieces of your assemblage is a bed, a place of births, deaths, lovemaking, art production, reading and writing, dreaming—a smooth horizontal plane of immanence, a life (Deleuze, 2001). Left behind are vibrations that might shimmer, close things in, affectively stick, linger and provide a ground for openings through which you might teach and learn literacies of the broadest sort. Where did life go, you were asked? It never left, and throbs inside the lines of possible worlds you produce and those yet to come.

References

Ahmed, S. (2010). Happy objects. In M. Gregg & G. J. Seigworth (Eds.), *The affect theory reader* (pp. 29–51). Durham, NC: Duke University Press.

Anderson, J. (2013). *Art held hostage: The battle over the Barnes Collection.* New York, NY: WW Norton.

Barthes, R. (2001). The death of the author. *Contributions in Philosophy, 83,* 3–8.

Bennett, J. (2010). *Vibrant matter: A political ecology of things.* Durham, NC: Duke University Press.

Bennett, J. (2015). Systems and things. On vital materialism and object-oriented philosophy. In R. Grusin (Ed.), *The nonhuman turn.* (pp. 223–240). Minneapolis, MN: University of Minnesota Press.

Berlant, L.G. (2011). *Cruel optimism.* Durham, NC: Duke University Press.

Berlant, L. (2012). *Desire/love.* Brooklyn, NY: Dead Letter Office. (Also found in *Critical Terms in the study of gender,* University of Chicago Press, 2013).

Bisland, E. (1906). *The life and letters of Lafcadio Hearn*. New York, NY: Houghton Mifflin & Company.

Braidotti, R. (2013). *The Posthuman*. Cambridge, UK: Polity.

Buchanan, I. (2015). Assemblage theory and its discontents. *Deleuze Studies, 9*(3), 382–392.

Carroll, L. (2012). *Alice's adventures in Wonderland*. New York, NY: Random House. (Original work published 1865).

Cvetkovich, A. (2012). *Depression: A public feeling*. Durham, NC: Duke University Press.

Deleuze, G. (1988). *Spinoza: Practical philosophy* (R. Hurley, Trans.). San Francisco, CA: City Lights Books. (Original work published 1970).

Deleuze, G. (1992). Postscript on the societies of control. *October, 59*, 3–7.

Deleuze, G. (1993). *The fold: Leibniz and the Baroque*. Minneapolis, MN: University of Minnesota Press. (Original work published 1988).

Deleuze, G. (2001). *Pure Immanence: Essays on a Life*.Cambridge, MA: Zone Books.

Deleuze, G. (2002). *Francis Bacon: The logic of sensation*. London, UK: Continuum. (Original work published 1981)

Deleuze, G. (2004). *The Logic of Sense*. London, UK: Continuum. (Original work published 1990).

Deleuze, G. & Guattari, F. (1986). *Kafka: Toward a minor literature*. Minneapolis MN: University of Minnesota Press. (Original work published 1975).

Deleuze, G. & Guattari, F. (1994). *What is philosophy?* New York, NY: Columbia University Press. (Original work published 1991).

Deleuze, G. & Guattari, F. (1987). *A thousand plateaus: Capitalism and schizophrenia* (B. Massumi, Trans.). Minneapolis, MN: University of Minneapolis Press. (Original work published in French, as Volume 2 of *Capitalism et schizophrenie*, 1980).

Deleuze, G. & Guattari, F. (2000). *Anti-Oedipus: Capitalism and schizophrenia* (R. Hurley, M. Seem & H.R. Lane, Trans.). Minneapolis, MN: University of Minneapolis Press. (Original work published in French, as Volume 1 of *Capitalism et schizophrenie*, 1972).

Derrida, J. (1996). *Archive fever: A Freudian impression*. Chicago, IL: University of Chicago Press.

Duberman, M.B. (1972). *Black Mountain: An exploration in community*. New York, NY: Dutton Adult.

Eakle, A.J. (2007). Literacy spaces of a Christian faith-based school. *Reading Research Quarterly, 42*(4), 472–510.

Eakle, A.J. (2015). Bodies with and without organs: The literacies of a true crime sex and violence drama. In G. Enriquez, E. Johnson, S. Kontovourki & C. Mallozzi, (Eds.), *Literacies and the body: Theories and research on teaching, learning and embodiment* (pp. 221–235). New York, NY: Routledge.

Eakle, A.J. (2017). Baroque, break out, and education without organs. *Qualitative Inquiry, 23*(9), 711–721.

Ellenzweig, A. (1992). The homoerotic photograph: Male images from Durieu/Delacroix to Mapplethorpe. New York, NY: Columbia University Press.

Emin, T. (2016). *Studio, homepage*. Retrieved April 21, 2016 from http://www.traceyemin studio.com/homepage/

Foucault, M. (1997). The masked philosopher. In P. Rabinow & R. Hurley (Eds.), *Michel Foucault: ethics, subjectivity and truth* (pp. 321–328). New York, NY: New Press.

French, D.C. (1923). Immortal love (aka *The sons of God saw the daughters of men that they were fair* [marble sculpture].

Heidegger, M. (1962). *Being and time*. New York, NY: Harper. (Original work published 1927).

hooks, b. (2000). *All about love: New visions.* New York, NY: Harper Collins.

Leander, K.M. & Rowe, D.W. (2006). Mapping literacy spaces in motion: A rhizomatic analysis of a classroom literacy performance. *Reading Research Quarterly, 41*(4), 428–460.

Leander, K. & Boldt, G. (2013). Rereading "A pedagogy of multiliteracies" bodies, texts and emergence. *Journal of Literacy Research, 45*(1), 22–46.

Massumi, B. (2015). *Politics of affect.* Cambridge, UK: Polity.

Maizels, M. (2014). Doing it yourself: Machines, masturbation, and Andy Warhol. *Art Journal, 73*(3), 5–17.

Mitchell, J. (1977). *Don Juan's Reckless Daughter.* [Audio Recording]. Asylum.

Nagel, T. (1974). What is it like to be a bat? *The Philosophical Review, 83*(4), 435–450.

The National (2010). *Vanderlyle crybaby geeks* [digital audio recording]. 4 AD. Retrieved April 21, 2016 from https://www.youtube.com/watch?v=1a1UoljLWrY

The New London Group. (1996). A pedagogy of multiliteracies: Designing social futures. *Harvard Educational Review, 66*(1), 60–93.

Nichols, J.M. (2016, February 2). ASSEMBLAGE: Meet queer artist and musician Neocamp. *HuffPost* (Queer Voices). Retrieved April 21, 2016 from http://www.huffing tonpost.com/2015/03/21/nepcamp-assemblage_n_6911512.html

Phillips, J. (2006). Agencement/assemblage. *Theory, Culture & Society, 23*(2–3), 108–109.

Piotrowski, M. (2016). Writing in cramped spaces: Doing interdisciplinary research in/ between the thousand disciplinary plateaus. Paper presented to the 12th Annual International Congress of Qualitative Inquiry. University of Illinois at Urbana-Champaign.

Rosenblum, C. (2010, February 19). Requiem for a jumble of artworks. *New York Times.* Retrieved June 22, 2017 from http://www.nytimes.com/2010/02/21/movies/21barnes. html

Saatchi Gallery (2016). *Tracey Emin, My bed* [assemblage of mattress, linens, pillows, objects]. Retrieved June 22, 2017 from http://www.saatchigallery.com/artists/artpages/tracey_ emin_my_bed.htm

Shaviro, S. (2010). Consequences of panpsychism. In R. Grusin, (Ed.). *The nonhuman turn.* Minneapolis, MN: University of Minnesota Press.

Shonibare, Y. (2011). *Girl on a globe 2.* [Dutch wax printed cotton, globe]. Retrieved June, 22, 2017 from https://www.nga.gov/collection/art-object-page.175808.html

Solomon, D. (2015). *Utopia parkway: The life and work of Joseph Cornell.* New York, NY: Other Press. (Original work published 1997).

Spinoza, B. (2003). *Ethica ordine geometrico demonstrata* (R. Elwes,Ttrans.). Retrieved June 22, 2017 from http://www.gutenberg.org/files/3800/3800-h/3800-h.htm (Original work published 1677).

St. Pierre, E.A. (2016). The empirical and the new empiricisms. *Cultural Studies↔Critical Methodologies, 16*(2), 111–124.

Verlaine, P. (1869). *Clair de Lune (Moonlight)* (C.F. MacIntyre, Trans.). Retrieved June 22, 2017 from https://gladdestthing.com/poems/moonlight

6

"IT'S SOMETHING THAT REQUIRES PASSION"

After-echoes of the Ethnic Studies Ban

Alyssa D. Niccolini

Nadie: There's really no training that can prepare everyone for this kind of work. It's something that requires passion. And that's something that a lot of teachers, or educators in general, a lot of times try to avoid because—I mean, I don't know, I get the sense that people feel that it's going to present problems. And it does.

Me: Passion?

Nadie: Yeah. [*laughs*] It can present problems.

Me: In what way?

Nadie: No, I just mean in terms of some—there's always going to be someone who takes it the wrong way when you're passionate about something. That's just how it is. I mean every great philosopher, I think, has probably spoken to those kind of ideas. But—

Me: What made you passionate about it?

Nadie: What made me passionate about it is that I grew up a student who was struggling with identity. That's ultimately what I see that Mexican American Studies is all about, is getting students to be confident and strong in their identity. I was going through a lot of identity issues as a young [person] in high school.

Taught to Resent or Hate

THE LEGISLATURE FINDS AND DECLARES THAT PUBLIC SCHOOL PUPILS SHOULD BE TAUGHT TO TREAT AND VALUE EACH OTHER AS INDIVIDUALS AND NOT BE TAUGHT TO RESENT OR HATE OTHER RACES OR CLASSES OF PEOPLE.

[. . .]

A SCHOOL DISTRICT OR CHARTER SCHOOL IN THIS STATE SHALL NOT INCLUDE IN ITS PROGRAM OF INSTRUCTION ANY COURSES OR CLASSES THAT INCLUDE ANY OF THE FOLLOWING:

1. PROMOTE THE OVERTHROW OF THE UNITED STATES GOVERNMENT.
2. PROMOTE RESENTMENT TOWARD A RACE OR CLASS OF PEOPLE.
3. ARE DESIGNED PRIMARILY FOR PUPILS OF A PARTICULAR ETHNIC GROUP.
4. ADVOCATE ETHNIC SOLIDARITY INSTEAD OF THE TREATMENT OF PUPILS AS INDIVIDUALS.

(State of Arizona, 2010)

Wayward Subjects

Let me begin by invoking a ghost.

Sor Juana Inés de la Cruz is considered the Mexican patron saint of intellectual freedom. She travels daily from hand to hand in Mexico as the face of the 200 peso bill, her portrait accompanied by a poised fountain pen and an open book. Her liquid circulation in the form of currency is ironic since it was precisely her "waywardness" that was condemned and ultimately censored by the Archbishop of Mexico in the late 17th century. A prolific author of poems, essays and "social manifestos," she was an autodidact who taught herself philosophy, music, science as well as *nahuatl*, the indigenous tongue of the central Mexican highlands (Ross, 2013, n.p.). Many consider her Mexico's premier literary figure. De la Cruz was also a teacher and ardent advocate for women's right to education, quite a feat at the time, as Oakland Ross (2013) puts it, in "a nation of matadors, mescal and machismo" (n.p.). However, her outspoken voice and passionate pedagogies were short-lived, after intense critique from church clerics and the Archbishop, "she sold her library, her musical instruments, her scientific equipment. She ceased to write on any subject at all and passed the final years of her life under an imposed silence" (Ross, 2013, n.p.).

This chapter explores the after-affects of the enactment of Arizona House Bill 2281, also known as the Ethnic Studies Bill. Since 2010, the law has stoked polarized passions around education, race and freedom of speech. The years following the invocation of the law have seen a proliferation of protests, national media coverage and legal action that has set off a cascade of lingering effects or perturbations, what I term here *after-affects*. In 2017, a federal judge officially overturned the ban declaring, "The Court is convinced that decisions regarding the MAS program were motivated by a desire to advance a political agenda by capitalizing on race-based fears" (quoted in Harris, 2017). In researching HB 2281, I follow Nathan To and Elena Trivelli (2015), not to undertake the impossible task of "'uncover[ing] the origin or foundation' of a critical situation," but rather, "to trace the conditions of existence and circulation of its aftermaths" (p. 306). I am interested in what Berlant (2009) might call the "affective hangover" of the law where "loss, belatedness, risk, overwhelmedness, shame, grief, trauma, paranoia and misrecognition" (p. 262) clamor within educational spaces (and beyond).

Perturbations

Perturbations are noisy backgrounds that refuse to shut up. They signal to bodies, stimulate, provoke, disturb. One of the chief arguments of the affective turn is that the body is porous, constantly signaling and being signaled to (Brennan, 2004). The body is "ceaselessly moving messages of various kinds" (Thrift, 2007, p. 236). It is important to keep in mind that a body within a Deleuzian figuration is more than a human body. As Deleuze (1988/2001) writes, "A body can be anything; it can be an animal, a body of sounds, a mind or an idea; it can be a linguistic corpus, a social body, a collectivity" (p. 127). Massumi (2015) uses a sound figuration to describe the transmission of affect. He argues that "our bodies and lives are almost a kind of resonating chamber" whereby perturbations "strike us and run through us, [. . .] strike us and strike beyond us simultaneously" (p. 114). Affect is the felt transition, the modulation (amplification or diminishment) of the body's capacities to act (Massumi, 2002).

Nadie, an interviewee I talked to in Arizona, captures this capacity when describing their own past educational experiences:

Nadie: [. . .] I had issues that I felt like, later on, looking back, they affected my grades, especially during my freshman year. And it was at that time when I was invited to a conference [. . .] I attended the conference and—I mean it was like a whirlwind.

Me: How old were you?

Nadie: I was 16. Or—I might have been 15. But I was about to turn 16.

Me: So young.

Nadie: Yeah. And I remember—I'm just getting—I'm getting goosebumps even thinking about it, the experience, being in that room. There was about a thousand participants. It was very—I mean, at that time, it was like a resurgence of—some would say a resurgence of the Chicano movement [. . .]. There were about a thousand kids in the crowd. You had all these speakers getting up there, very passionate speakers, evoking like, I don't know, like *vibrations of the crowd* [. . .] I'm sure there's various names for it because I've heard sports teams use the same kind of clap we do, too. But it's like a clap that starts real slow and then it— everyone claps together and it gets faster and stronger. It's supposed to represent the rhythm of the movement, as people are coming together, it becomes one.

Nadie illustrates the capacity of affect to travel through a crowd. It refuses to stay contained. At the conference, they describe affect resonating between bodies making an auditorium of over a thousand people "become one." Like affect, the *vibrations of the crowd* charged the space and moved between and among bodies. In Abby Kluchin's (2012) words, affect has a "has a deeply un-Cartesian lack of respect for or knowledge of the membrane of the skin, the boundary between the self and the world" (p. 14).

Like the vibrations *Nadie* describes above, which move from the past to prickle skin with goosebumps in the present, this chapter dwells within echoing rhythms and resonances (Henriques, 2010) of the ethnic studies ban. Tapping into an assemblage of data—media reports, interviews, images, political rhetoric, a letter, legal documents, fictionalizations and sketchings—I work to dwell in the "virtual remainders" (Massumi, 2002, p. 25) that result when bodies (here humans, books, institutions, laws and an assemblage of texts) encounter and *move* each other. Affect theory may help us find new modes of feeling out how literacies act on bodies in ways that don't privilege individualized bodies, contained texts or single sources. *Affect is the body reading the world.*

This brief chapter is then not an attempt to exhaustively cover the event of HB 2281. Instead, I follow Sara Ahmed (2014) who declares in *Willful Subjects*, "I have relied on the sound of connection to build up a case from a series of impressions and have thus imagined the writing as poetic as well as academic" (p. 19). Toward this end, I take up Kevin Leander's and Gail Boldt's (2013) "strategic sketch" as a methodological tool. As they write, "[w]e offer the strategic sketch as an invitation to an alternate means of experiencing data—to think and feel within the possibilities of the data and not 'over' them toward conclusion" (p. 26). In contrast to the ethnographic tradition of thick description that seeks to flesh out a scene through an accumulation of detail, a sketch is the offering of an impression. By definition, a sketch is "a rough or unfinished drawing or painting, often made to assist in making a more finished picture" or to "[p]erform (a gesture) with one's hands or body" (Oxford Dictionary, 2016). We might think of affect itself as a sketch—an initial bodily responsivity, a vague hunch (Hickey-Moody, 2013) that assists in making "a more finished picture" of the world. Sketching refuses to complete an image and bears the impulse of movement—a pencil that hurries off to another line, a clumsy hand smudging past marks as it follows. Because of the highly politicized nature of this topic as well as to protect the identities of my interviewees, I mobilize sketching and fiction as a form of ethics. Sketching cottons the data, providing a buffer or filter, an intentional smudging or blurring. *Nadie* is a composite subject comprised of many voices I encountered in Arizona. I offer no contextual information about these voices and use the name *Nadie* (no one) and the plural pronoun *they* to signal to the "crowd" that is at work in all identity formations (Deleuze & Guattari, 1987).

Nadie then is a sketch, an echo, an intuition, a filter, a sense, an impression—a ghost.

I find haunting an apt metonym for researching the after-affects of HB 2281 since, as Avery Gordon (2008) writes, "haunting is one way in which abusive systems of power make themselves known and their impacts felt in everyday life, especially when they are supposedly over and done with [. . .] or when their oppressive nature is continuously denied" (Gordon, 2008, p. xvi). Haunting underscores the sketchiness of representation, as well as the refusals of histories and social violences to disappear. The brief fictional sketches I conclude with are intended to serve as affective jumps (Stewart, 2007), ghost stories, to produce sensations in addition or excess of narrative coherence.

Sensations are sketchy. As Ahmed (2017, p. 22) writes:

> A sensation is often understood by what it is not: a sensation is not an organized or intentional response to something. And that is why sensation matters: you are left with an impression that is not clear or distinct. A sensation is often felt by the skin. The word *sensational* relates to both the faculty of sensation and to the arousal of strong curiosity, interest, or excitement. If a sensation is how a body is in contact with a world, then something becomes sensation when contact becomes even more intense.

These sketches operate perhaps through a sonic and sensory connectivity—resonances, vibrations and echoes. Like filters used on images they are intended to be blurry, diffuse, incomplete.

Sounding

Haunting is often experienced as a terror of sound. The creaking of walls, a whisper, a wailing, a piercing scream in the night. Rather than giving voice to the multitude that makes up *Nadie*, which positions me as the researcher as the source of signifying agency, this chapter attempts to offer a sounding of data. To sound, as a verb, is:

> *to give forth*
> *to give forth a sound as a call or summons*:
> *The bugle sounded as the troops advanced.*
> *to be heard, as a sound*
> *to convey a certain impression when heard or read*
>
> *(Dictionary.com, italics added)*

In many ways, Arizona called to, perhaps even haunted me. As I researched book banning for my dissertation, friends and colleagues repeatedly forwarded me articles on the events in Arizona. Initially, I actively avoided researching HB 2281, fearing doing so would be a form of academic trauma tourism. I felt intensely uncomfortable about the coloniality of my white US-born middle-class New Yorker gaze in researching an event so far removed from my own teaching and schooling experience. But the event gnawed at me and kept returning in images, messages and media. It interrupted, impinged, made itself known. It made an impression. What was the greater violence, the risks of replicating the colonial gaze in my research or actively ignoring one of the most politicized curricular debates around books in contemporary schooling history? How could I *not* address HB 2281 in a project on contemporary school book bannings?

Affect—encounters that bother, irritate, provoke and move us—is a researcher's tool. Affect cues us in, urges us in certain directions, unsettles us. My body literally felt off as a New Yorker in the dry swallow of the desert when I finally travelled to Arizona. I was immediately struck by the "the affective fecundity of place" (Duff, 2010, p. 882). For Arun Saldanha (2010, p. 2414) affect *is* a form of geography:

> [A]ffect can then be said to refer to the constant self-refreshing of bodies go through their inevitable sensory and proprioceptive embedding in the world. This conception of embodiment is intrinsically geographical, as it requires tracing a body's *encounters* with objects, conditions, and other bodies, which are possible only in particular places.

This affective imprint of objects, conditions, histories and bodies in Arizona is evident in my fieldnotes:

> *I'm surprised to see a 10-foot cactus when I step out of my rental car. It seems otherworldly, the ghost of black-and-white Westerns on the TV in my grandparent's cold back bedroom. My body feels off—my hands moving a millisecond behind or ahead of how they should. The sauna heat, jet lag and the fatigue of travel shifts my relation to the world. I set the GPS to The Oasis Motel a short distance from the cafés where I'm scheduled to meet interviewees. I can feel my skin. The heat gives me a body. My phone vibrates with an unfamiliar number. "Are we still doing the interview? I'm here at the café." I'm mixed up. I've lost a day in travel. "Yes, yes. I'm on my way." I consider, for a second, cancelling, then reset my coordinates and move through the desert.*

Suspension

> "Isn't that the book graveyard where they send all the old books, never to be seen again?"
>
> "Yes."
>
> *(Korina and Lorenzo Lopez quoted in*
> *Biggers, 2012, p. 182)*

So since we're talking about ghosts, let's move to a graveyard of sorts. In 2012, a district PR statement declared that "seven books that were used as supporting materials for curriculum in Mexican American Studies classes have been moved to the district storage facility" (Rene, 2012, n.p.). The seven books were listed as:

1. *Critical Race Theory* by Richard Delgado
2. *500 Years of Chicano History in Pictures* edited by Elizabeth Martinez
3. *Message to AZTLAN* by Rodolfo Corky Gonzales
4. *Chicano! The History of the Mexican Civil Rights Movement* by Arturo Rosales
5. *Occupied America: A History of Chicanos* by Rodolfo Acuna
6. *Pedagogy of the Oppressed* by Paulo Freire
7. *Rethinking Columbus: The Next 500 Years* by Bill Bigelow

The statement was intended as a corrective for media exaggerations of prohibited materials, some claiming that as many as 50 books had been banned including, to public outrage, Shakespeare's *The Tempest* (Golgowski, 2012). Media and public confusion spread. A headline capturing public uncertainty declared, "Neither banned nor allowed: Mexican American Studies in limbo in Arizona" (Planas, 2012). To set the record straight, the PR statement refuted that any books were officially banned:

> NONE of the above books have been banned [. . .]. Each book has been boxed and stored as part of the process of suspending the classes. The books listed above were cited in the ruling that found the classes out of compliance with state law.
>
> **Every one of the books listed above is still available to students through several school libraries.** Many of the schools where Mexican American Studies classes were taught have the books available in their libraries. Also, all students throughout the district may reserve the books through the library system.
>
> *(Rene, 2012, n.p., bold and capitalization in original)*

According to the official statement, the books were not banned but were *moved* and *contained*. I find the distinction between banning and containing intriguing for thinking about affect. Affect affronts the notion that the "individual is an energetically self-contained or bound entity, whose affects are his or hers alone" (Brennan, 2004, p. 24). Affect then bears an impulse of movement between bodies, both human and non-human. In the statement above, we see that the affective capacities of books needed to be contained ("boxed and stored") in order to comply with state law. The law then is curiously predicated on seeking to foreclose affect by barring curricula and materials that may move bodies or promote resentment and revolutionary impulses. The law in part legislates affect.

One Unhappy Case

"Republicans hate Latinos." Many trace the origins of HB 2281 to these three charged words (Biggers, 2012; Harris, 2017; Kunnie, 2010; Phippen, 2015). They were delivered in a 2010 speech at a high school by a United Farm Workers leader. In "AN OPEN LETTER TO THE CITIZENS OF TUCSON," the then school superintendent recounted the moment the words were spoken:

> My Deputy [. . .] who is Latina and Republican, came to refute the allega-
> tion made earlier to the student body, that "Republicans hate Latinos."
> Her speech was non-partisan and professional urging students to think for
> themselves and avoid stereotypes. Yet a small group of La Raza Studies
> students treated her rudely, and when the principal asked them to sit down
> and listen, they defiantly walked out. [. . .] In hundreds of visits to schools,
> I've never seen students act rudely and in defiance of authority, except in
> this one unhappy case. I believe the students did not learn this rudeness at
> home, but from their Raza teachers.
>
> *(Horne, 2007, p. 2–3)*

In the scene above, teachers are charged with instilling "rude[ness]" and a "defi-ance to authority" in students. Indeed, one of the chief objections of opponents to the MAS program was the perceived political overzealousness, or affective excess, of its teachers and students. The students' act of silent protest is perceived as a form of incivility. Incivility, as Joan Wallach Scott (2015) elaborates, is often invoked in politics to invalidate particular claims. She writes:

> [T]he dissident claims of minority groups go unheard in the public sphere
> when they are tagged as departures from the protocols of style and deco-
> rum—dismissed as evidence of irrationality and so placed outside the
> realm of what is taken to be reasoned deliberation. They are, by defini-
> tion, uncivil, and thus beneath contempt. Once a certain space or style
> of argument is identified as civil, the implication is that dissenters from it
> are uncivilized. "Civility" becomes a synonym for orthodoxy; "incivility"
> designates unorthodox ideas or behavior.
>
> *(2015, n.p.)*

Charges of incivility cast speakers outside of "reasoned" political debate. The state and its agents are then figured as sites of bounded and contained rationality while the MAS program is a space of unchecked affective excess. These notions of the state as a site of bounded rationality serve as a foil to imaginaries about the Mexican–American border as "a badlands that is out of control—an unruly space in dire need of containment from the ravages of criminals, illegal aliens, terror-ists, and other undesirable threats to the national body" (DeChaine, 2012, p. 8).

The Mexican–American border "gives form to a constellation of normative and often prescriptive ideas about where America ends and something 'other' begins" (DeChaine, 2012, p. 7). Mirroring these fears, a perceived danger of the MAS program was that it dissolved borders between individuals, *desubjectifying* bodies from individually contained units ("individuals" in the words of the law) that are by proxy easily managed and governed into unruly affective collectives.

An Angry Tone

Opponents to the program frequently imagined unruly affective collectives being produced through the "tone" of MAS classrooms. For Sianne Ngai (2005) tone is "a global and hyper-relational concept of *feeling* that encompasses attitude: [the] affective bearing, orientation, or 'set toward' its audience and world" (p. 43). In the open letter above, the author relies on the words of a former teacher whom he assures readers "despite his name, is Hispanic" (Horne, 2007, p. 3). In selected quotations, the former teacher describes an affective transmission that works outside of direct language:

> But the inference and tone was anger. (They taught students) that the United States was and still is a fundamentally racist country to those of Mexican-American kids.
>
> Individuals in this (Ethnic Studies) department are *vehemently* anti-Western culture. They are *vehemently* opposed to the United States and its power. They are telling students they are victims and that they should be angry and rise up.
>
> . . .
>
> By the time I left that class, I saw a change (in the students), he said. An angry tone.
>
> *(Horne, 2007, pp. 3–4, emphasis added)*

In this statement, teachers are imagined as engineers of affect with teachers' affect spreading mimetically to students. Affect is imagined as transmissible, moving unidirectionally from teacher to student as well as being uniformly received by passive bodies. In particular, teachers' affective excess is presented as setting students against the US and Western culture writ large. Rather than *moving with* a triumphalist or feel-good narrative of US history, it is implied students are being *vehemently* set against teleologic notions of national progress and pride. This opposition was perceived as intense and affectively excessive.

I emphasize *vehemence* in the quotes above because the word was often used by opponents to describe the program's teachers, their politics and their pedagogies. Similar to how Nadie describes passion as being perceived as problematic in our opening exchange, vehemence is portrayed as pedagogical passion gone too far. Grammatically, vehemence is usually used as an intensifier—as in *vehemently disagree*. There is a cut of violence in vehemence's etymology; Google Dictionary defines it as "great forcefulness or intensity of feeling or expression." Vehemence is an apt word for thinking about affect since it could in many senses be thought of as an unstructured *intensity*. Repeated claims of MAS teachers' *vehemence* come to stand in for a diffuse marker of unchecked affective intensity.

Resenting Resentment

While vehemence was frequently mentioned, resentment was the affective state most prominently cited within opposition to the MAS program. In the open letter (Horne, 2007), the program is even termed a "resentment-based program" (p. 4). Resentment works two ways in this formulation—the program is charged with breeding resentment in students and, we might also argue, opponents to the program resented the resentment the program was thought to produce.

Resentment has a long history of being theorized as an especially political emotion (MacLachlan, 2010; Smith & Schurtz, 2013). Resentment is a socially accepted response to injury and injustice:

> Resentment is an emotion we feel when we suffer a perceived wrong. It can be a powerful, motivating state, characterized by a blend of anger, bitterness, and indignation. The hallmark of resentment is that people feeling it believe that they have a justified moral complaint against another person or general state of affairs. They believe they have suffered undeservedly.
>
> *(Smith & Schurtz, 2013, p. 658)*

Resentment names a source of harm. As MacLachan (2010) has it, "in resenting, I reject your message of disvalue and communicate the wrongness of your act" (p. 426). Likewise, in *Hard Feelings*, Macalester Bell (2013, p. 162) cites the "liability" of hard feelings which:

> hold persons accountable for their actions and faults. When I resent you [. . .], my resentment addresses a demand to you: you should not have treated me in that way, and I demand you take responsibility for your wrongdoing and attempt to make amends.

Foreclosing resentment, or *resenting resentment*, can be seen as an affective weapon to reconfigure the site and source of injustice. If I resent your resentment, *I* become the site of injustice, not you. I, at least temporarily, am relieved of an accountability of harm. Resentment then can be used as an affective weapon or "an emotional riposte" (MacLachan, 2010, p. 426) to charges of inequity.

Nadie maintains, however, that resentment was not a pedagogical goal of the program as the law alleged:

> I guess that they're saying that [learning the history is] going to create some kind of resentment. But to me, it has nothing to do with resentment. [. . .] The ultimate goal is harmony. So although that could be one of the first stages that students go through is being angry—I mean it's something that you may revisit different times in your life when things come up [. . .] But the ultimate goal is for the kids to feel confident in who they are and feel like they could live in harmony with everyone around them. Regardless of what race that person is, that we could all work together. That's ultimately what it's about and ultimately it's not even about any kind of race.

Nadie suggests that resentment is not an endpoint, a static bodily reaction, but a process that is worked through non-teleologically. It may "revisit," or perhaps using another lexicon *haunt*, bodies, but it is a temporary guest. MacLachlan (2010) explores how "many instances of resentment directed toward long-term, systemic, and collectively sustained injustice will most likely fall outside of 'reasonable' boundaries" (p. 432) and thus remain unheard. For example, the students' act of silent protest is positioned as "unreasonable" (MacLachlan, 2010) while the state politicians' resentment of the protest is presented as reasonable. The law then creates a hierarchy of reasonable (politicians') versus unreasonable (MAS teachers' and students') resentments.

Controlled Substances

Casting certain affects and emotions outside of reason while legitimizing others is part of larger processes whereby affect marks and unmarks citizen bodies (Cisneros, 2012; Muñoz, 2000). Cisneros (2012), for example, argues that Arizona's Senate Bill 1070, which was passed the same year as HB 2281, "operate[s] under an affect that the immigrant body [i]s dirty, dangerous, or disruptive. Notice that the method chosen to combat human trafficking is to target the immigrant body (rather than the crime of trafficking) as a dangerous substance that is transported, moved, concealed, or harbored" (p. 141). In a similar move, the prohibited books listed above were treated as controlled or toxic substances whose very proximity to students' bodies needed to be controlled and contained.

Mel Chen (2012) explores the growing prevalence of toxicity in popular discourse, arguing that fears about being in-toxic-ated "suggest a shift in national sentiment that registers an increasing interest in individual bodily, emotional, and psychic security" (p. 190). Intoxication, be it from lead, alcohol or toxic politics and pedagogies, underscores the body's permeability and receptivity to other bodies. Chen (2012) submits that notions of toxicity are thus tied to "ideas of vulnerable sovereignty and xenophobia" (p. 168) "reflect[ing] an effort to externalize—but also to indict for [a] threatening closeness (to home)" (p. 191). If affect reveals the porosity of the body, we can see why opponents to the MAS program so vehemently sought to stop and contain affect. Affect crosses borders. In many ways, the MAS curriculum and the affects it produced were imagined as a stable body, a fixed set of content to be governed much like a geographical region or nation state. But like ghosts, affects don't respect the boundary of the skin (Kluchin, 2012; Zembylas, 2007).

And bodies, texts and affects indeed failed to stay contained.

Packing Up

Nadie: I started packing up my material, a lot of material that I had. Some of these students came in and they asked: What are you doing? I said: I'm packing everything up since it's illegal. And I was putting away some curriculum I had. And they requested it. They wanted it. And I said: Well, I'm not going to be able to teach it now, so I might as well give it to you guys. So a lot of the stuff that was my personal copies, I gave to them.
[. . .]

Nadie: But this girl, she was real passionate about it. I mean, I forgot when it was, but one of the days during all of this struggle, she said I'm going to be symbolic. I'm going to put tape over my mouth, and I'm going to write—she got a blank shirt and she wrote: *You can silence my voice, but never my spirit.* I guess it was symbolic of the censorship she felt was being dealt to us.

Rental Car

It's Friday night, my last day in Arizona. I have a few hours until I have to head to the airport. I write fieldnotes, look at my phone. I pay my check at a local restaurant and enter a swarm of bodies on the street. It's getting dark and there's a buzz in the air. Excitement, energy. An event. Drums pulse. I hear mariachi music. Trumpets blast and an ululation echoes against the concrete wall I'm parked behind. Heyayay a yayayaa a yayayayaa! The call is a grito, a shout that can signal at once a cry of despair, a call to battle and a laugh. As I get into my car to head to the airport, I watch a silver balloon in the shape of a heart lift into the sky. I trace its path across the streetlights and then higher into the blue darkness above. I sit in the dark calm of my rental car not sure if it's occasion to hope or despair to laugh or to cry.

How Much There Is to Be Said

In a box of books rests Sor Juana Inés de la Cruz's (1691/2008) lauded *Respuesta a Sor Filotea.* A passionate girl picks it up and takes it home. She reads these lines:

I returned to my studious task (I misspeak, for I never stopped); nay, I mean, I continued reading and reading more, studying and studying more, with only books themselves for a teacher.

(de la Cruz, 1691/2008, p. 7)

(Or perhaps these:)

> According to St. Augustine, some things are learned as a tool for action, whereas others are learned only for knowledge: *Discimus quaedam, ut sciamus; quaedam, ut faciamus.*
>
> *(de la Cruz, 1691/2008, p. 29)*

(Or perhaps these:)

> I've nearly decided to leave the matter in silence, yet silence would be a negative choice even though it explains a lot by placing emphasis on no explanation; therefore, it is necessary to put a short label on this so that you understand what silence is meant to convey; for if I fail to label it, silence will say nothing, because such is its proper function: to say nothing. [. . .] Therefore, it is even necessary to say that those things that cannot be said so that we understand that keeping quiet is not not having anything to say, but rather that words cannot convey how much there is to be said.
>
> *(de la Cruz, 1691/2008, pp. 2–3)*

A Grito

A passionate girl goes to the bathroom on the first floor. She slowly takes out the contents of her backpack. They echo on the metal shelf above the sink. The smell of bleach mingles with Sharpie and makes her dizzy. From a classroom down the hall there is the faint sound of clapping.

She looks into the mirror, the rhythm of her breath mixing with the rhythm of hands. She speaks quietly at first, her voice strange against the white tiles

discimus quaedam, ut sciamus; quaedam, ut faciamus
the clapping and her voice get louder and stronger

the clapping is everywhere and nowhere
some things we learn to know, some things to do

she has to yell to be heard amidst the many hands
some things we learn to know

the walls vibrate
some things to do

somewhere
a cry that can signal at once despair, a call to battle, and a laugh
some things—

she covers her mouth.

References

Ahmed, S. (2014). *Willful subjects*. Durham, NC: Duke University Press.

Ahmed, S. (2017). *Living a feminist life*. Durham, NC: Duke University Press.

Arizona, State of (2010). House Bill 2281. Retrieved from: http://www.azleg.gov/legtext/49leg/2r/bills/hb2281s.pdf

Bell, M.(2013). *Hard feelings: The moral psychology of contempt*. Oxford, UK: Oxford University Press.

Berlant, L. (2009). Neither monstrous nor pastoral, but scary and sweet: Some thoughts on sex and emotional performance in *Intimacies* and *What do gay men want? Women & Performance: A Journal of Feminist Theory, 19*(2), 261–273.

Biggers, J. (2012). *State out of the union: Arizona and the final showdown over the American dream*. New York, NY: Nation Books.

Brennan, T. (2004). *The transmission of affect*. Ithaca, NY: Cornell University Press.

Chen, M. (2012). *Animacies: Biopolitics, racial mattering, and queer affect*. Durham, NC: Duke University Press.

Cisernos, J.D. (2012). Looking "illegal:" Affect, rhetoric, and performativity in Arizona's Senate Bill 1070. In D.R. DeChaine (Ed.), *Border rhetorics: Citizenship and identity on the US–Mexico frontier* (pp. 133–150). Tuscaloosa, AL: University of Alabama Press.

DeChaine, D.R. (2012). Introduction: For rhetorical border studies. In D.R. DeChaine (Ed.), *Border rhetorics: Citizenship and identity on the US–Mexico frontier* (pp. 1–18). Tuscaloosa, AL: University of Alabama Press.

de la Cruz, I.J. (2008). Answer by the poet to the most illustrious Sister Filotea de la Cruz (W. Little, Trans.). Retrieved from: http://dept.sfcollege.edu/hfl/hum2461/pdfs/sjicanswer.pdf (Original work published 1691).

Deleuze, G. (2001). *Spinoza: Practical philosophy*. San Francisco, CA: City Lights Publishers. (Original work published 1988).

Deleuze, G. & Guattari, F. (1987). *A thousand plateaus: Capitalism and schizophrenia*. Minneapolis, MN: University of Minnesota Press.

Duff, C. (2010). On the role of affect and practice in the production of place. *Environment and Planning D: Society and Space, 28*, 881–895.

Golgowski, N. (2012). Shakespeare's work axed in Arizona schools as law bans "ethnic studies." Retrieved from: http://www.dailymail.co.uk/news/article-2087667/Shakespeares-The-Tempest-banned-Arizona-schools-law-bans-ethnic-studies.html

Gordon, A. (2008). *Ghostly matters: Haunting and the sociological imagination*. Minneapolis, MN: University of Minnesota Press.

Harris, T. (2017). Arizona ban on ethnic studies unconstitutional: U.S. judge. Retrieved from: https://www.reuters.com/article/us-arizona-education/arizona-ban-on-ethnic-studies-unconstitutional-u-s-judge-idUSKCN1B32DE

Henriques, J. (2010). The vibrations of affect and their propagation on a night out on Kingston's dancehall scene. *Body & Society, 16*: 57–90.

Hickey-Moody, A. (2013). Affect as method: Feelings, aesthetics and affective pedagogy. In R. Coleman & J. Ringrose (Eds.), *Deleuze and research methodologies* (pp.79–95). Edinburgh, UK: Edinburgh University Press.

Horne, T. (2007). AN OPEN LETTER TO THE CITIZENS OF TUCSON. Retrieved from: http://nau.edu/uploadedfiles/academic/cal/philosophy/forms/an%20open%20letter%20to%20citizens%20of%20tucson.pdf

Kluchin, A.S. (2012). *The allure of affect: Rigor, style, and unintelligibility in Kristeva and Irigaray*. Doctoral dissertation, Columbia University.

Kunnie, J. (2010). Apartheid in Arizona? HB 2281 and Arizona's denial of human rights of people of color. *The Black Scholar. 40*(4), 16–26.

Leander, K. & Boldt, G. (2013). Rereading "A pedagogy of multiliteracies:" Bodies, texts, and emergence, *Journal of Literacy Research, 45*(1), 22–46.

MacLachlan, A. (2010). Unreasonable resentments. *Journal of Social Philosophy, 41*(4), 422–441.

Massumi, B. (2002). *Parables of the virtual: Movement, affect, sensation.* Durham, NC: Duke University Press.

Massumi, B. (2015). *The politics of affect.* Malden, MA: Polity.

Muñoz, J.E. (2000). Feeling brown: Ethnicity and affect in Ricardo Bracho's *The sweetest hangover (and other STDs). Theatre Journal, 52*(1), 67–79.

Ngai, S. (2005). *Ugly feelings.* Cambridge, MA: Harvard University Press.

Planas, R. (2012). Neither banned nor allowed: Mexican American Studies in limbo in Arizona. Retrieved from: http://www.foxnews.com/world/2012/04/19/neither-banned-nor-allowed-mexican-american-studies-in-limbo-in-arizona.html

Phippen, J.W. (2015). How one law banning ethnic studies led to its rise. Altantic.com Retrieved from: http://www.theatlantic.com/education/archive/2015/07/how-onelaw-banning-ethnic-studies-led-to-rise/398885/

Rene, C. (2012). Reports of TUSD book ban completely false and misleading. Press release. Retrieved from: http://www.tusd1.org/contents/news/press1112/01-17-12.html

Ross, O. (2013). Celebrated Mexican nun was baroque sensation, but Catholic Church put a stop to that. Retrieved from: http://www.thestar.com/news/insight/2013/03/16/celebrated_mexican_nun_was_baroque_sensation_but_catholic_church_put_a_stop_to_that.html.

Saldanha, A. (2010). Skin, affect, aggregation: Guattarian variations on Fanon. *Environment and Planning A, 42,* 2410–2427.

Scott, J.W. (2015). The new thought police. Retrieved from: http://www.thenation.com/article/204481 /new-thought-police

Smith, R.H. & Schurtz, D.R. (2013). Resentment. In H. Pashler (Ed.), *Encyclopedia of the Mind.* Thousand Oaks, CA: SAGE.

Stewart, K. (2007). *Ordinary affects.* Durham, NC: Duke University Press.

Thrift, N. (2007). *Non-representational theory: Space/politics/affect.* New York, NY: Routledge.

To, N.M. & Trivelli, E. (2015). Affect, memory, and the transmission of trauma. *Subjectivity, 8*(4), 305–314.

Zembylas, M. (2007). The *specters* of bodies and affects in the classroom: a rhizo-ethological approach. *Pedagogy, Culture & Society, 15*(1), 19–35.

7

THINKING AND FEELING THE INTERVAL

A Few Movements of a Transnational Family

Ana Christina da Silva Iddings and
Kevin M. Leander

In this chapter, we take up questions of feeling and language learning by drawing on data gathered in a research project by the first author, Chris, who is an immigrant from Brazil, a native speaker of Portuguese and who came to the US and learned English as an adult. As an immigrant, as a mother of two sons and as a language researcher, Chris often struggled with the possibility of her children growing up not speaking her native language, and therefore not fully knowing her. Also, because Brazil is geographically far from and non-contiguous with the US, to come and go across borders can be challenging. Therefore, she wondered about the impact of her sons growing up far away from their extended families, left in her native land, and feared that they could be fracturing important familial and emotional connections. She also pondered upon what could be the implication of her children not having literacy in Portuguese and thought they could be missing significant social and cultural aspects of being.

So, for the larger study, which took place in Arizona, Chris inquired of other Brazilian immigrant mothers how they went about raising their children across a language boundary. In addition, she asked about how ties with remote native lands and family members influenced the development of bilingualism and biliteracy.

In the following, we provide an account of one mother, "Neide,"—a Brazilian/American transnational—who expressed a strong desire to develop bilingualism/biculturalism and biliteracy for her children, "Ben " and "June," and attempted to do that through book-making practices, among many different ways which we will expand on. For this specific portion of the larger project conveyed here, we want to think and feel our way into understanding language learning and language being for families who are living transnationally and cross culturally. In the research process, we don't just find languages-in-context, in some kind of relationship of figure to ground ("context"). We don't just find language to be merely indexical to an (established) world that gives it meaning, anchoring, reference, authorial grounding. And we don't just find culture as a system of established signs and artifacts which, together, form Brazil, or America, or even some kind of syncretism of Brazil-America—a hybrid thing to be decoded.

Rather, what we find is that languaging (Swain, Lapkin, Knouzi, Suzuki & Brooks, 2009; Swain & Lapkin, 2011) is dynamically related to a project of sense-making. And, this affective field of sense-making is played out in the between spaces of language-to-language, in the between spaces of mother-to-child or person-to-person, in the between spaces of language-to-materiality, in the between spaces of language-to-place. These between spaces, as we sense them, are forms of differentiating through movements of relations between languaging, relating as persons, materializing and place-making. What pulls us here is not the production of language nor the production of culture, as a historical or microhistorical process, but the everyday flows of signs and bodies that make differences in their forms of contact and in their movements. Sense-making practices (concurrently making meaning and feeling), which are also played out in their in-betweenness (e.g., mother/child relations), are carried forward in the differences produced by contact, by ongoing movement in an unstable, highly active and affectively charged manner of being translingual and transnational.

Thinking and Feeling the Interval

> From the complex flow of time we produce ordered wholes—such as the notion of the human self. We then imagine that this self *preceded or grounded the flow of time rather than being an effect of time.*
>
> *(Colebrook, 2002, p. 41)*

The work of putting being before becoming is part and parcel of much of social science, considering, for example, identities of persons as things, noun-like, with differences marked between them on the front end according to their qualities or characteristics. So, as the story goes, a Brazilian is different from an American in ways that, when made explicit, provide an understanding of these two identities—make these identities a concept. A blend or hybrid of these identities might also then be predicted or understood, based on the blending of known qualities. For Deleuze and Guattari, however, difference is difference in intensity as produced through the formation and deformation and reformation of assemblages. Difference is about virtuality, about what could happen that is unplanned, undesigned. Difference provides force, momentum, life. In other words, difference is proliferation: " . . . the interval takes all, the interval is substance" (Deleuze & Guattari, 1987, p. 478). For our purposes, a Deleuze-Guattarian approach to thinking and feeling the interval is valuable for sensing the affective intensities of the flows and rhythms of differentiating raw energy in the evergoing creation of people and places.

Affect is intensive rather than extensive. Extensive thinking is representational: "Ordered and synthesized perceptions give us an exterior world of varying
extended objects, all mapped onto a common space, differing only in degree"
(Colebrook, 2002, p. 38). Such extensive spatiality absorbs geography in the
study of points, their identification, their distribution and the measurements of
distances and spaces between them (critiqued by Doel, 2000). In thinking and
feeling the interval, spatially, we might think and feel place not as an identity
undergoing change, but a "differential equation: flow upon flow; variation upon
variation; differential upon differential" (Doel, 2000, p. 125). In this case, the
local and the global no longer represent a difference in kind or scale; glocalizing
is rather understood and felt through its folding and constriction. The point—as
illusion—is left behind for lines (direction, orientation) and movement.

How might we sense these rhythms of difference-producing in the lives of
bi/multilinguals? How might we, as researchers, come to affectively engage in
such linguistic landscapes? How might we sense and feel language, place and
cultural materials as they are co-constructed in dynamic relations?

The idea of the human self or the identity of place always becoming, as an
effect of time, and through affectively charged movements across intervals or
gaps also signals something of how a reconsideration of time is key to Deleuze's
philosophy. While we tend to think of time chronologically—as the connection of equivalent units within some kind of given whole, and while we tend
to think of persons and places as going through time, (as being before time),
Deleuze's affect-saturated concept of time, developed especially in his works on
cinema (1986; 1989), considers how time differentiates and interrupts synthesis
and order. Time is split in two—memory lives as virtuality alongside the actual
lines of present, lived time. In cinema, Deleuze thinks of these virtual/actual splits
as "irrational cuts," affectively charged, but his interest in cinema is a means of
understanding the experience of time in modern social life more broadly. Time
is intensive, affective flow. The multiplication of possibilities of intervals of time
is described by Ashton (2008) as follows:

> I propose that there is an *interval/gap triumvirate*, particularly as they relate to
> film, that applies to both movement-images and time-images. This inter-
> val/gap can be thought of as existing: 1) as the mind/body of the spectator,
> 2) "between" image and image "in" a film or on the screen, and 3) as a film
> character's mind/body.
>
> *(2008, section 30)*

Shifting the modality from film to social life (a move invited by Deleuze), and
considering ways of observing and researching social life, such as through ethnographic observation, we might create a parallel proposition that there are
affectively charged time intervals or gaps in the mind/body of the researcher,
between images inscribed and ordered in data and in the mind/body of

the researched. Moreover, there are intervals of time—irrational cuts—between the three of these entities, creating their own affects.

As such, in feeling alongside Neide's becoming through time, and in participating in it, in this venue, we desire to remain intensive—eschewing gross level categories that predefine space–time, such as transnational or transcultural. How do we keep movement—her movement—on the move?

Overview of the Larger Study

For this study, ten women were interviewed who had emigrated to the US from Brazil and who had American-born children five years old or younger. The children were also interviewed. The in-depth interviews took place in the families' respective homes, where the research team (including Chris) visited, on average, three or four times a semester for an entire academic year. Each visit lasted about an hour. We engaged with both the mother and the children. Interactions with the mothers involved their telling of their life histories from the time before and after emigration. The children's interviews were focused on what they might know about their mothers' histories and experiences in their native land. In addition, the mothers and the children collaborated to compose a digital storybook with the purpose of familiarizing the children with the mother's pre-immigration life history, using old family album photographs of their extended family and native land, while developing biliteracy for the children.

In part, our intentions as researchers were to take note of the ways the mothers and children would be languaging (Swain, Lapkin, Knouzi, Suzuki & Brooks, 2009; Swain & Lapkin, 2011) together as they composed the digital storybook. Languaging, as we use the term here, refers to the process of shaping knowledge and experience through the use of languages, in this case Portuguese, while remembering, attending, narrating and so on. The mothers looked through their family albums together with their children, speaking Portuguese, while explaining the various photographs, talking about individual relatives, telling pertinent stories and memories about the different contexts and people included. Together they selected the photographs they wanted to use for their digital story book and the mothers helped the children compose a simple storyline for the book, speaking and writing in Portuguese throughout the composition process.

Congruently with the more general purposes of this study, we aimed to understand the experiences of the children as they were developing bilingualism and biliteracy and of the mothers in creating opportunities for their offspring, not only to make meaning from language and print, but also to connect affectively with their native tongue and land. In addition, we were curious as to how the children were learning Portuguese through the process of composing a digital story, talking about their mother's native history, identifying sociocultural elements and material objects relative to Brazilian daily practices and listening to stories that were pertinent to their extended family and places.

We noted, during our visits to the homes, that all mothers who participated in this study went through significant efforts to reproduce to some degree the socio-cultural context of the native culture and land. In addition, they all seemed to have a particular desire to provide opportunities for affective experiences for the children that might also promote emotional ties with the mother's remote family and homeland. For example, in our observations, many of the households had objects that were recognizable as being from Brazil and others from the US. In many instances, entering these spaces was especially appealing to me (Chris), as a Brazilian, as the sense of home that they exuded, through scents, colors, lighting, space distribution and inside/outside flow, resonated with my own experiences of homes in Brazil. There were, of course, many things that were more familiar to me with respect to homes in the American context. The homes of these Brazilian-American families were not merely a sum of the parts, but a wholesome new homespace where Brazil was, in some sense, also living.

We were (and still are) moved by the tremendous efforts of the mothers to create linguistic and cultural ecologies in, with and across their homes. We were also moved by the mixed affect of the children in response, including their ambivalence. In the following, we tell the story of one of the mothers we interviewed, Neide, and her children, Ben and June, in order to provide a case example from the research.

The manner in which we offer Neide's story is intentionally set up to show something of the difference-producing intervals created by our different encounters with it. We move across various dimensions of Neide's life, with Kevin first offering commentary on the data as he feels and thinks about it, and as he imagines this woman he has never met, her home and her family. We term this work—an attempt to push past analysis and to raise questions of affective possibility—"Interval 1." Next, Chris engages the data as she feels them in her experiences of conducting the visits, also relating them to her own memories as an immigrant. We term this work "Interval 2." Each of these intervals raises the specter of multiple other intervals (spatial, temporal, material) within them, as suggested earlier. Morever, we want to bring movement through the energies created by the juxtaposition of our two movements, disrupting the "we" of much of this chapter with a gap created in the betweenness of our experiences.

Neide Creating a Homespace as Interval

Neide was a 39-year-old mother at the time of the research, born in Brazil and emigrating to the US in her early 30's. She had two children: Ben, who was six years old, and June, three. Neide came from a family who had strong ties, an unconventional structure, and struggled in deep poverty. Her formal schooling ended at Grade 5, yet she placed a very high value on education. Emigrating to the US after falling in love with an American man who was visiting her hometown, Neide was working as a housecleaner at the time of the study. She spoke only Portuguese with her children at home and spoke English with a beginning level of proficiency in her daily interactions outside of the home.

Home Décor

Neide filled her family home in Arizona with material objects from Brazil in ways that were deliberate and extraordinarily effortful. Her house was replete with Brazilian symbols and emblems, including, for example, national flags, displayed inside and outside of the home. Also, world maps with the map of Brazil saliently marked were pinned on the walls and each child had a globe in their bedroom. The mother would often use those to refer, roughly, to places where their relatives lived. Photographs of the extended family were abundantly on display throughout the house.

Interval 1. The Brazilian flag pinned to the walls of the house is not a recontextualization of Brazil in America—few Brazilian homes would post national flags on their walls. Rather, the flag, as a symbol, is a compressed narrative of another place, another set of colors, another time, another way of being. The objects she was using and the language she was using were brought into a sense-making relationship of differentiating energy—Brazilian native foliage as American and not-American, Portuguese words as-sung-in-America. The flag literally is pressed out onto the walls of the house—this simple Arizona

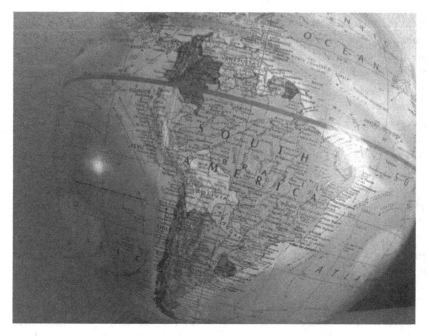

FIGURE 7.1

FIGURE 7.2

ranch home, with its eight-foot ceilings and plainly painted sheetrock walls, unlike those of Neide's Brazilian apartment. The flag and wall differentiate one another—the flag does not transform the wall, but enters into relationship with it, a relationship further mobilized in myriad interactions of family members and guests around the flag-wall, in subtle and not so subtle ways. The map differentiates itself from the wall in similar ways and, internally, sparks differences across its surfaces and its attachments to this place—Brazil is here on the surface, while America is over there; Brazil (map) is here in America (place); America is here (map) and here (place). Even before a human presence, the materiality of symbols, colors, words, mapped dots, lines and regions, scaled relations, wall texture, wall height, wall color and lighting enter into differentiating relations, playing off one another, pushing and pulling against one another, showing up their own fissured relations.

Then, there's the family in the space, of the space. How might we think the interval with respect to family photos? How might we make them not simply a project of identification (e.g., "This is your uncle Eduardo and your Aunt Carolina,") to a process of differentiation? What are the ripe potentials of differentiation? Lived out in the relations of family, the photos are not static representations of others, but rather felt in the intervals of now and then, here and there, self and other, older and younger, specific memories (for the adults) and story (for the children). For the mother, the photos offer memory fragments of self along with fragments of other. Affective intensities live in the and . . . and conjuncture of here and now and then and there:

> [M]emories of who we are now, who we were, who we wanted to become, are wrapped up in memories of where we are, where we were, and where we will be (would like to be). This makes the connections between geography and memory inseparable but also dynamic and very slippery.
> *(Jones and Garde-Hansen, 2012, p. 4)*

Representationally, the family photos speak of another time and place. But that representation is only *good for* or valuable to the analyst outside of the space, outside of the family. As images living in the difference-producing intervals of life as *and* (here *and* there, here *and* now, etc.) the affects and meanings of the photos morph. The ghosts speak, and are spoken to.

Interval 2. Walking into that space felt to me like being suddenly transported into my native country. The colors of the walls, the amount of natural light coming in through the windows, the openness of the floor plan and especially the mosaic-style, flaming red, some tiles laid on the floor blending the inside areas with the outside spaces. The tiles were sort of the same as the ones in my grandparents' beach house in Brazil. When walking on those tiles with my bare feet (as I was invited to do), I felt the coolness of the earth giving ground to my body. Through that sensation, I was reminded of my own longing for that kind of open living space, for the earth tones contrasting with the bright wall colors and especially for the coolness of the tiles against my feet. Interestingly enough, each time I was in her home, Neide inevitably pointed me directly to the photographs of her relatives hanging on the wall and often began to tell stories about them. Since I didn't really have a relationship with any of them, it was difficult for me to keep track of those stories, faces and names. Also, I was usually distracted by how good it felt to be barefoot on those tiles and by the called-up sensations and memories of being a young girl, and later a young woman, in my grandparents' beach house in Brazil, where I spent holidays and summer vacations.

Food

Food was also a significant material connection and reproduction of Brazilian culture: Neide cooked only traditional Brazilian dishes at the house and reproduced Brazilian meal times and practices in the day-to-day.

Interval 2. The scents of particular Brazilian spices, like *malagueta peppers* and *dende* oil filled up the rooms and, like a time machine, transported me to the open street markets of Brazil. When I asked Neide (with a kind of self-interest) where she had found these spices in Arizona, she explained that she had brought them from Brazil inside her luggage.

FIGURE 7.3

In addition to cooking for the everyday meals, Neide would also plan and host Brazilian-style parties often. For example, she would host birthday parties for her own children and also for other Brazilian children, friends of the family. Children's birthday parties are especially elaborate and labor-intensive events in Brazil. They are particularly recognizable for the colorfully wrapped handmade candies and handcrafted table decorations. These are important multigenerational celebrations and times for bonding, which are normally attended by grandparents, aunts, uncles and family friends, as well as children.

Interval 1. *Feijoada* is a traditional Brazilian dish stew made of beans with beef and pork, cooked for hours and served over rice. *Bobo de camarao* is a dish made of shrimp, traditionally in a puree of cassava meal with coconut milk and other ingredients. *Pao de queijo* are delicious savory small cheese bread rolls. This is the life of Brazilian food on the page—its representational life. Yet, even as representation, the food escapes, fills the senses with odors, textures, color, taste. The food on Neide's table is sensory pedagogy. In the experience of languaging/eating, the chain is not sign–object–interpretant. Food is not interpreted. Neither is food the background context for language learning. Rather feijoada (the word) and feijoada (the thing) enter into an interval of difference and repetition.

Here, the qualities of connection and heterogenity with respect to relations between bodies come to light. For Deleuze and Guattari (1987), a body is broadly defined as a whole composed of parts and characterized by the relations among its parts. Deleuze and Guattari (p. 7) describe how "semiotic chains of every

FIGURE 7.4

nature" are formed by connections among things of different phenomenological status. The gap between the discursive and the nondiscursive is bridged by force, which Deleuze describes as a productive movement toward the formation of new multiplicities (Massumi, 2002). The word is made flesh, or at least the word and flesh chase one another, push on one another, enter into dynamic movements. At Neide's table, her children digest food-words, on the shopping list, she and they taste the items. These are the assemblages of meaning/feeling the world, the essential synaesthesia of language learning, where senses stand in for one another and bleed together to make sense, to feel the world of things/words.

Interval 2. Either by coincidence or by shameless strategy, I often came by to Neide's house close to dinner time. Each time, I was invited to stay for dinner. She often prepared some of the foods I had mentioned in passing to be my favorites—mostly savory fried stuff I never made for myself because it would take too much labor and time. These meals were a feast for my senses. I often left Neide's home with my clothes and hair smelling like the delicious food she had prepared, and in those scents, I lingered.

Toys, TV and Music

In addition to the many social relationships she established with other Brazilians in the neighborhood and community at large, Neide also attended the Brazilian church in the area each Sunday, which would also provide opportunities for other Brazilian children in the community to have weekly playtimes with her children, often using Brazilian toys. The toys or figurines often represented folkloric characters, such as the *Banda Sertaneja* (cowboys' band) or depicted a scene from the circus *mambembe* (a type of low-budget, small-town, amateur circus), which are emblematic of Brazilian musical entertainment or folk comedy.

Interval 2. It was strangely heartwarming to see the kids playing with these physical toys. I think what called my attention mostly was the fact that I don't often see kids playing with physical objects any longer, but, it was also interesting to remember that those wooden and paper toys were somewhat timeless. I too had played with things like that as a kid.

FIGURE 7.5 Characters of Mambembe Circus

FIGURE 7.6 Brazilian cartoon playing on DVD

Neide's house was often filled with her native language—she spoke only Portuguese to her children, the satellite TV was constantly playing Brazilian telenovelas (soap operas) or cartoons, which her family in Brazil would send to her on DVD in the mail. Also Brazilian music—specifically music genres typical of her region of Brazil—was frequently playing on the stereo every time we visited the home. Occasionally someone in the household, most often the children, would begin to move to the beats and encourage me to join in with them (which I often did).

The Yard

Moreover, cultural emblems flowed from the front yard to the back. Even though she lived in southern Arizona, where backyards are generally barren or display a desert landscape, Neide had planted grass and a variety of trees and plants, which were native to Brazil, and also had hung a Brazilian-style hammock in her yard.

Among other plants, Neide had started a row of palm trees in her backyard. As the palm trees began to grow, she could see them from her living room and bedroom windows, reminding her of the views of common landscapes in the region where she grew up.

FIGURE 7.7

Interval 2. Reminding me of my grandparents' home on the beach and of the swaying motions that called me for a nap on the hammock.

Interval 1. On a calm day, the palm appears to be still, but it survives in movement, some of which is hidden to the observer. With heavy fronds and a heavy trunk, we might assume that the palm has a heavy root structure for anchoring and stability. Yet, the palm's roots are strong in their lightness, in their abundance, and in their responsive flexibility. The thin roots—rhizomes—stretch away from the trunk in search of moisture and nutrients, stabilizing the palm as well. Because the roots grow and die, grow and die, they remain nimble, small and flexible. These rhizomes break off in irregular patterns, pushing through the soil, breaking off here, continuing there, rising up and then dropping down when they begin to cluster in the soil.

The rhizome is not an end in itself for Deleuze and Guattari (1987), but rather functions in their creation of a philosophy of immanent relations or, in other terms, an approach to the active potentials of performance in everyday life to create something new and unpredictable. Rhizomes spread in every direction and are contrasted to hierarchical or "aborescent" relations—like those of most trees. In nature, rhizomatic (root-like) relations are seen in crabgrass, tubers, mosses, many palms and "when rats swarm over each other" (Deleuze & Guattari, 1987, pp. 6–7). In his appreciation of Deleuze and Guattari, Ingold (2011) prefers the fungal mycelium, apparently because it emphasizes, even more, the fluid character of life and/or the idea that the rhizome produces multiple bundles of lines as it consumes.

Another key principle of the rhizome is multiplicity: Lines extend in all directions (Deleuze & Guattari, 1987). The choice to focus on rhizomatic connections functions as a critique of point-driven, either/or, dichotomous thinking. Deleuze remarked that it is not "beginnings and ends that count, but middles" (1995, p. 160). The movement and betweenness among objects (the line) is the focus rather than the identification of what is connected (the point) and where it is located (the position) (Deleuze & Guattari, 1987). Deleuze and Guattari push against representational modes of thinking that focus on foundations or "roots." Unlike representational views that describe foundational configurations (e.g., identities, meanings, categories) in *a priori* ways, Deleuze and Guattari move us to consider how social life and social foundations are an outcome of dynamic connections. Thinking in terms of lines and movement among heterogeneous objects is a means of thinking toward difference.

Neide had brought seeds, bulbs and palm seedlings to the US in her luggage. She felt bringing those items in was *inocente* [an innocent thing to do], as it wasn't harmful to anyone and was important for her sense of home to have those planted in her backyard. She determined that, if caught by customs, she would simply give those up. As a result, the flora displayed in her Arizona backyard was a literal movement of flora from Brazil as well as a movement of affective energies across Brazil-Arizona-yard space-plant-weather relations.

Neide, on the other hand survives in movement, some of which is hidden to the observer. With the weight of parenting, two countries, work and acculturation in various forms, we might assume that Neide has a heavy root structure for anchoring and stability. Yet, Neide's roots are strong in their lightness, in their abundance, and in their responsive flexibility. Emergent living/feeling at the transnational interval takes up movements that it could well be overblown to call strategies or even tactics. Rather, they are felt turns of the body one way or another, quick and slow movements, thin roots, multiplying over the surface, reaching for moisture and nutrients. At the interval of the border, there are emergent possibilities—roots that may grow or die. Stability is movement over permanence, felt emergence over structure. And, border crossings are continuous, so new growth cannot rest.

Interval 2. Being in that homespace was at once food for my starved Brazilian being and salt in my immigrant wound. In some respects, Neide's family's place drew forth in me some strong sense of being Brazilian and of being *not American*. In visiting that space, I felt less of a researcher, a university professor or a speaker of English. There, I felt relaxed and comfortable, like my guard was down and I had stepped into a different realm of being. I felt as though I too was home, where I didn't have to perform anyone other than myself. There I was frequently reminded of myself or a self that is no longer or that was in memory or perhaps even lost in the deeper nooks of me. Upon leaving that space I often felt a kind thirst for more, for a next time and took with me the colors, the scents, the lingering sense of being Brazilian. For me, perhaps as a function of time or need to acculturate, the Brazilian-American spaces were heavily etched in place and emotionally separate, more like two different camps.

The book-making project

As a culminating part of the original larger research project, all of the participating mothers and their children were asked to co-author a digital storybook, speaking and writing Portuguese and using photographs of their remote family in Brazil and retelling of the mothers' experiences regarding their lives before emigrating to the US. In the case of Neide, she had multiple photo albums depicting her nuclear and extended family in Brazil and also some albums of photographs pertaining to the family's trips, with her children, to her homeland to visit relatives. For about three weeks toward the end of the engagement in the study, Neide spent some time each day going over the pictures with the children. She would name the people featured in the photos, would point to different practices and activities that may have been occurring during the time the pictures were taken (e.g., carnival; a trip to the beach; dinner at the grandparents' house), always using Portuguese for her descriptions. Ben and June would mostly repeat the language of Neide's statements, while pointing and selecting some pictures to include in their stories. The digital stories that entailed were simple picture books of about ten pages each with one sentence descriptions of the photographs, written in Portuguese, on the bottom of each page (see example below).

Interval 2. [Observing the book-making project made me feel some regret in not having been more diligent in creating opportunities for my sons to engage with their family members (even in photographs) or to use the language and culture as they were growing up. Mistakenly, when they were young and in the years of their growing up I assumed that presenting them with my Brazilianness and my Portuguese language was not interesting and, further, it was irrelevant to their upbringing since they were going to be living in the US as adults and, therefore, needed to learn the ways of being American. I, of course, believe differently now.]

From the digital version, we printed paper versions to be shared with the family. Neide read the print book to June each day for about two weeks. She believed that the digital storybook she and June composed during our visits, speaking and writing Portuguese and using photographs of her remote family in Brazil, were helpful toward the goal of affectively connecting her children with her past life in Brazil, while developing bilingualism and biliteracy. Curiously, however, when we returned to their home, about two weeks after the end of the study to revisit the digital storybook, June used mostly English in engaging with the book and describing the pictures.

From a linguistic standpoint, we were surprised that June retold her story to us in English, even though she had composed it with her mother in Portuguese. Our first impression is that although the sociocultural context of Brazilianness was somewhat reproduced through the story, in its actual content, the affective and emotional connections with the mother's language seemed remote or disconnected on this occasion. Although we are not certain of why the children were not responding to Neide's effort to connect directly with the text in Portuguese, we speculate that this project, as a kind of intervention, got caught up in its own forms of representationalism, freezing print texts and images in ways that were disconnected from embodied flows of experience experienced elsewhere in Neide's own pedagogy of her home.

Interval 1. In contrast to static analysis of the image or text, movement is placed at the center of Ingold's (2011) thought, by which he means not only that texts are on the move, but also that perception is caught up in movement (mobility) as well as being moved (affected). Perception of this kind of not distanced from the object, but is immersed within it, and sensations and meanings that emerge from these movements or disturbances. Mediating on Deleuze, Ingold invokes a strong image: researchers tend to focus their attention on the banks of the river (that which is solid, form and substance) and entirely lose sight of the river (that which is fluid): "To regain the river, we need to shift our perspective from the transverse relation between objects and images to the longitudinal trajectories of materials and resources" (2011, p. 14).

In researching language and literacy, we might ask ourselves what the rivers or flows are and, in contrast, what the river banks are that capture our attention (but which would not even exist without the river!). Perhaps, in this case, the book that June made, with Neide's intensive involvement, was a kind of river bank for June. Although situated in the house, and in the content of her life as a transnational child—moving in the interval—the book somehow froze or locked down the movements that made languaging and materializing feel connected, feel alive.

Critical reflections on Neide's case and research methodology

Henri Lefebvre, in his magnum opus *The Production of Space* (1991), described a triadic relationship between perceived space (*espace perçu*), conceived space (*espace conçu*) and lived space (*espace vecu*). Lefebvre argues that space, as it is produced in the living of it, is formed through triadic relations of the perceived, conceived and lived (c.f. Soja, 1989). While not engaging fully in the nature of this triad and its dialectics, Lefebvre's triad signals something of how spatial understandings get locked into a dimension of space while forgetting the fullness of spatial understanding and life, as it is lived spatially. In particular, a tendency in research methods, by their own representational practices of production, is to focus primarily on space as it is perceived and especially on space as it is perceived, and fixed, through representations. Time differentiates and interrupts static space, breathing affective life into (still/not) life. Memory as virtual time creates its own intervals with lived time—sometimes irrationally splitting open the moment. These intervals split static space, as well as images of life-as-timeline.

Text-centric or discourse-centric perspectives on the production of subjectivity ignore movement and sensation, favoring instead the story of ideological apparatuses or subject positions that "structured the dumb material interactions of things and rendered them legible according to a dominant signifying schema into which human subjects were interpellated" or that "opened a window on local resistance in the name of change" (Massumi, 2002, pp. 3–4). Such theories of positionality, as Massumi (2002) argues, captures bodies in "cultural freeze frame," removing movement from the picture. "The notion of movement as qualitative transformation is lacking. There is a displacement but not transformation; it is as if the body simply leaps from one definition to the next" (p. 3).

Much of our present work on this case is an attempt to recover bits and pieces from our earlier data collection and put them on the move—to ungunk the ways the research was gunked up. The original data collected were field notes, interviews, photos and video clips. Returning to the concept of meshworking, with a critical eye to our method, in many ways this study reproduced traditional ethnographic means of classification: observing and recording material objects, social practices and relationships and categorizing them within a framework of culture-as-collection. In Ingold's (2011) terms, the study took a genealogical approach. But how do we feel the river and not focus on the banks? How to feel movements, how to feel the intervals of transnational life?

Our partial answer to this question has been to engage, in different ways, interval movements along with Neide and her family. For us, this meant not merely interpreting or reading gaps, cuts or intervals, although we tried to suggest the possibilities for movement in as a way of sensing and feeling the data. This process also meant drawing attention to the value of the intervals created by feeling alongside, by knowing alongside and by doing this as a couple, with intervals between us. Rather than being experienced as losses of veracity—gaps keeping us from Neide's true story—we draw out these intervals as affectively charged movements that engage us, apart and together, in ways of feeling Neide's movements of becoming.

References

Ashton, D. (2008). Feeling time: Deleuze's time-image and aesthetic effect. *Rhizomes, 16*. Retrieved from: http://www.rhizomes.net/issue16/ashton/index.html

Colebrook, C. (2002). *Gilles Deleuze*. New York, NY: Routledge.

Deleuze, G. (1986). *Cinema 1: The movement image* (H. Tomlinson & B. Habberjam, Trans.). Minneapolis, MN: University of Minnesota Press.

Deleuze, G. & Guattari, F. (1987). *A thousand plateaus: Capitalism and schizophrenia* (B. Massumi, Trans.). Minneapolis, MN: University of Minnesota Press.

Deleuze, G. (1989). *Cinema 2: The time-image* (H. Tomlinson & R. Galeta, Trans.). Minneapolis, MN: University of Minnesota Press.

Deleuze, G. (1995). *Negotiations, 1972–1990.* New York, NY: Columbia University Press.

Doel, M.A. (2000). Spatial science after Dr. Seuss and Gilles Deleuze. In M. Crang & N. Thrift (Eds.), *Thinking space* (pp. 117–135). New York, NY: Routledge.

Ingold, T. (2011). *Being alive: Essays on movement, knowledge, and description.* New York, NY: Routledge.

Jones, O. and Garde-Hansen, J. (2012) *Geography and memory: Explorations in identity, place and becoming.* New York, NY: Springer.

Lefebvre, H. (1991). *The production of space* (D. Nicholson-Smith, Trans.). New York, NY: Wiley-Blackwell.

Massumi, B. (2002). *Parables for the virtual: Movement, affect, sensation.* Durham, NC: Duke University Press.

Soja, E.W. (1989). *Postmodern geographies: The reassertion of space in critical social theory.* New York, NY: Verso.

Swain, M., Lapkin, S., Knouzi, I., Suzuki, W. & Brooks, L. (2009). Languaging: University students learn the grammatical concept of voice in French. *The Modern Language Journal, 93*(1), 5–29.

Swain, M. & Lapkin, S. (2011). Languaging as agent and constituent of cognitive change in an older adult: An example. *Canadian Journal of Applied Linguistics/Revue canadienne de linguistique appliquée, 14*(1), 104–117.

PART III

Coming to Know

Movement 3: Affectively Charged Foldings of Literacy and Coming to Know

Bruno Latour, the sociologist, claims that coming to know in science and technology is inextricably linked to writing and imaging (1990). His arguments are largely developed through extensive ethnographic and sociological studies of scientific and technical practices, including those of laboratories. Without inscriptions and paperwork, Latour argues, science and technology as practice fall apart. In order to understand scientific work, we must avoid both "materialist" and "mentalist" accounts of science and seek that which is "so practical, so modest, so pervasive, so close to the hands and the eyes," (p. 24) or rather, writing and imaging craftsmanship. The advantages to scientific work of such craftsmanship—qua Brahe, Boyle, Pasteur and others—is that paperwork allows the world to be made flat, modified in scale, reproduced, reshuffled and combined, superimposed, made consistent and converted into diagrams and numbers.

In this part, "Coming to Know," a group of scholars consider the shifting science of their field—the changing ontologies of coming to know affectively—and somewhat inevitably return often to writing, to imaging, to reading. Like Latour, they invoke the "systems" of knowledge production in changing formations (e.g., Perry's invocation of Becker's (1982) *Art Worlds*,) but just as much, the chapters follow the entanglements of feeling with writing and imaging, and feeling through them, at every twist and turn of research practice. As one of my colleagues commented recently about university life, "We can change systems all we want, but if we don't change the DNA of what we're up to, nothing changes." These papers wrestle with, feel with and unravel pieces of the DNA assemblage of literacy practice/research—research on literacy practice that is, at every turn, saturated with literacy that is, at every turn, affectively charged.

I read and experience these papers as three different stirrings or *foldings* of time-space and affect in literacy research. More conventionally, we could roughly associate these foldings with periods of time in relations of research, as it is produced and moves out into relations with readers and audiences. However, these time periods (e.g., "interpreting data" in Ehret & D'Amico, for instance, or later, "presenting findings" in Burnett) are in no way linear to a process or system, but are rather occasions of folded or *scrumpled* time, where present-past-futures of reading, imaging and researching come into contact, where here-and-nows are visited by there-and-then's or imagined-there's-and-could-be's.

In the first folding, the chapters by Ehret and D'Amico on the one hand and Hollett and Dudek on the other consider writing and imaging, respectively, as affective practices that happen "with" others, in "subject–subject" relations. Here we are situated with something like "data collection" or "data interpretation." However, unlike in Latour's (1990) vision, writing does not merely provide a "trace" of activity elsewhere—a moveable reduction. Rather, "[l]anguaging [. . .] is material" (Ehret & D'Amico, this volume). Rather than being mere re-presentations of life elsewhere; writing and imaging are rather the and-and creations of new forms of (material) life, put into contact with other enunciations, other bodies, yielding new possible meanings and intensities. Literacy practices built the assemblage of relations in curious ways—relations of present to past, body to body, image 1 to drawing 1—creating openings and emergences for relations well outside of mimesis. These chapters engage with the possibilities for writing (Ehret & D'Amico) and sketching (Hollett & Dudek) to become more than merely representational and analytic. In Hollett and Dudek, for instance, sketching becomes of means of feeling the ebbs and flows of energy in video data with their own bodies. Both chapters ask of this moment of research, How can we be moved, across time and space, alongside that which we are coming to know, and moreover, how can we use literacy practices as energies to sustain such movements?

In a second folding, Perry's chapter takes us to the encounter of reading research reports. The chapter blows the doors open on Rosenblatt's famous *The Reader, The Text, the Poem*, (1978) with an examination of how the practice of reading research of whatever genre—"no matter how coded to smithereens or danced to abstraction it might be" (Perry, this volume)—is always the creation of an assemblage, is always a process of bringing into relation the world of research production (things, people, texts, practices, methods of reduction or amplification) with a reader who is affected by this world, who is moved. While research texts may not make affect evident within themselves (and in fact may eschew any such leakage), practices of reading research are affectively charged—persuasion succeeds or fails, readers are moved or not, illustrations and arguments gather together and push and pull on readers. The reader herself brings a host of her own affectively laden assembled relations to the research text: Reader-World, Text-World, and Poem-World are assemblages that move, in the present moment of a particular reading, toward some newly emergent configuration or pull back into some familiar one. Either way, the movement is rich with affective energy and potential. Perry invites us to pull back the curtain on our own desires and affective energies, as we enter a particular reading of research, and move with our own energies more fully, as we also enter into the affective movements of the researcher. Reading, in this manner, is not a practice located in the moment *after* research, but rather practiced and even celebrated as an encounter of a reader stretched and expanded across a field of relations and positions, including the positions of the researcher.

Burnett takes us, in a third folding, across episodes of what would be more conventionally considered data collection–presentation–re-interpretation, yet upsetting these conventional understandings by bringing us back to the body—her body—as a researcher, reader and sense-maker of the world. Burnett troubles over the sense of loss of life as a story—an affectively charged account of two girls— travels across time–space. Latour's (1990) "immutable mobile" in conventional scientific research—the stable and combinable representation—perhaps terrifies Burnett as she seeks for a living, becoming sense of affective experience that is not merely recovered but affectively re-lived. Across this time-travel and foldings of time, Burnett feels again both loss and life, sensing how the rhythms of an earlier occasion (two girls at play, in a classroom) comes into contact with the rhythms and structure of a research presentation at a conference. In the middle of it all, Burnett's body, in another "iterative reassembling" of self-data-reader/audience. How could it be otherwise? The room space of conference (re)presentation— with its microphone, notes on paper, furniture, researcher/audience relations and projector converge with Fran and Sophie's play, and their rhythms, in some classroom years back. Something new is made in this convergence—something uncertain, something with hope and loss and movement. Burnett captures experience with a wonderful line as she describes going back to her video data following her conference presentation: "Going back in via video troubled my story, but it also chucked me out again." Here, in this present moment, we get a sense of the past moment/data intra-acting on the body—"chuck[ing]" the body into some unknown, but rising, felt potential.

Deleuze and Guattari (1987) and Guattari (1995) understand semiotic and narrative practices or refrains as powerful organizing or territorializing representations of chronos. However, their account challenges analyses that posit humans as primarily or exclusively organized through narrative or meaning in chronos and by the refrain. Rather, aiôn breaks into chronos; time is bent, folded, torn and reassembled. Research practices and literacy practices (reading, writing, imaging) are powerful organizers of subjects in time, of events through time, of the world of things made mobile across time in its translation to text. In Latour's (1990) vision, scientific knowledge would not be possible were it not for the work of literacy practices that mobilize it, systematize it, create specific forms of literate and optic craftsmanship to shape and steady the world. And yet, the world leaks, bleeds, folds, reassembles anew. As a more complete Latourian (1993) account would say, we have never been modern. These chapters explore and even celebrate the implosion of the conventional research story-on-the-move that leaves the world behind, and the possibilities for stories that move along with us, and that drift along, unpredictably, with the flotsam and jetsam of researching bodies and knowing.

References

Becker, H.S. (1982). *Art worlds.* Berkeley, CA: University of California Press.

Deleuze, G. & Guattari, F. (1987). *A thousand plateaus: Capitalism and schizophrenia* (B. Massumi, Trans.). Minneapolis, MN: University of Minnesota Press.

Guattari, F. (1995). *Chaosmosis: an ethico-aesthetic paradigm.* Bloomington, IN: Indiana University Press.

Latour, B. (1990). Visualization and cognition: Drawing things together. In M. Lynch & S. Woolgar (Eds.), *Representation in scientific practice* (pp. 19–68). Cambridge, MA: MIT Press.

Latour, B. (1993). *We have never been modern.* Cambridge, MA: Harvard University Press.

Rosenblatt, L. (1978). *The reader, the text, the poem: The transactional theory of the literary work.* Carbondale, IL: Southern Illinois University Press.

8

WHY A MORE HUMAN LITERACY STUDIES MUST BE POSTHUMAN

Encountering Writing During and After the Holocaust

Christian Ehret and Daniella D'Amico

Perhaps it is ironic that we begin a chapter titled so strongly in favor of posthumanism with a quote from an eminent humanist's essay, "Humanism:"

> There are so many works of the mind, so much humanity, that to disburden ourselves of ourselves is an understandable temptation [. . .]. So many voices, so many worlds, we can weary of them. If there were only one human query to be heard in the universe, and it was only the sort of thing we were always inclined to wonder about—Where did all this come from? or, Why could we never refrain from war?—we would hear in it a beauty that would overwhelm us. So frail a sound, so brave, so deeply inflected by the burden of thought, that we would ask, Whose voice is this? We would feel a barely tolerable loneliness, hers and ours. And if there were another hearer, not one of us, how starkly that hearer would apprehend what we are and were.
>
> *(Robinson, 2015, pp. 15–16)*

Yet we do so to evoke tensions arising in the field related to literacy researchers' renewed attention to developing posthuman theory (e.g., Boldt & Leander, 2017; Ehret, Hollett & Jocius, 2016; Kuby, Rucker & Kirchhofer, 2015). Robinson's reflection resonates with tensions we have felt through comments in conference rooms after presenters posit posthuman positions, for instance, "People have agency, not things," "I'm not ready to give up a central commitment to humanity," "What does equity matter for matter?" Just one provocation of posthuman theory elicits feelings that we, as literacy researchers, risk disburdening ourselves of ourselves, of avoiding the most difficult *human* questions: The provocation that matter matters (Barad, 2007), and that human beings, only one form of matter, should be decentered in academic inquiry. And so, the worry might go that, in advocating the "vibrant" new academic theory *de rigueur* (Bennett, 2009), literacy researchers risk pushing aside essential questions about, for instance, the power and politics that produce inequities for human beings living and learning with texts.

The nascence of the posthuman conversation in literacy studies is perhaps the primary contributor to this worry, given that early insights are emerging mostly from an emphasis on materiality and multiplicity. Given this early focus, researchers have yet to fully realize the ethical and ontological implications of decentering the rational, humanist subject, which drives posthuman perspectives well beyond a turn toward materiality and multiplicity alone. For well over a century, philosophers have critiqued narrow conceptions of the rational, humanist subject (St. Pierre, 2016), and these critiques have illustrated how agency exceeds "the human," or an autonomous being acting on an inert, external world (see also Ingold, 2013). From the "will to power," to an irrational subconscious, or a collective, historical dynamic of social class, the perspectives of Nietzsche, Freud and Marx, respectively, started the swirl of late 20th-century posthuman theory that has done away with the separation and elevation of the rational human from and over the world.

However, despite over a century of philosophical critiques that extend well beyond these early figures, the Enlightenment's enduring rationalism continues to manifest in social science through representational logics that separate knowing from being (St. Pierre, 2013). With a nonrepresentational perspective contemporary posthuman theory meets language, power and discourse in their materialities and in how they actively affect human and nonhuman bodies in the world's constant unfolding. Agency is therefore not a matter of human power *over* the world, but of nonhuman and human bodies' emergent capacities to affect and to be affected as becoming *parts of* the world. Furthermore, affect is not an individual state, feeling or emotion, but the very force of movement that makes life *feel*, "that give[s] everyday life the quality of a continual motion of relations, scenes, contingencies and emergences" (Stewart 2007, p. 4). Questions of how life feels in becoming relations with texts and how those feelings move bodies toward more, or less, just acts of doing, making and being together have not been fully explored in literacy research. How might literacy research itself become in new material forms that affect living and doing education differently as an ethical charge? And how might the academic writing constitute one such material form?

Recently these questions have been central to our own struggles to avoid the over-knowing tendencies of conventional humanist qualitative inquiry (St. Pierre, 2014). This struggle began in an everyday office conversation about affect and writing when Daniella told Christian a story she had read about Janina Heshele's experiences with writing before and after surviving imprisonment in a Nazi concentration camp as a 12-year-old girl. This conversation grew into a year-long inquiry process through which we read about Janina's life, read her poetry and autobiographical writing and talked with her online. As we continued to read affect theory and process philosophy throughout the same time period, we slowly came to a seemingly paradoxical insight: A posthuman perspective may bring inquiry closer to more human expressions of literacy and social life. We believe that in resisting an overly rational, constructivist analysis and interpretation of Janina's experiences, we may actually come closer to her and to ourselves, especially in our writing.

Therefore, rather than analyze her writing and our conversations as *data* (how could we?), we wrote multiple, short *movements* that focus on writing in the camps, on how Janina's writing moved herself and others during and after the Holocaust, and how Janina's writing moved us. These are movements because the process of writing itself moved us, made us feel differently about writing and about doing literacy research. In fact, we feel closer to understanding how writing moves precisely because our inquiry is *not* determined by an overly rational process that feigns to know completely and, here unethically, turns life into data. The ethical movements in our writing process required us to reflect on how our writing was one amongst multiple material actors, including ourselves, our histories, Janina writing, Janina herself and so on. The movements we present in this chapter emerged from our struggle (1) to bring all of these living materialities into relation without interpreting one through the other, and (2) to express something about affect and writing that is not in our writing itself, but that moves our readers toward a new quality of experience in their reading, a quality that, for them, is a coming to know how writing moves, affects and produces intensities and desires that we cannot predict in advance. Laying out these materialities on a relational plane, acknowledging their intense relations but refusing to interpret one through the other, is, we argue, an ethical charge for non-representational research writing. We describe this emergent writing experience before presenting six movements that gesture toward affective dimensions of writing—for research reports, in the everyday, during the unimaginable.

Through this writing process, we produced short movements about singular experiences of writing—ours, Janina's and others'—that form a whole expression that is more than the sum of its parts. Brought into relation with each other, these movements affect a quality of our inquiry together that is not available through any one movement alone. Remove any one movement and this quality fades. Across movements, we wrote in search of this quality, of how writing moved us all, desiring through our writing to "feel a barely tolerable loneliness, hers and ours" and to bring "another hearer, not one of us" to "apprehend what we are and were" (Robinson, 2015, p. 16) in the process of coming to know each other differently: Us, the authors and Janina. This is how the radically relational ontology of posthumanism, here as a process of inquiry that includes writing, may actually bring us to a more profound and humble humanism. Writing modest stories in search of something. Stories together reaching for something. Something moving. A quality of life.

Writing in Search of Something During and After the Holocaust

"I don't want you to interpret my story. Be humble."

Janina Heshele, Jerusalem, June 2016

Janina was 12 years old when the Germans overtook Lvov, a town in Poland. Her mother and father died soon after the occupation, and Janina was sent to Janowski, a Nazi concentration camp. Janina began writing poems about her experiences in the war before being brought to the camp, and once in the camp, she kept writing. One night, the women of her barracks stepped outside to sing songs. Janina joined them and recited poetry she had composed in the camp. Later, the head of her barracks spoke of her poems to Michal Maksymilian Borwicz, the organizer of clandestine cultural events in Janowska, who would later invite her to one such secret event. At that event, Janina recited her poetry and captivated Borwicz, who later helped her escape Janowska. Outside of the camp, Janina changed identities and hideouts several times in order to survive. In her first hideout, Mariasnka, her safeguard, asked her to write an account of her experiences. Both the journal she produced thereafter and her poems were kept safe through the end of the war.

We were captivated by the event of Janina's poetry recitation in Janowski, and by Janina's story, because she owes her life to writing, to poetry, and to its capacity to move even in the most inhuman of circumstances. Writing-voices-suffering-singing-Janina acted through the event to produce a quality then, a quality now and a quality again below that feels like something essential in writing's unique relation to humanity. Talking to and corresponding with Janina, we learned more about her experiences of writing during and after the Holocaust, and we were touched in ways for which we could not always find adequate words. The experiences of writing to and talking with Janina, and then to each other about Janina and her experiences of writing, touched us because we felt the experiences in our bodies, in nervousness, disgust, beauty, gravity, qualities of experience of our coming to know something vital about writing. Experience touches because it moves our bodies in ways that force us to rationalize and find the language for a feeling: nervousness, disgust, beauty, gravity. Words touch, but touch is not *in* words. Languaging itself is material.

So moved with words, we were forced to consider how we might use our own writing not as a mere report of her experiences, as she, her journals and her poetry related them to us, or as a rationalized analysis of some*thing* we abstracted from those experiences, *a* word, *a* category of emotion ready-made. At best, we feared that to decompose Janina's experiences into explanations of atrocity, of structures of power, politics or discourse, would evacuate our expressions of the very intensities of living experience that make it feel. At worst, we thought that this process of analysis would be unethical, an overly academic interpretation of

Janina's experiences that claimed *truth, our* truth. In this case, we felt that such scientism would perpetrate a small violence complicit with the larger, incomprehensible violence that horrifies us.

How then, we wondered, could a posthuman theory of writing help us to avoid the Scylla and Charybdis of scientism and silence? How could a posthuman approach to writing bring us into a humbler, more ethical relation with Janina that honored her desire that we not interpret her story, yet also searched toward our questions about how writing moves? What composition of words would resist rationalization? What composition of words would affect an apposite texture of touch?

Writing Movements, Writing-Gestures

We wrestled with our predetermining rational impulses in order to become more aware of how and when we felt moved while reading Janina's poetry and journals, while talking with her and while talking with each other. Across the project we desired opening ourselves to moments when we were moved to write and search for answers to questions that seemed impossible to answer, "Where did all this come from?" or, "Why could we never refrain from war?" When did we desire writing, to write desire, when thinking-feeling for affective dimensions of writing, in experiences with Janina, with each other, and desires to write? When we were moved and aware of our desires, we paused and wrote, sometimes to each other, sometimes to ourselves, sometimes inside ourselves. Because if "to human" is a verb in posthuman theory (Ingold, 2016), then writing, too, should always be a verb in posthuman literacy research: Here, writing entangled in our embodied struggles to feel and to know something of Janina's writing life.

However, more than a mere artifact of our own experiences of coming to know and feel in relation to each other and to Janina, we wanted our writing, active verb as it is, to gesture toward semblances of feeling that might move readers without their knowing exactly why or toward what. Our desiring writing is both a search toward something itself, and a writing-gesture that brings us into relation with readers, "another hearer, not one of us," who through the affects generated across our composition of words might "apprehend what we are and were" in the process of our searching, much in the way we worked to apprehend something of Janina's own searching through writing, though poetry. This writing process was therefore not a searching for answers and then coming to those answers, but a nonrepresentational approach to research writing that, for readers, opens to a new experience that can only be felt, a feeling of a feeling of writing for which there are no words (Ehret, 2018b). Words-bodies-histories-stories producing difference through their relations that exist in no one materiality alone. A writing-gesture toward knowing and expressing affective dimensions of writing.

Writing through the desire to know the unknowable can make a material gesture that affects knowing more of ourselves in our humble relations to each other and to history: a writing-gesture. Writing-gestures are therefore a kind of force through which bodies understand each other because they desire toward an apposite texture of touch through the materiality of language: its sound, arrangements, perspectives (first, second, third person), metaphors and rhythms. These relations between materialities of language, between the movements in the next part, for instance, affecting a quality of life that is more than the sum of its parts. The balancing effects of affects and reason. The paradoxical fitting and exceeding of traditional images of thought and writing. The posthumanly humble humanity. A minor gesture below the surface of scientism (Manning, 2016), disrupting it and its major tendencies (Ehret, 2018a).

Answers to our questions, "How might literacy research itself become in new material forms that affect living and doing education differently as an ethical charge?" and "How might academic writing constitute one such material form?" are nowhere to be found *in* our writing. We don't desire certainty in answers. We desire because the question is one that gestures toward a dimension of literacy as a phenomenon deeply entangled in what makes us human. To gesture toward a semblance of an answer is posthuman. And how starkly we appended ourselves in the writing.

Writing During and After the Holocaust

Writing on the Wall[1]

Condemned to death 24-7-43 (cell 154).

Walk with me to Fresnes prison in Paris. It's still too dark to see clearly, but you might make out three long corridors, each with 506 cells. Cell 154 was mine.

Place your hand on the cell wall and slowly run your fingers across it. Do you feel the indentations in the stone? The letters and numbers, I carved with my nails: "Condemned to death 24-7-43 (cell 154)."

Where is my name?

Oh, I see what you mean. Mine wasn't the only life condemned on 24 July 1943. Perhaps I wrote namelessly for everyone who perished that day. An I and Thou beyond the borders of naming, sharing oneness in bodiless existence, keeping names always on the inside.

[Scratches]

Let's keep going. I want to show you the search room. It's larger, yet it remains a suffocating darkness. I spent hours in this room, before entering Cell 154.

Place your hand on the wall and slowly run your palm through it. Feel again the scratched stone. If you allow yourself, you will hear the different voices of the past, the sounds of fingernails carving walls, verbalizing doubts of panic: Are they going to shoot us? Gas us? Bury us alive?

"Pierre, my dear, do not forget me."

Feel again. Listen with care to this woman's voice, as it echoes pain and gasps for air. Feel how before the woman gives way to sobbing, she tightens her stomach, fights her distress and carves a message to her husband, "Pierre, my dear, do not forget me." The pain is written into love. Listen beyond the torturing and squelching sound of the carving fingernails: love is rewritten anew. These are words of a murdered love.

Underneath, a name this time. Praxiya Dimitrak—murdered, but still alive, in the here-and-now, though differently than in the there-and-then.

Look also to the right of her name. I'll read it aloud, "You too, Praxiya, were you sad to die like that—without significance and without a voice? You, too, wanted to leave, something that would stay and remind? I understand you."

We wrote in togetherness, here, in the time when we waited for our uncertain fate, but closest to death. The drawings and symbols are us, still, absent, present, in this material specificity. In these rooms, there was someone, many some-ones, many lives, sometimes desiring to write life into these walls for proof: WE WERE HERE.

We produced carvings over older carvings, over much older carvings. We cre-ated a chain of living semiosis. We linked past worlds to present and to future ones. We wrote our voices and sufferings into these walls. Something that carried forward.

"Important notice, Paul, the doctor, was here." A voice against oblivion.

Who am I?

I am the writer and the writing. You are not alone.

Written into Adulthood[2]

"When were you born?"

These are the first and only words addressed to the arriving. For some, their answer will hasten death. For others, their answer will prolong life. In Janowski,[3] this question does not celebrate being born into life.

"When were you born?"

There are Akser and Bronek, two inmates writing down fake birthdates instead of deathdates. Janina's turn: instead of 1931, they write her history into 1929. A child would be killed, gassed, shot . . . useless for labor. These numbers change

Janina's history and future. Instead of walking the left line, the one to death, she becomes with temporary life in the right line.

Now in her right line, Janina thinks of her mom, whom she was forced to abandon, just a few streets away from Janowski camp. She struggles to evade the thought that she might forever follow a line without her mother. Akser and Bronek's written lie, these numbers on paper, grant Janina life, but the life this lie writes is not that of a child.

[Two weeks earlier]

Janina's frail mother lies on a hospital bed.

There is no one to care for her. Most have been deported to Piaski—killed. The ghettoes are deserted. Dead. Janina and her mother escape deportation until this point because of her mother's position as a nurse. But life is now threatened not just by the Nazis. There are weakened and starved bodies, illnesses frantically infecting; if not the Nazis, then disease murders. With time, her mother could recover, her illness is not one that would naturally kill. But time is what makes this illness so threatening. The Nazis will not afford time to the weak, the ill or the child. Such bodies cannot serve the economy of the war, to Piaski they go—to be disappeared.

Her mother's baggy, red eyes and wrinkled face cannot hide her illness. On her rests Janina's destiny: If she is deported, so will Janina be—a child who will burn with her. The agony in her eyes makes her look older. She worries: how might I protect my child? Every effort to keep Janina alive, to bring her out of this barbarity alive seems useless. There is an agonized mother, lying on a hospital bed, realizing that she can no longer do much for her child, to keep her little girl alive.

"*Pourquoi tu es triste? 'L'action' n'a pas encore commencé.* "

A mother's broken heart. Her tender eyes, desiring to wrap Janina with protection. Her tears, externalizing what she struggles to do and say to her little girl:

"*Pour moi 'l'action' est déjà en route. Et malgré la cyanure, ma mort va être dure parce que toi, tu es là. En ce qui me concerne moi, je n'ai pas à hésiter.*"

"*Est-ce que ce n'est pas mieux d'en finir une bonne fois pour toutes, dans les bras l'une de l'autre? Que vaut la vie pour moi si je dois vivre seule?*"

"*Il faut que tu y ailles! Il faut que tu nous venges, moi et papa!*"

What could be said? What words could undo the inevitable separation of this mother and this child?

There is only goodbye.

[Janowski camp]

Each day, Janina shakes through physical labor that punishes her 12-year-old body before it collapses in the Wäscherei barrack, where she sleeps with older bodies. Her routine is always the same: after a piece of bread and a coffee which the inmates fight over at 3:30 am, the women of Wäscherei make their way to the DAW[4] workshop. There, they must meet a daily quota of four pants or jackets to be spared prolonged hours of work, carrying bricks and polishing toilets the following day.

To get to the DAW workshop, they traverse deadly terrain. They must pass through the "bunker" where those condemned await their death. Ears ring with the sound of an orchestra that plays the "Tango of Death." The condemned are humiliated before being killed: Walking to this music—to its mocking rhythms, directed by the barbarous SS officers—the condemned arrive to their graves: BAM BAM! Then burnt.

In the meantime, work begins at 6 am, and ends at 6 pm. Janina is only a little girl: In fact, 12 years of age; in the camp, 14. 1929 instead of 1931 gives her this life of a fabricated slave. Does she consider this fabrication? Is death in her thoughts? Perhaps, perhaps not. But these hours allow Janina to remember experiences and to rewrite them into thoughts, then questions: Is her mother still alive? When will she see her again?

This searching inner monologue is interrupted by Bauer's sporadic orders. Janina's overseer in the DAW workshop, berates her with scoldings.

Work harder!
Work faster!
Work . . .!

But nothing stops her from going back inside of herself where the possibility of her mother's existence lives. Her search continues until one day, two women tell her that her mother died in the dispensary of this camp, so close to, so far from. The story the women tell her becomes an endless reel in her mind: Her ailing mother, lying on the floor of the dispensary room and forming a circle with three other women. They ingest cyanide potassium in protest at dying at the hands of the perpetrators.

Janina cries only when she is alone.

That night sleep is impossible. Words want to escape, perhaps she yearns to share. Her mother is gone, but she feels her close: she writes her mother, they write together.

Everything seems heavy, the paper, the pencil, but not the words, which have been written and rewritten into heart and mind and soul throughout waking life. They float, and touch, and project. In verse, Janina writes the lasting wound of when she was forced to leave her mother in the hospital, to face their fates apart.

"Pourquoi . . . m'as tu laissée seule
Parmi tant d'étrangers?"

She remembers a child. Herself? Perhaps, the child's mother will come when everything is quiet and peaceful, to kiss her goodnight, to, momentarily, take away the painful image of her mother's ashes, of the smoke consuming her instead of being consumed by the love of her child.

"Viens maman, viens."

The moment moves the letters, words, verses. Altogether, there is Janina, her mother, the barrack and the older bodies, the memories, the loss, the yearning for her mother—these are not just words.

["Maman" p. 120, lines 12–16][5]

But Janina is no longer the child in her writing, of that moment, of that happy once upon a time. The comfort of this sofa—her *grabat*—of a goodnight kiss, of having her mother. Gone. Burnt. Yet alive, somehow, in written experience.

Her poem searches to account for this tension, just as she must now account for herself, a child written into adulthood, stripped of her mother, by the horrors of history, the inmate at intake and now her pencil in the night. She searches through writing and with writing, noting words that desire an impossible present. Holding the pencil point close to the paper, she admits candidly the dread that stalks her:

"Je cherche de quoi me consoler . . . j'espère que tu reviendras
Que tout s'est réellement passé."

But resolved, she writes:

Goodbye, Mama.

Poetry that Moves Camp

Unable to sleep in the suffocating, lice-infested barracks, six to ten women from her unit step outside in the June night. Janina considers the courage it takes, this decision to walk outside the barracks after 9 pm. Life is at stake. Their barrack is set on a muddy hill, surrounded by an electrified fence and towers where soldiers guard with spotlights and guns.

Then, she hears the women chanting. Harmonizing? Singing. Something about their singing urges her to join them, despite the dangerous nature of this decision. She can't go back now; her body is absorbed into this unifying movement. At a short distance, the rising smoke of Piaski singes the sky in the name of those who perished.

Janina's frail fingers grasp something precious. She wants to share it and to keep the moment alive as long as possible. Her eyes plunge into the words that hold a part of her. She recites the poem meant for her mom; it is the first time that she shares it. The women listen quietly. The song stops but continues.

Belzec, Weisesenhoffa prison, Piaski, Death, the loss of her mother, the concentration camp—these are her poetry's topics. As she continues reading, Janina appears older, mature, her young spirit consumed by a life that shouldn't belong to a child. A new type of togetherness, of unity, is formed, and in the days to come, the women, as well as the head of her division, Lucy Hasenus, plead to Borwicz to save this them in her.

Uncontained

Michal Maksymilian Borwicz, a prisoner with a background in literature and connections to the Polish Socialist Party (PSP), organizes illegal cultural events and communicates with members of the PSP and Zegota council, an underground organization outside Janowski that aids Jews. At first, the exchanges are written letters brought in and out of the camp. But later, with other inmates' help, Borwicz meets with the council outside of the camp. Borwicz moves in and out of the camp, sharing in the mission to save words on stained paper: as human authors, they will perish, but together, they smuggle their writings outside the camp to the PSP. Whether within or beyond the camp, they will not die without saying. The barbed wire limits of the camp are no less deadly, metal, real. But in this instance, fences cannot contain the desire to write, a desiring that chooses to move in mortal danger beyond, and then toward the smoldering evil back inside.

Tonight, at a cultural meeting Borwicz organizes inside the Janowski fences, silence sets in. Distant memories are felt in the quiet, forging an alone-togetherness amongst the prisoners. Borwicz's voice breaks the silence, his words flowing from a scrap of paper stained with mud. Togetherness slowly becomes less alone, mud-stained words taking form amongst these inmates, who have also been stained with mud: Beatings and insults, kicks and slaughters, scorns and spite. Stained alone together.

Janina stares, listens. The alone-togetherness she feels in the present includes singing with the women outside barracks. Could she share herself here, too? But the question is rhetorical. She wants to share so the moment stays alive, for as long as possible. Her eyes plunge into the words that withhold a part of her. In this way, this togetherness continues . . . and there isn't a sound, just her voice that appeases the night.

["Piaski-Dunes" p. 117, lines 1–22]

Words that speak of pain, portray strong affects, vacillating between life and death: "Where to go? Does liberty still have the power to seduce us after all this suffering?" Tears stumbled down dirty faces. That a 12 year old could express, so acutely, the reality in which they live, slowly to perish, moves them, awakening, feeding a less alone-togetherness that moves beyond the camp, that exceeds its sharp-edged metal borders. These poems, simple and without detours, embody a life richer than that imposed by the perpetrators: Poetry is no trivial thing, especially not in hell.

Neither her writing nor the child-poet shall perish in the Nazis' ovens: Borwicz-poetry-voice-movements in and out—a feeling that this does not belong here, a feeling in excess of hell, saves her.

Writing Atmospheres

Fall is around the corner. Along with nature, faces, attitudes and feelings change. They know: Winter kills more than other seasons. Bare skin exposed to cold. No refuge, even their beds frozen in the barracks. And winter loves illness. It has become complicit in the extermination effort—this is evil's reach. Bodies—more tired than ever. The Nazis—grumpier and meaner. Winter loves beatings and assaults. Together, they weaken bodies quicker. What is the point of life when the forces of life feel allied against you?

Morale collapses in on itself, again. No strand of hope escapes the chasm. Fewer smiles. The freezing weather gives way to quiet curfews. Songs and recitations cease. What once was a strong sisterhood now dissipates, the feeling frozen somewhere in the past.

Janina has less patience for poetry. Her bones, spirit, writing . . . stilled. Will Borwicz keep his promise? Will he save her? She no longer believes that he will bring her to Krakow, to the Aryan side, where she will be safe. Darker days take over, making the camp entirely a cemetery. Without hope, prisoners begin to rebel—to look for death. More and more executions take place. The half-alive are forced to watch with a clear message: Let this be a reminder of what awaits if you defy our orders.

Dead end.

A man is about to be executed. For what? Soup. For wanting more soup. Janina breaks her line and walks away. She does not want to watch. But a guard prompts her to return. It's first time that Janina watches an execution. She had shut her eyes before . . . the man puts the rope around his own neck—no reluctance. He is resigned. Quiet voices comment on the man's heroism. This is not the first time that she hears comments about dying quietly, indifferently, heroically. She used to prefer to suffer hunger and loss, but live, because she loved life despite it all. Now, as the man hangs, her longing for life also dangles. Perhaps dying stoically is better than living this hell.

And no words or poems or writing or sharing or songs can undo what has now settled in the camp and in Janina. Writing atmospheres—frozen.

Dead end.

Forced into Words

"Boruchowicz nous emmène à Cracovie. On part demain!" says Rena.

————

[In Krakow, the Aryan side]

Janina's first hiding place is with Mrs. Wanda, an aesthetician during the day and a fabricator of false papers to help conceal Jews' identities. Janina's new name is Marysia.

Here Janina has her own little room and bed. The privacy that she longed for in the camp finally allows her to rest physically and emotionally. The tiny room jogs memories of what once was her happy, ordinary place with mom and dad. Words unfreeze this place laminated with memories. Now, here, she writes away from the past, from the camp, and toward it, her parents.

["Apaisement" p. 125, lines 13–19]

She looks up to see Marianska at her door. Marianska is a member of the Zegota council and she is responsible for finding Janina's hideouts. She compels Janina to put on paper her memories and experiences, to record them. But Janina has never written prose. Where will she start?

Prose does not provide her with the refuge of poetry. Prose forces facts of the past onto Janina's body. She must account for it all, must remember the detail as detail was. Prose makes sense in a way poetry does not. Poetry provides a refuge from a forced sense of sense; poetry is sense-making on her own terms.

The story that Prose writes begins when Janina enters Janowski camp and ends with this writing, in this room. But Marianska pleads with Janina, again, to write more sense about her experience before she was locked in the concentration camp. Suddenly, the walls of her room suffocate her, trapping her with memories of when her nightmare began, with her father's death.

[1939]

Janina is 10. First come the Soviets.

As the leader of a Polish journal, her father's life is endangered. He thinks that the Soviets will not harm women and children, and so he flees to Romania for safety.

But soon, the Nazis arrive, and her father flees back to Lvov. Before he can get to Janina and her mother, the Soviets apprehend him at the border of Poland.

[1941]

Janina is awoken by an abundance of kisses. She doesn't recognize the man in front of her: Her father. He looks older. His head is bald.

"Papa, is that you?"

For a second, the little girl thinks that her father could only appear in dreams. But the joy of a child takes over. Her father is different, but he is still hers.

Happiness does not last.

Ukrainian children beat up elderly Jews.
People scream.
There are beatings.
People are detained.
Chaos everywhere.

As Janina and her father make their way back home, Madame Niunia Blaustein begs her father to turn back. To help those who have been detained. What is about to happen, Janina understands already. Her father's gaze is sad. He kisses her, and Janina tears up.

"*Si tu m'aimes, vas-y et sois courageuse. Il ne faut jamais pleurer. Pleurer n'est qu'une humiliation dans le malheur, comme dans le bonheur. Vas-y, rentre à la maison et laisse-moi seul maintenant.*"

This is the last time Janina sees her father.

[Struggling writing-now]

Now, Prose forces Janina to write this memory into words. She struggles with herself. Everything feels heavier: The paper, the pen, even the words. She pushes through. She writes through. The pencil's point glued to the paper. The paper becomes wordier. The letters take shape faster. And when the hustling of recording is over, so is Janina's willingness and capacity to write.

It takes her two weeks to be able to write anything again.

Undone in the Writing

I'm not sure how to begin this movement. Part of me wants to ask our readers if they were moved and in what ways did this writing undo them, if at all. But it would be impossible to get straight answers to this question—how could anyone define their experiences experiencing?

The limits of language are undoing me, too. I think back to moments writing this chapter, and I still feel dissatisfied with the words on paper. Janina's story moves me in ways that verbalize in my thoughts, almost without asking for the words, and I can feel them move around and throughout my body. But then I try to communicate how I am moved—sometimes to Christian, at times to Janina, and of course, through my own writing here—but then I find myself wordless.

When I finally do write, I un/write; when I speak, I mostly ponder and stutter. I just can't find the words that I was first forced to feel-think in moments of encounter with Janina's story.

I un/write because words trick me. One moment they lend themselves to be written, and so I type them. Letters take their place in words, and words in sentences. There are paragraphs on paper. Soon after, an orchestra of words populates the white surface that makes up this document. It looks pretty. I become a spectator to my own words. I read them, sometimes quietly and at times aloud. Often, I am left with the question: Have I colonized Janina's story? Interpreted out of history and into something academic, something less human?

Words orchestrate their becoming-with-screen by colonizing the force of feeling that circulates in me. Suddenly, there is war. Language on the one side, and feeling on the other. Language's allies—first words, then letters, later phrases and finally a product of symbols—fight to sound pretty. They want to be the force that moves because that is what good writing is expected to do. Soon, feeling's allies—nonrepresentation, affect and humility—fight to be given space to move without pretension.

The result is tension, struggle, more feeling. There is also frustration: Externalizing this movement within cannot be saved from being lost in translation. Translation to thoughts and translation to language. Voices in my head:

So, what is truth?
Is truth definable?

Whose truth? Definable by who?

Janina's truth.
What is Janina's truth?

How could you ever know?

I never could. No matter how much attention to Janina's writings. Despite our conversations. Regardless of my efforts to feel her story, to feel how writing moves and to express that movement. In the end, how could I ever know what Janina's truth is, or was? How could I ever write any truth of feeling into words? The most that my desiring humanity could do is to accept that there could never be an answer to *how writing moves*, and yet to let writing move me, and to move with the feeling that compels it, and to know that as one truth. Here.

Finding History's Feeling in the Minor Key

It's a rainy day in Israel. Janina is 65 years old and newly retired from her professional life as a chemist. It's strange, thinking about her life—its beginning, middle and now, toward its *natural* end. Where did the years go? Now, with her loving husband and a cup of tea at hand, she contemplates her life in the immediate years after the war.

[After the war]

A letter is delivered to Janina from Israel. It's from her aunt, her father's sister. A surviving relative? She decides to travel to Israel to meet her, but cancer gets to her first. By her hospital bed, Janina cares for her aunt. In her grey eyes, Janina sees her father, but that tender stare leaves her only a day after her arrival to Israel. Again, Janina is alone.

She desires studying literature, but first, she must learn Hebrew.

There is a Hebrew program that offers a five-hour work shift and a five-hour period of language education. It's the perfect opportunity for her to work, to sustain herself and to study. Her dream of studying literature lies in a near horizon, but soon, it dissipates. Was the program a scam? Janina ends up working the hours meant for her Hebrew education and is forced to abandon her dream of studying literature for chemistry.

[Israel: 1950s and 1960s]

Despite her career change, this young chemist desires publishing her accounts of the war, but the barrier against literature continues throughout a decade of denial. Israel denies the Shoah's terrible experiences until the trial of Adolf Eichmann, an SS officer. Publishers reject stories of the war.

Still, Janina's bond with literature persists.

1964: Janina writes *They Are Still Alive*, a novel partially based on her diary and complemented with fiction. The Association of Writers and Composers accepts it and awards it second prize for best novel: Money that serves as seeds for growing her love for literature.

1967: The seeds of money buy Janina a private publisher. She publishes her novel. Janina should be happy, but she is overcome by the sadness of knowing that her real accounts of the war remain unwanted.

In Israel, the world of literature continues to reject writings of the war.

[Europe: 1950s and 1960s]

Here, things are different because the world of literature welcomes accounts of the war. People want to know. Researchers want to make History out of the Holocaust. They want to interpret it. To make a certain sense.

Borwicz, Janina's savior, is now a researcher who hopes to give the World ears to his and others' experiences of the war. Where has his mastery of literature gone? Where is his belief in literature for re/humanizing victims?

Compacted into a majoritarian History, its structures, its evidential certainties.

Along with Janina's accounts of the war.

In 1946, Borwicz publishes Janina's accounts, written in that little room just freed from Janowski.

[History Book]

Two journals,
By Janina.
One of Janowski camp.
One since her father's death.
Both about the war.

A crime committed and:
Lost their wholeness,
Broke their original form,

Made the two journals into one.
Adding, omitting, changing and remaking.
Borwicz and Marianska
Make Janina's felt-experiences
Fit their lens of the war.

Claiming to change simply
Some words,
To rearrange and reformulate
For clarity's sake,
Borwicz and Marianska
Add, omit, change, and remake
Two into one.

1946,
One year after the war.
Janina's felt-experiences,
Thoughts and words,
Memories and sufferings,
Colonized into the grips of majoritarian History.

What is the point of a testimony if History silences it by playing in the major?

Now, there are the testimonies of twenty surviving children
Known by Janina
From the orphanage
Where she remained after the war.

These children don't recognize the enemy:
History in the major key,
Ready to slaughter their testimonies.
Historians' systematic questions
Smother the children's testimonies
Make them into one
Universalize and camouflage them
In the name of history's promise:
To keep the Holocaust from re-happening.

Writings produced, disseminated, shared with the world.
Let the world know,
That this is the experience of the victims,
Of all surviving and all who perished.
Let the world know,
This heartbreaking story.

What is the point of a testimony
if a majoritarian History decides what these unique experiences mean and do to
the world?
But, who can object to this act of humanity?
Seemingly well intended and subtle?

"I'm under the impression that the child tells the truth,"
Says a historian.
"Stop, slow down, pause, wait and continue,"
Pleads another.
Fingers typing quickly,
Hand noting everything
so that nothing is lost.

But everything is lost:
The sound of the testimonies,
The voices, the faces, the moving bodies telling you just what was
Gone.

This alone is a barbaric act.
Children's wounds reopened,
Unhealed,
Objectified.

Children become objects.
Words become objects.
Felt-experiences become objects.

Tears become objects.
Wounds become objects.
Memories become objects.
Writings become objects.

A majoritarian History makes objects of histories.

[2015]

It's 2015. Janina's journal exists outside of History in Spanish, Catalan, Russian, Ukrainian and Hebrew. Sixty-five years to emancipate from the tentacles of History. The words, the order, the feeling through the eyes of 12-year-old Janina, finally intact.

When her father says goodbye, when she knows that this goodbye is forever, when her father's words, "to cry is but a sign of weakness," force her to hold her tears—all this expresses Janina's first accounts of the war. Words that are no longer touched. Words that are, from the moment they came to be, in the very instant that they left Janina's heart and engraved the paper at Marianska's request.

Her writing now lives. It is untouched by a majoritarian handed History. And no one/thing can omit her father's goodbye because it happened under the Soviet occupation, and not the Nazis'. Her journal will not be deconstructed to fill the gaps of other books, nor will it be assembled into parts of other testimonies to complete the story of a struggle—of how the children of the Holocaust grew up, matured and suffered. Her picture will not be taken to complement a testimony to prove its place in a majoritarian History.

Her experiences are hers, and hers only.

Surviving children may have been shaved, maltreated, starved, but their story belongs to them, and it shall not be made into one. A History shall not undo to redo.

Janina's perseverance, or perhaps, love for literature, or perhaps both, has thrived. What her young ears heard, the words that her mother uttered in their last exchange, she avenged:

"*Il faut que tu y ailles! Il faut que tu nous venges, moi et papa!* . . . *Supporte la souffrance, tant de peines!!*"

And now . . . In the comfort of her home, side by side with her loving husband, a cup of tea at hand, she contemplates these words, still with an open wound, one that shall never recover. But today is as beautiful as ever. She is immune to History's majoritarian tendencies, to all those who have dared, dare and will dare to universalize her experience.

For her mother and her father, for her writing and her 12-year-old self. For the young poet who did not perish in the Nazis' ovens.

Writing Without an Object

Humans continue becoming: A part of the Anthropocene (Connolly, 2013), augmented through emerging technologies (Hayles, 2008). But these recent becoming-withs do not make humanity newly posthuman, in the sense that our enduring fragility and the metaphysical horror inflected by the burden of unanswerable questions, "Where did all this come from? or, Why could we never refrain from war?" are inescapable reminders of our own limitations. From time to time across the centuries something forces us to reflect on this fragility; something in history forces us to think. Something, not always of human making, forces us to reconsider what humans can do (Hayles, 2008), what humans are doing (Connolly, 2013), how humans know each other (Manning, 2016), or even humanity's physical location, and thereby meta-physical future, in the universe (Galilei, 1610/2016). Horrors are perpetrated that force us to ask whether we deserve the humanity we live. But through the horror of horrors a 12-year-old girl writes, says and moves us toward why we must live. We feel it through her even though we cannot quite put it into words. We are forced to remember that we have always been posthuman, and that we will continue being reminded.

We began this chapter with the argument that the primacy of scientism and rationalism in academia has welled up over years and has now broken out, forcing us to try and think differently about even—especially—the small moments that escape being pinned down as an "object" of analysis. Working from this energy in the field, we proceeded with writing not about how writing moves as a rationalized object of study. We wrote instead in a subject–subject–subject (. . .) relationship desiring to express what moves in the process of writing about writing *with each other*, with Janina, with Christian-Daniella, with his-tories coming into new relations. In this way, coming to know how writing moves through Janina's stories, our talks with her, our exchanges with each other as co-authors and our writing process is part of our own struggle to live while remembering our fragility, our own limitations as always posthuman beings. This was a struggle because the majoritarian tendencies of representa-tion and interpretation challenged us at every strike of the keyboard, at every turn of talk. The impulse to get the truth of the matter; to find the right histori-cal detail; to interpret back upon the experience of a young girl to whom none of us, even Janina, have access any longer. Most importantly, our relationship with Janina was threatened by the binary of subject–object, by making her past the object of our study.

Because of this, we wrote and revised the above movements while *forcing ourselves to feel like we had never quite gotten to something* about how writing was moving between us. This meant that our writing process—our process of com-ing to know through our experiences of writing—required, at first, failing to be purely affective, purely nonrepresentational (as if such a thing is even possible, especially in words). For Daniella, this often involved feeling herself pushing and shoving words onto the screen because she just couldn't find the right words, or the right number of words, or the right combination of words, or the right anything needed to say just what. But this failure of adding unnecessary and overlong descriptions of emotional experiences, and then realizing it, meant simultaneously realizing the impulse to over-write, over-explain and over-know affect, as if it were an object. It is not rational that feeling explains itself, and so reason does its work to explain. When reason kicks into overdrive, you know you are onto something about feeling.

The affect of feeling pushing back became the small moments that forced us both to think, to reflect on the inescapable fragility of our shared us-ness, to know it, and to become with it in more ethical relations in our writing-with each other. Feeling along each other's writing for moments of over-knowing and over-explaining helped put the unsayable into fewer words. Christian reviewed Daniella's drafts, over and over, cutting explanations and writing indirect descriptions of experience to open new potentials of being moved without explaining why the reader ought to be. This meant describing materiality—weather, mud, scratches, pencil—all around the scene of feeling. A material dancing around something. After each rewriting, we talked about what we thought the movements were becoming-about, and we returned to the screen. All along this collaboration with each other as authors, with Janina, with histories, it felt like something of Janina's experience was actually getting (to) us. It felt like we had come to know what we hope you have felt, too: A more human literacy studies must be posthuman.

Notes

1 All language in quotes within this first movement are paraphrased from Borwicz (1954).
2 All language in quotes from this point onwards are from Janina's poems and/or journals, including one published work (Hescheles 2016).
3 Janowski was primarily a labor camp dedicated to the production of German weapons. Ukranian, Jewish and Polish prisoners were brought here to work. In 1942, Janowski was extended and divided into three sections. In the first section, there was the camp's administration, SS housing and processing for deporting and killing inmates. The second section was jagged and held the prisoners' barracks and kitchens. Finally, there were the workshops where the inmates were brought to work every day.
4 DAW is a Deutsche term that refers to German weapon factories, this one situated close to the camp (not within). Janina and the women of her barracks needed to traverse the camp to get to the DAW, and because it was outside of the camp, some women would risk escape attempts.
5 In working to publish this chapter, we have found ourselves entangled in, and resisting with little success, publishing processes through which language becomes industry capital. Traditional publishing processes value language as a capital object, necessarily objectifying language, here Janina's poetry as unrelated to Janina herself,

as a speaker, and as unrelated to you, as a reader. This speaker/hearer interaction, and these poetic words, become objects in the representation of value-as-capital. They are not subjects in relation to the affects of speaking or writing, hearing or reading, that language expresses. As we have argued in this chapter and throughout this book, affect theory forces thinking without an object, and this move alone compels a reconsideration of value in singular and emergent subject–subject relations. We therefore pause in this footnote to highlight three sections where we are not permitted to quote from Janina's memoir, given that such a quote would include lines of poetry. We ask you to find these poems via our citations in brackets that mark these sections. We ask you to read them, hear them and become through language's tendency to move us unexpectedly toward imagining otherwise. How might affect theory inform theories of language and literacy that reclaim language from capitalization?

See: Hescheles, 2016.

References

Barad, K. (2007). *Meeting the universe halfway: Quantum physics and the entanglement of matter and meaning*. Durham, NC: Duke University Press.

Bennett, J. (2009). *Vibrant matter: A political ecology of things*. Durham, NC: Duke University Press.

Boldt, G.M. & Leander, K. (2017). Becoming through "the break:" A post-human account of a child's play. *Journal of Early Childhood Literacy, 17*(3), 409–425.

Borwicz, M. (1954). *Ecrits des condamnés à mort sous l'occupation allemande (1939–1945): étude sociologique*. Paris, France: Presses Universitaires de France

Connolly, W.E. (2013). *The fragility of things: Self-organizing processes, neoliberal fantasies, and democratic activism*. Durham, NC: Duke University Press.

Ehret, C. (2018a). Propositions from affect theory for feeling literacy through the event. In D.E. Alvermann, N.J. Unrau, M. Sailors (Eds.), *Theoretical models and processes of literacy* (7th Edition) (pp. 563–581). New York, NY: Routledge.

Ehret, C. (2018b). Moments of teaching and learning in a children's hospital: Affects, textures, and temporalities. *Anthropology & Education Quarterly, 49*(1), 53–71.

Ehret, C., Hollett, T. & Jocius, R. (2016). The matter of new media making: An intra-action analysis of adolescents making a digital book trailer. *Journal of Literacy Research, 48*(3), 346–377.

Galilei, G. (2016). *Sidereus Nuncius, or the sidereal messenger*. Chicago, IL: University of Chicago Press. (Original work published 2016).

Hayles, N.K. (2008). *How we became posthuman: Virtual bodies in cybernetics, literature, and informatics*. Chicago, IL: University of Chicago Press.

Hescheles, J. (2016). *À travers les yeux d'une fille de douze ans*. Paris, France: Classiques Garnier.

Ingold, T. (2013). *Making: Anthropology, archaeology, art and architecture*. New York, NY: Routledge.

Ingold, T. (2016). *The Life of Lines*. New York, NY: Routledge.

Kuby, C.R., Rucker, T.G. & Kirchhofer, J.M. (2015). "Go Be a Writer:" Intra-activity with materials, time and space in literacy learning. *Journal of Early Childhood Literacy, 15*(3), 394–419.

Manning, E. (2016). *The minor gesture*. Durham, NC: Duke University Press.

Robinson, M. (2015). *The givenness of things*. New York, NY: Picador.

St. Pierre, E.A. (2013). The posts continue: Becoming. *International Journal of Qualitative Studies in Education, 26*(6), 646–657.

St. Pierre, E.A. (2014). A brief and personal history of post qualitative research: Toward "post inquiry." *Journal of Curriculum Theorizing, 30*(2).

St. Pierre, E.A. (2016). Rethinking the empirical in the posthuman. In C. Taylor & C. Hughes, (Eds.), *Posthuman research practices in education* (pp. 25–36). London, UK: Palgrave Macmillan.

Stewart, K. (2007). *Ordinary affects*. Durham, NC: Duke University Press.

Thiel, J.J. (2015). Vibrant matter: The intra-active role of objects in the construction of young children's literacies. *Literacy Research: Theory, Method, and Practice, 64*(1), 112–131.

9

AFFECTIVE SKETCHES

Writing, Drawing and Living with Analysis

Ty Hollett and Jaclyn Dudek

The Story of Sketching

In the spring of 2016, Ty taught a graduate course on interaction analysis (IA); Jaclyn was enrolled as a student. The course used Jordan and Henderson's article (1995) as an anchor, drawing on a key phrase in the article as an overall metaphor for the course: "Ways of Seeing." As a class, we talked a lot about how to see data—how to identify interactive hot spots, for instance, or how to review video with collaborators, how to trace conversational turns, how to analyze how people arrange themselves spatially to achieve intersubjectivity, and more. We read articles on conversation analysis and ethnomethodology in order to further help us refine our ways of seeing.

A few weeks into the semester, and inspired by a citation to Goffman's dramaturgy (1982), we, Ty and Jaclyn, began talking about drama—something on both of our minds given Jaclyn's background in acting and her future dissertation project studying dramatic interpretations of Shakespearean plays in outdoor settings. We discussed how much of our readings were focused on seeing, but feeling seemed to be missing, and the fact that, as researchers, we are continuously called to see data, but rarely asked to feel it. The following week in class, in hopes of introducing a methodology of feeling, and in order to activate our own bodies as researchers, Jaclyn led a mini-lesson on improvisation. Students partnered and performed a variety of drama exercises—what Jaclyn called "awareness training"—closing their eyes, for instance, as their partner circled around them and made various sounds with their hands, like rubbing or snapping, from various distances.

Later in the semester, Ty challenged Jaclyn to *feel* some data that he had previously collected of middle-school youth making a digital book trailer for the book *Holes*. Jaclyn, at the time, had recently finished a course with Gail Boldt (see chapter 2, this volume) on post-structuralism and literacy, thus Jaclyn was primed to experience her data in ways that belied the representational logic of IA. Moreover, inspired by the class's reading/viewing of Sousanis's graphic novel *Unflattening* (2015a), as well as his take on "Grids and Gestures" (2015b), Jaclyn began to develop sketches of her experience, both seeing and feeling this data in new ways, often tracing out the rhizomatic nature of youth's production of the digital book trailer, its ebbs and flows, starts and stops. Jaclyn produced more mimetic representation of specific instances from the video data. Her sketches dreamily floated between the reality of the digital book trailer's production and fictional elements from the narrative of *Holes*. The sketches enabled her to play with time as well, as she collapsed minutes into moments, following one student, for instance, as he clenched a fist or leaned back in a chair.

Ty, in contrast, took Sousanis's "Grids and Gestures" (Sousanis, 2015b) as a starting point, a short piece that the class read alongside the opus, *Unflattening*. In his description of grids and gestures, Sousanis urges artists to sketch "marks of some sort" which signify "physical or emotional activity within and across those frames of time" (p. 3). He especially urges artists "to do their best not to draw representational things," instead nudging artists to consider how various marks and lines can depict movement over time. Inspired by this focus on "emotional activity," Ty represented the production of the digital book trailer through lines and shapes, working to move with waves of energy as they ebbed and flowed across participants, within and across production settings. His sketches then were not produced through bursts—thus only focusing on the loud, or chaotic, moments, but were sometimes slow and faint, tracing lulls and silences too. Furthermore, whereas Jaclyn created detailed drawings of participants in the book circle, focusing particularly on students' embodied orientation toward the passing of the novel from hand to hand, Ty followed movement of affective energy at that moment by drawing energy spirals, especially as those energies began to dissolve outward and away from the circle itself. This process entailed not just watching video, but listening to it—hearing the experience without visual cues. Conversely, an additional layer of the process included watching data—without sound—an overlapping analytic experience that led Ty to etch new "marks" and "lines" on paper.

We then met to share our sketches, new energy emanating from them— and us—as we found and questioned their divergences and overlaps. Using the sketches as starting points for our discussion, we re-experienced the production of the digital book trailer together, recognizing similarities and differences in how the data moved and put us into motion. This conversation, then, enabled us to revisit previously experienced moments in our data, to talk through what we saw, or felt, and how it moved us.

FIGURE 9.1

In our collaborative dialogue, Jaclyn, for instance, described how she sketched various moments of the data and then juxtaposed the images to see if "something else could emerge through their juxtaposition." Thus her act of sketching was also an act of (re)combination. For example, Jaclyn's drawing of a shovel led Ty to share his sketch's focus specifically on the energy of "things," especially how those things—shovels, shoes, hats—"began to move bodies in new ways," as he put it. The conversation ebbed and flowed, resting briefly on the experience of feeling the data, of the differences between sketching and coding and our desires to sketch-in-the-moment when in the field in the future. Even more broadly, and inspired by these sketches, we began to ask: How does affect theory permeate how we, as literacy researchers, go about our research? How do we feel the bubbling up of a moment, how it creeps (or bursts) into our presence, rests and dissolves? How does one live research, as opposed to conduct it?

Chapter Contours

Through these sketches, and our subsequent collaborative dialogues about them, we consider the affective intensities that move, put into motion, a group of middle-school students throughout their production of a digital book trailer. Affect, animated through our sketching, ebbed and flowed as a group of five middle-school students collaboratively produced a digital book trailer for the novel *Holes*. In short, this small group of students worked alongside two graduate student reading masters candidates (RMCs) to produce their trailer. Book trailers, as a genre, blend elements from book reports with the audiovisual nature of movie trailers, serving both to inform viewers about the novel as well as strive to convince them to read it. Over eight weeks, the original research team collected video and audio data of production sessions, as well as artifacts created by students. Because participants often split up to distribute production of the book trailer (e.g., filming, drawing scenes) researchers moved with participants as they moved across settings (e.g., a gymnasium, a stairwell.)

FIGURE 9.2

Our sketches underscore (intra)activity across a book circle, a stage, stairwell and athletic field, especially as we move alongside two students—Domiana and Marcus—as they collaborate to produce pivotal scenes for the trailer.

Our sketches do not strive for verisimilitude; they are not strictly visual depictions and they do not, necessarily, seek to represent. They are efforts to sense and feel movement, to trace energy emanating from bodies, human and nonhuman.

We present the following as an *affective sketch*, playing with that phrase in two ways: First, we employ drawn sketches to visually display how our data moved us throughout our analysis. Second, we recall improvisational sketches, associated with comedic acting, especially how those sketches could be played, and re-played differently each time, with new actors, new props, new settings. In the following, we use this initial story of our sketching as an entry point toward addressing these questions, thinking and feeling anew through, what we will call, analytical sketches. We briefly bring the theoretical history that influenced our thinking-feeling to the fore before homing further in on how the experience of sketching adjusted our analytic approach. This chapter, then, is about *method*, not in the doing of it, but in the feeling of it. Specifically, it expands representational, ocularcentric approaches to data visualization as a form of inquiry through an overt focus on sketching as one form of living with data. Living with the data through sketching, we argue, offers a methodological means for the body-in-research to attune itself to life in-the-moment. Perhaps, in a future academic conference, audience members will not ask questions such as "What were your methods?" Rather, they might ask: "How did this experience feel?" We offer these analytical sketches as one way to pivot towards this feeling.

In producing this affective sketch—both in writing and in drawing—we let theory guide us (St. Pierre and Jackson, 2014). Specifically, we attune ourselves to the rhythmic capacities of affect through an emphasis on accelerations and decelerations, when things feel like they are speeding up or slowing down (Rosa, 2013; Henriques, 2014). We question what—including people and things—catalyzes those accelerations and decelerations. We find accelerations and decelerations important because of the constant presence of affective energy in both, including energy rising and falling. Moreover, by feeling—and sketching in terms of acceleration and deceleration—our own analytic bodies are constantly in motion themselves, attuning equally to lulls and spikes of activity.

Through reflections on sketches and sketching video data of adolescents making a digital book trailer in school, our chapter complements recent efforts in literacy studies to move beyond static representations of data visualizations and toward a deeper engagement with the "process of visualization as analysis itself" (Smith, Hall & Sousanis, 2015). With this focus, it also participates in a larger, ongoing conversation in literacy studies surrounding nonrepresentation (Deleuze & Guattari, 1987), affect (Massumi, 2002), and the intra-actions among humans and non-human bodies (Barad, 2007). As St. Pierre (2015a) argues, "We have to learn a new language that is incompatible with the ontological grids of intelligibility that structure humanist methodologies" (p.79). Unfortunately, there are no methods to follow or textbooks that offer, say, "four handy research designs for new empirical research" (St. Pierre, 2015a, p. 78). Perhaps, however, researchers do not need only a new language, but also a new way of experiencing data, of seeing, feeling, listening, engaging with it and conveying that data to others who do not just *read*, but see, feel and experience it as well. In doing so, this affective sketch interrogates the experience of data analysis, with an explicit focus on analysts' embodied engagement with data through the production of animated affects (Niccolini, 2016). In the end, we consider these analytical sketches—at this moment in time—to be a means to be "living with" the data (St. Pierre, 2015a), not simply visualizing it in new ways, but (re)feeling it, (re)experiencing it.

"Living with It"

We bring our sketches into contact with thinking about the "new" in "new empiricisms, new materialisms, and postqualitative inquiry" (St. Pierre, 2015a). St. Pierre (2015b) implores researchers in the social sciences to break the shackles of positivist qualitative research. Rather than stopping with data (i.e., coding it, framing it, representing it) she encourages moving with it: "living with it" (p. 92). So-called research practices do not start and stop—at a computer, with a book or article, with a literature review, or a coding scheme—they are continuous, evolving, becoming: When on a run, talking with friends, washing hair, cooking dinner *and-*. In a reference perhaps familiar to readers, St. Pierre (2015a) notes the steady flood of emails she receives inviting her to "learn how to code qualitative data using various software programs" (p. 76), a practice, she argues, that is unthinkable in interpretative social science. Furthermore, of course, coding is unthinkable when performing non-representational analyses. Coding halts motion. It straps in that which is animated. In fact, as Barad (2007) writes, "We do not uncover pre-existing facts about independently existing things as they exist frozen in time like little statues positioned in the world. Rather, we learn about phenomena—about specific material configurations of the world's becoming" (p. 90–91).

Our sketches help us come to know the affectively charged movement that was integral to students' production of the digital book trailer, when the book trailer itself began to take form (Ehret, Hollett & Jocius, 2016). The sketches are one way forward toward expanding our capacities to relate (Adey, 2008), especially to feel and sense the "energetic outcome of encounters" (p. 440) that students had with one another, with the things they employed and with the spaces they inhabited. That said, we do not crystallize individual moments-in-time. Rather, with a nod toward studies of movement in dance and choreography, we think, feel and draw in terms of movement and flow. Manning (2014, p. 165) writes of this effort to become alongside "movement-moving," inspired by the choreographer Forsyth, noting:

> Forsythe speaks not of hitting a form ("do this figure") but of dancing the very force of movement-moving ("find the movement in the figure, and move with it"). He asks his dancers to body, not to "represent" a body. From noun to verb, what movement does is make apparent that nothing is quite what it seems.

An affective method must, then, be moving as well. It must take, as a starting point, that "nothing is quite what it seems." Thus, through our sketches, we seek to "find the movement [. . .] and move with it." Tracing accelerations and decelerations, specifically, helps us do this: when things pick up speed and slow down, only to reignite again. Our drawings act as visual expressions of our efforts to "body"—from noun to verb—in analysis. We move with movement: We body. And through this bodying analysis, we explore the movement that makes up the production of a digital book trailer—the ways in which bodies—those we study as well as our own—are affected, moved, put into motion.

In step with this orientation, we began with a general theme of movement—of bodies, things, being put into motion. Thus, after an initial meeting to discuss how we would (re)enter into the analytic experience, we (un)settled on movement as our theme, curious about the spikes and lulls that propel, and perhaps halt, new media making. Guided by Davies' (2014) assertion that "ideas and concepts are not innocent or neutral, but actively engage in the diffractive entanglement of any research," (p. 734) we sought to move alongside the things, bodies, people, ideas that became entangled in the experience of new media making, how they affected and interfered with one another.

Still, we were also entangled in our own experiences, histories and research engagements. As Davies continues:

> just as ripples and waves and drops of foam do not exist without the body of water, or the wind, of the other matter they encounter (stones, sand, rocks, human bodies . . .), we, as researchers, are part of, and encounter, already entangled matter and meanings that affect us and that we affect in an ongoing, always changing set of movements.
>
> *(2014, p. 735)*

This orientation toward movement, however, ripples back into Ty's nascent career as a researcher—from recent work on the relationship between rhythm (Hollett & Ehret, 2015; Hollett & Ehret, 2017) to initial work related to youth's literacies moving with mobile devices (Ehret & Hollett, 2013; Ehret & Hollett, 2014). Much of thinking (and feeling) stems from his relationship with a mentor, Kevin Leander, who encouraged him early on in his graduate career to look beyond learning and literacy research and toward research from human geography exploring moving bodies (Spinney, 2009), affect (Thrift, 2008), rhythm (Edensor, 2014) and more.

Jaclyn's emphasis on movement stems from her early work in theater and visual arts training. Her theater work has been heavily influenced by body-electric technique, mask-work, clowning and place-based theater. Moreover, her study of Ancient Greek language, drama, modes and meters informs her study and interest in rhythm, and collective performance. When taking the aforementioned class on IA with Ty, Jaclyn would frequently doodle when watching snippets of video, creating sketches and other forms of marginalia in lieu of taking notes. Noticing this practice, Ty encouraged Jaclyn to build her work around her sketches and doodles—and thus their partnership began.

Sketching: Scale, Time, Energy and Overlaps

In the following, we reflect on our sketches and what they enabled us to feel, see, sense and desire when reviewing video and audio footage of the students' production of the digital book trailer. We do not offer the following as findings. Rather, we work to articulate what our sketches offered us by focusing on three emergent areas of interest: the sketch, the dialogue and the movement. The first section, for instance, acts more as a commentary on the sketch itself, especially in terms of how we began to integrate aspects of scale and time in our sketches, themes that emerged as we joined up for our dialogue. From there, we emphasize our dialogue, especially how the overlaps we encountered when collaboratively reviewing our sketches led us to use those overlaps to sense and feel our data differently. That section, then, dovetails with our final section, as we describe how we both sought to move with the generation and dissolution of energy as students produced their book trailer

Still, and even in writing this now, we know that new sketches, at a new time, even perhaps in a new place, would lead us to produce new interpretations of this data, and our dialogue would push us to feel, and see, in new ways. However, given the nature of the book chapter, we freeze the following sections here, awaiting future sketches and future dialogues.

Scaling and Temporalizing Through Sketches

Our sketches enabled us to play with both scale and temporality as we re-engaged with the students' production of the digital book trailer. More specifically, the sketches enabled us to *feel* at different scales and temporalities. The temporal elements of analysis are likely familiar to researchers inspired by methods like IA (Jordan & Henderson, 1995). IA gained momentum alongside video capture technologies which enabled analysts to scrub back and forth through video recordings to revisit analytic "hot spots." Still, in terms of scale, IA methods tend to operate at the scale of the body, video cameras, for instance, standing in as *de facto* humans, capturing interaction from the corner of a classroom. Video cameras, then, mounted on tripods, simulate human vantage points, human perspectives. Of course, while emerging video capture technologies—from wearables, like the GoPro, to drones—are altering the scale of data capture, researchers continue to privilege human-centric perspectives.

The depiction of time in comics is well documented (McCloud, 2000). Readers, McCloud notes, *feel* time, for instance, through the shortening or elongation of specific panels. A longer horizontal panel, for instance, situated between two smaller panels, gives off the feeling of a longer period of time (McCloud, 1994, p. 101). Jaclyn's depictions of the book circle began to play with time—not by elongating it, but by shortening it. After a quick sketch of the book circle as a whole, her sketches begin to zoom in on Marcus.

This alteration of scale—from group to individual—enabled her to shift her analytical feel further as she continued to focus on Marcus, who began to give off an air of frustration when sitting in the book circle. Inspired by his repetitive opening and closing of his fist, Jaclyn then zoomed in further,

FIGURE 9.3

FIGURE 9.4

sketching staccato-like images—quick, small frames—that depicted split-seconds throughout the book circle discussion. Viewed individually, these frames signify frozen moments; viewed collectively however, they signal Marcus's irritation as moments of inspiration dissolved into moments of frustration.

While playing with time, Jaclyn also simultaneously introduced issues of scale, as she felt-sensed a growing frustration by Marcus. Through her sketch, Jaclyn began to attune herself to the scale of the hand, rather than the scale of the body.

By focusing on multiple sketches of Marcus's hand opening and closing, she began to sense the growing frustration that he was emitting when sitting in the reading circle, especially as his voice continued to be overwhelmed by the group's general focus on the book-as-thing. As researchers, we can easily freeze video our data, make screenshots, cut it up, zoom in and, generally, manipulate it as much as we want. But how can we further attune ourselves to moments?

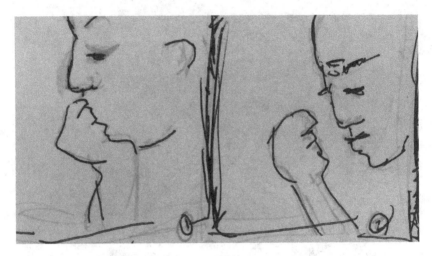

FIGURE 9.5

How can we, potentially, not just *see* but *feel*? Certainly, we can see Marcus grow frustrated as he sits in the circle. Marcus's growing frustration was evinced as he leaned back in his chair and put his face in his hands and, inevitably, stood up. Jaclyn's sketch, however, scaled down even further, shifting from scale-of-body to scale-of-hand.

Jaclyn did not just zoom in however, but also began to zoom out. Thus, our reflective dialogue led Jaclyn to discuss other instances that she sketched when re-experiencing the initial brainstorming in the book circle discussion. Picking up on other energies evident in the auditorium, Jaclyn sketched one student dancing along the stage in the background.

FIGURE 9.6

While this student was not formally ratified as a participant in the digital book trailer project, Jaclyn's emphasis on this student led us to further question how energies—produced by the human and the nonhuman—potentially reverberate within and across spaces: How did this student's exuberance, for example, potentially leak into students' production of the book trailer? This is not to say that everything that moves necessarily factors into production. We are curious, however: What becomes entangled in the production of new media projects, such as the book trailer? In particular, we wonder about the scale of the tangle in question—what bodies count? And further, in this push toward a more affectively attuned experience of analysis, what scales of activity (both human and nonhuman) are included in analysis?

Sketching to Reflect: Overlaps Between Depictions

While our sketches allowed us to engage with our data in (un)related ways, the subsequent conversation about those sketches was perhaps the richest part of the experience. The conversation led us to shift from overreaching theoretical ideas (i.e., intra-action) to discussions about the finer, granular details that we sought to integrate into our sketches. In the following, then, we convey an instance in which our sketches overlapped, but differed in significant ways. While this was a common occurrence—we never sketched out exactly the same thing—we underscore this instance in particular as a means to focus on specific components of each sketch. Thus, in the following, we emphasize the overlaps between our portrayals of students' movement outside of the confines of the school as they sought to portray the "desert" landscape described in the book in an outdoor athletic field adjacent to the school. In particular, we both targeted Marcus's enthusiastic running across the landscape as he sought out the perfect location to film.

Following his theme of energy spirals, Ty sought to depict Marcus's movement—his sprints to various set locations across the athletic field. Thus, in his gesture, Ty illustrates Marcus akin to a spinning top, brimming with energy, careening from one location to another. In doing so, Ty began to consider the ways that Marcus's movement fueled visions of what was possible for them to film. What potential,

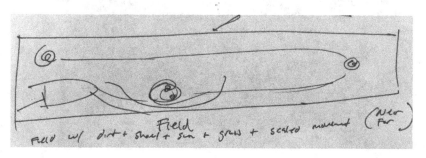

FIGURE 9.7

for instance, did certain patches of grass hold for their book trailer? Certain backdrops? Certain ways in which the sun hit the ground?

Ty's dialogue with Jaclyn, however, was important, as her depiction of Marcus overlapped with Ty's, yet differed significantly. Rather than focusing on Marcus's movement in and of itself, Jaclyn illustrated what Marcus—now taking on the role of setting scout—envisioned as he ran across the field.

Marcus, who ran off exclaiming, "I'm going to be a scout," sets off on his journey, leaving the school in the distance as he enters new, imaginative territory. Where Ty questioned what Marcus might have imagined, Jaclyn illustrated it—including cacti, jackrabbits, scorpions, lizards, holes and shovels. While the eponymous holes were chosen for the book trailer, we wonder what arguments Marcus might have made for various locations in relation to events from the novel if given the opportunity. Jaclyn's sketch, for instance, shows the school far off in the distance, Marcus peering toward it through his binoculars. Together, in our dialogue, we reinterpreted this part of her sketch together, especially the way in which Jaclyn provided such distance between the school and Marcus. Marcus, in that moment, we began to claim, inhabited the world of the novel: He was no longer a school student, but an aspiring director, the athletic field his own personal green screen over which he wanted to add CGI tumbleweed, lizards, holes. Instead, he was called in, back to the group, back to quotes from the novel, back to a not too far distance from the school.

FIGURE 9.8

While the students and RMCs settled on depicting Domiana-as-Stanley, our overlapping sketches inspired us to think more about Marcus's movement, about all that he saw in his mind's eye as he ran from one location to the other. From the perspective of improvisational actors, Marcus was *yes and*'ing as much as possible, creating *something* out of what seemingly appeared to be nothing. Yet, those ideas—except a single hole—were left on the cutting-room floor. When do we—as educators, or researchers—commit the singular improvisational faux pas of saying no, of breaking ideas down before they can even be built up, before they have been given life?

Generation and Dissolution of Energy

In thinking with theory related to movement, our sketches initially drifted toward depictions of both the generation and dissolution of energy among group members. We attuned ourselves to the rise and fall of energy in a number of ways, often sensing the production of an affectively charged atmosphere (Ash, 2013), one that felt thick with excitement or boredom or confusion or frustration. In sketching these atmospheres, then, we felt these atmospheres as moving bodies and things; shouting voices or whisper words, frustrated fingers and declarative fists became entangled together.

Both Ty and Jaclyn, for instance, were drawn to the energy emitted when participants sat, leaned and squirmed when their chairs were put in a circle. Whereas Jaclyn depicted the book circle more realistically and then zoomed in on Marcus, as described in our first section, Ty's depiction of the book chapter was—at least visually—quite different. Ty deliberately did not represent actual people or things. Instead, he used spirals of various sizes to signify the energies that he felt present in the circle.

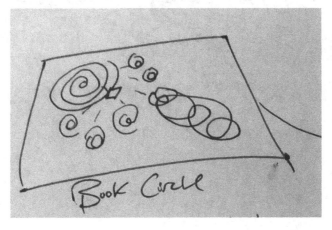

FIGURE 9.9

The larger energy spiral on the left represents Domiana, her hands firmly grasping the book, nearly all attention and energy focused on her. On the right, in contrast, energy spirals outward. This is Marcus, his physical body often leaning out and away from the group, his imaginative body too, bubbling with ideas, scenes, possibilities, which Jaclyn portrayed in one of her sketches.

Jaclyn's sketch imagined Marcus's energy—and his creative ideas—leaking out and away from the group. While others in the circle focused on the text, his visions—a sunset over the desert landscape, lizards, large holes—all spilled out and away, unheard.

The generation, or even dissolution, of energy was a leitmotif for Ty, as he followed the ebbs and flows of energy across students' production settings,

FIGURE 9.10

including a stage, hallway, stairwell and outdoor athletic field. He was moved, for instance, to depict energy levels on the stage like the lines of a heart rate monitor, with spikes and lulls over time.

His notes point toward the energetic pulsations that built up among the students, especially through the introduction of various things, tangible props, that further inspired the students as they brainstormed ideas to film. Various shapes (floating square, circle and triangle above) represented props brought by the RMCs, including shoes, hats and shovels. The props, Ty notes, signaled motility for students, or the potential to move. Shovels inspired students to mimic shoveling motions, hats prompted them to act as specific characters, shoes transported them to an important scene in the novel, which they would subsequently act out.

In his dialogue with Jaclyn, Ty noted that the objects seemed spring-loaded with narrative potential, like a jack-in-the-box waiting to be released. Ty was particularly reminded of theory related to passengering with which he had

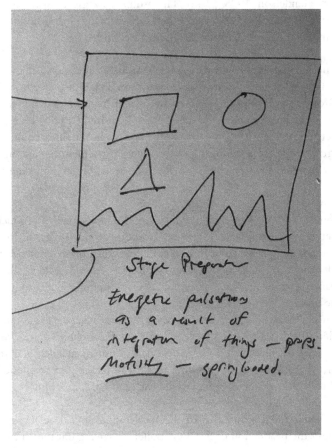

FIGURE 9.11

previously thought—how people, things, sounds and more—were in a constant state of becoming together. On the stage, then, this "becoming with" (Bissell, 2010, p. 270) stretched across students and things as the improvisational *and/and-ness* propelled students toward their next scene, one in which the shoe would play a critical role.

Moving On

After our dialoguing session, there was a new energy emanating from both of us. New ideas, connections to previous work, intentions to sketch in the field emerged. For Ty, especially, there was a stark contrast between how he approached his sketches and how he approached IA (Jordan & Henderson, 1995), and the teaching of it, in his most recent course. Even though IA shies away from preconceived coding schemes, analysts expect "categories to emerge from [their] deepening understanding of the orderliness of the interactions of participants" (Jordan & Henderson, 1995, p. 43). The group work aspect of IA, in which an owner (in IA terminology) brings a previously thematically logged bit of data to share, can begin to feel regimented. As described in IA:

> The tape is played with one person, usually the owner, at the controls. It is stopped whenever a participant finds something worthy of remark. Group members propose observations and hypotheses about the activity on the tape, searching for specific distinguishing practices within a particular domain or for identifiable regularities in the interactions observed. Proposed hypotheses must be of the kind for which the tape in question (or some related tape could provide confirming or disconfirming evidence.
>
> *(Jordan & Henderson, 1995, p. 44)*

While both Ty and Jaclyn certainly drew on IA methods when producing their own sketches—viewing and re-viewing portions of video data, for example—their sketches invited a kind of flexibility and imagination that extended beyond the evidence on the tape, such as Jaclyn's efforts to enter Marcus's creative mind as he leaned back in his chair, possible cinematic options spilling out and away from the group.

Much like Marcus's, as scout, improvisational *and-and'ing* as he ran through the athletic field, there was an excited energy that bubbled up as we collaboratively shared our sketches. It was, honestly, fun to imagine and reimagine together, to musically riff on one another's ideas, picking up on subtle portions of the sketch—the dancing student in the background, for example—and playing with possibility. We said yes to one another.

Our sketches also attuned us to the accelerations and decelerations evident throughout the production of the book trailer. In feeling out these instances, we began to focus particularly on the introduction and movement of things—like shovels and shoes—as well as dramatic changes in scale—like shifting production to an athletic field. Still, while energy spirals began to take new form as new things led to new possibilities, we want to be careful not to pretend that the world is "awash in fluidities" (Marston, Jones & Woodward, 2005, p. 423). As Marston, Jones and Woodward caution, an overt emphasis on fluidity "fetishizes movement in a way that makes invisible its blockages and coagulations" (p. 425). Thus, we could imagine another attempt at sketches, guided by related theory, in which we attuned ourselves to those blockages and coagulations. Drawing on Cresswell's (2010) "politics of mobility," for instance, we could shift our bodies to feel not when things begin to start, but rather when they begin to stop, working to respond to Cresswell's query: "What kind of friction does the mobility experience?" (p. 17).

Finally, our sketches were inspired by Sousanis's *Unflattening* (2015a) and his call for readers to see the world differently. Sousanis, however, does note that his focus throughout *Unflattening* is ocular-centric:

> Permit me to pause briefly here to note that while the discussion has been restricted to the visual, this is not meant to exclude other modes of perception. Rather it is intended that our literal ways of seeing metaphorically serve to encompass other ways of making meaning and experiencing the world.
>
> *(2015, p. 40)*

Much of this focus on alternative ways meaning making, especially in literacy studies, reflects back into the classroom. Vasudevan and Rodriguez Kerr (2016, p. 457), for instance, urge educators to

> [c]onsider what it would mean to open up a space for graphic novels in your classroom to encourage graphic note-taking in your meetings, to show the connections that emerge from your data through graphic displays, and to create assignments that do not privilege the word over other modes of representation.

Throughout this affective sketch, we've sought not only to see, but to feel differently. Thus, our call is not simply for researchers to deploy sketching as an innovative means to engage with analytical experiences. Rather, we deployed sketches to tap into alternative ways to engage with the energies that, in this case, rose and fell throughout experience of new media making. These sketches also enabled us to engage with one another differently, to follow impulses.

Still, this affective sketch, in recalling the work of improvisational artists, is just that: A sketch—one of many that could be produced as new props, new people, new settings entered the scene. What other sketches could have emerged through this analytical experience? Could we, as St. Pierre (2015a) writes, "make a movie, paint a picture, run a marathon?" (p. 91). What if we let feeling guide us rather than methods and the language we have inherited—triangulation, field notes, observations, interviews, etc.? What if we take a lesson from sensuous researchers like Spinney (2006), who, when studying the kinesthetic experience of cyclists, trained with a cycling club to experience the "challenge of researching the saddle" (p. 716), or Pink's (2007; 2008) practice of sensory embodied engagements, which encouraged her and her colleagues to engage with the with the nonmaterial dimensions of towns, "as [they] tasted local foods, felt the sun over [their] heads and the ground beneath [their] feet" (p. 457)?

Perhaps the act of sketching circles us back to the concept of the (improvisational) sketch and the practice of saying "yes . . . and." Analytical sketches, then, provide a revitalized temporal component to the experience of data analysis, a means to both re-visit and re-feel data over time, to say yes to what that data was and yes to what it is yet to become. That is, analytic sketches provide one way to "live with" data, and to let it live as well rather than bury that data—that life—in locked drawers, secure hard drives, conference proceedings and even book chapters.

References

Adey, P. (2008). Airports, mobility and the calculative architecture of affective control. *Geoforum, 39*(1), 438–451.

Ash, J. (2013). Rethinking affective atmospheres: Technology, perturbation and space times of the non-human. *Geoforum, 49,* 20–28.

Barad, K. (2007). *Meeting the universe halfway: Quantum physics and the entanglement of matter.* Durham, NC: Duke University Press.

Bissell, D. (2010). Passenger mobilities: affective atmospheres and the sociality of public transport. *Environment and Planning D: Society and Space, 28*(2), 270–289,

Boldt, G. Lewis, C. & Leander, K.M. (2015). Moving, feeling, desiring, teaching. *Research in the Teaching of English, 49*(4), 430.*

Cresswell, T. (2010). Towards a politics of mobility. *Environment and planning D: Society and Space, 28*(1), 17–31.

Davies, B. (2014). Reading anger in early childhood intra-actions: A diffractive analysis. *Qualitative Inquiry, 20*(6), 734–741.

Deleuze, G. & Guattari, F. (1987). *A thousand plateaus: Capitalism and schizophrenia.* Minneapolis, MN: University of Minnesota Press.

Edensor, T. (2014). Rhythm and arrhythmia. *The Routledge Handbook of Mobilities* (pp. 163–171). London and New York: Routledge.

Ehret, C. & Hollett, T. (2013). (Re) placing school: Middle school students' countermobilities while composing with iPods. *Journal of Adolescent & Adult Literacy, 57*(2), 110–119.

Ehret, C. & Hollett, T. (2014). Embodied composition in real virtualities: Adolescents' literacy practices and felt experiences moving with digital, mobile devices in school. *Research in the Teaching of English, 48*(4), 428–452.

Ehret, C., Hollett, T. & Jocius, R. (2016). The matter of new media making: An intra-action analysis of adolescents making a digital book trailer. *Journal of Literacy Research, 48*(3), 346–377.

Goffman, E. (1982). The interaction order: American Sociological Association, 1982 presidential address. *American Sociological Review, 48*(1), 1–17.

Henriques, J. (2014). Rhythmic bodies: Amplification, inflection and transduction in the dance performance techniques of the "Bashment Gal." *Body & Society, 20*(3–4), 79–112.

Hollett, T. & Ehret, C. (2015). "Bean's World:" (Mine)Crafting affective atmospheres of gameplay, learning, and care in a children's hospital. *New Media & Society, 17*(11), 1849–1866.

Hollett, T. & Ehret, C. (2017). Civic rhythms in an informal, media-rich learning program. *Learning, Media and Technology, 42*(4), 483–499.

Jordan, B. & Henderson, A. (1995). Interaction analysis: Foundations and practice. *The Journal of the Learning Sciences, 4*(1), 39–103.

McCloud, S. (2000). *Reinventing comics: How imagination and technology are revolutionizing an art form.* New York, NY: Perennial, New York.

Manning, E. (2014). Wondering the world directly–or, how movement outruns the subject. *Body & Society, 20*(3–4), 162–188.

Marston, S.A., Jones III, J.P. & Woodward, K. (2005). Human geography without scale. *Transactions of the Institute of British Geographers, 30*(4), 416–432.

Massumi, B. (2002). *Parables for the virtual: Movement, affect, sensation.* Duke University Press.

Niccolini, A. (2016). Animate affects: censorship, reckless pedagogies, and beautiful feelings. *Gender and Education, 28*(2), 230–249.

Pink, S. (2007). Sensing Cittàslow: slow living and the constitution of the sensory city. *The Senses and Society, 2*(1), 59–77.

Pink, S. (2008). An urban tour The sensory sociality of ethnographic place-making. *Ethnography, 9*(2), 175–196.

Rosa, H. (2013). *Social acceleration: A new theory of modernity.* New York, NY: Columbia University Press.

St. Pierre, E.A. (2015a). Practices for the "new" in the new empiricisms, the new materialisms, and post qualitative inquiry. *Qualitative Inquiry and the Politics of Research, 10,* 75.

St. Pierre, E.A. (2015b). Refusing human being in humanist qualitative inquiry. In K.N. Denzin & M.D. Giardina (Eds.), *Qualitative inquiry—past, present, and future: A critical reader* (pp. 103–120). Walnut Creek, CA: Left Coast Press.

St. Pierre, E.A. & Jackson, A.Y. (2014). Qualitative data analysis after coding. *Qualitative Inquiry, 20*(6), 715–719.

Smith, A., Hall, M. & Sousanis, N. (2015). Envisioning possibilities: Visualising as enquiry in literacy studies. *Literacy, 49*(1), 3–11.

Sousanis, N. (2015a). *Unflattening.* Cambridge, MA: Harvard University Press.

Sousanis, N. (2015b). Grids and gestures: A comics making exercise. *SANE Journal: Sequential Art Narrative in Education, 2*(1), 8.

Spinney, J. (2006). A place of sense: a kinaesthetic ethnography of cyclists on Mont Ventoux. *Environment and Planning D: Society and Space, 24*(5), 709–732.

Spinney, J. (2009). Cycling the city: Movement, meaning and method. *Geography Compass, 3*(2), 817–835.

Thrift, N. (2008). *Non-representational theory: Space, politics, affect.* London, UK: Routledge.

Vasudevan, L. & Rodriguez Kerr, K. (2016). "Unflattening" our ways of seeing, reading, and writing. *Journal of Adolescent & Adult Literacy, 60*(1), 103–105.

10

CODED TO SMITHEREENS AND DANCED TO ABSTRACTION

Forms of Affect in the Industry of Research

Mia Perry

Are you sitting comfortably? Are you reading this on a screen? Are you scanning this for reference or curious about the title? What do you expect next? In the context of thinking analytically about the affordances and absences of affect in literacy research, this chapter lends a focus to research as product as well as process and research in the hands of the reader (who may be the reviewer, the student, the peer or the policy maker). However, research doesn't land on your desktop by chance, and in order to look at the reading of research, the impact, the affects, or the absences therein, we need to take into account the commissioning or conception of research, as the two (conception and reading) can be connected by dots. This chapter then, considers reading research (and the affects and subsequent impacts of research) in the context of the broad project and industry of research. Drawing on various theoretical strands, this chapter identifies the affective dimension across paradigms of research and teases apart some of the influencing factors in the creation and reception of research. Why does some research read as sterile or as if the life has been lost? And why does some research make us tingle with empathy and vicarious lived experience?

In curating this volume, an invitation was issued to "write toward where life [was] going with literacy and affect" (Ehret and Leander, p. 00). This was like music to my ears, and I took the invitation to heart. I realized quite quickly that what was escaping me was a sense of common ground with the significant body of work and field of practice in scientific and rationalist research in literacy education. Was the growing pull of affective research pulling away or protecting me from something else; something that has been produced regardless of affective forces? I am on high alert for binaries emerging because they are good for making a point, good for planning a journey, good for building an identity, but typically counterproductive or harmful for much else. Here I was seeing, perhaps only in my own understanding, a binary emerging between research that captures, traces and engages with affect, and research that doesn't. So, this is where my inquiry began.

This chapter is grounded in an understanding of research as something like an industry, in that the conception, production and application of research occurs within an economy of, and relations between, knowledge, ideas, finances, power systems and social dynamics. Similar to Howard Becker's examination of art in *Art Worlds* (1984), I consider research as relational and always indicative of the broader cooperation of social, political and economic forces. Echoing sociologist, Mariam Fraser (2012), I wonder, "Where, or when does a project begin?" (p. 86). It is in this ontological context that I take up affect in literacy research. I explore the context further through three main premises, and from there, this chapter explores and questions the place and role of affect in the various components of the research endeavor, but particularly in the context of the research in encounter with the reader.

Premise #1: Research Revolves Around the Researcher, Until the Encounter with Its Reader

Since a seismic shift in research theory in the 1970's and 80's that is best known as "the crisis of representation," social scientists have troubled and reframed ethnographic and anthropological research outputs as being inevitably entangled with personal and political positions and movements, be they colonial, patriarchal or cultural (Denzin & Lincoln, 2005). Like all waves of theoretical critique, the subsequent development, rethinking and positioning that has emerged since the crisis of representation has happened at different paces and in various disciplinary contexts. The emergence of the "affective turn" in literacy research is no exception (Leander & Boldt, 2013), and although the very nature of affect helps us to look to *relations-between*, rather than *centres-of*, the approach shares and relates to the same inherited past of knowledge production.

Arguably the shift of awareness to the role of the researcher began in the field of anthropology, where research was critiqued for colonial undertones or indeed overtones; worlds, cultures, societies being represented as "real" through the perspectives of the outsider, privileged, and typically white western, researcher (Fabian, 1983; Hymes, 1974; Said, 1989). Cultural studies, sociology and theories of research have contributed many other critiques and propositions regarding the project and politics of research. Concepts such as researcher lens, gaze, bias and subjectivity have all been developed to support the treatment of the relationship between the researcher and his or her subject. More useful to note here though, are frameworks and methods of research that have evolved to acknowledge, incorporate and account for the pivotal, if not contentious, role of the researcher, in all of his or her colors, in the research. Traditional humanist qualitative research for example might include positioning statements, member checking and co-researching strategies. Posthumanist approaches might incorporate agential realism or actor-network theory, and affective research resides comfortably in this space too. Directly or indirectly, researchers are rarely blind to their substantive role in the production of knowledge today; indeed, research can often be distinguished paradigmatically through the manner in which the researcher is revealed in the work. This is not to say that all contemporary research has responded to the crisis of representation or adopts an onto-epistemological perspective that foregrounds the viewer in the viewed. As we know, research isn't a neat or coherent journey that can be recognized in terms of era like fashion; the paradigms that people use in research span across influence and objective much more so than time or historical movement. The fact that we have a plethora of recognized approaches and methods in qualitative and quantitative research today equates to a *larger diversity* of truths/findings, rather than a *better* or more *appropriate* set of truths/findings. In the face of that diversity, the reader has choices, perhaps more choices than earlier eras of research prior to the crisis of representation.

With the substantial scope of frameworks in literacy research to understand the encounter and engagement with, and interpretation of, texts of all descriptions, it seems only right to foreground here the role or presence of the reader in literacy research. The reader of research on an unknown context of life in the early 1900's might depend on the paradigm and methods of one person, let's use Margaret Mead for example. Mead's assessment of Samoan sexuality (1928/2001) for a Western audience may have been the only option (other than to simply disregard) for contemporary readers of that research. Research carried out today will almost always exist in the context of other research on similar questions, done in other ways, resulting in other outcomes. Similarly, "reading" research today can span reading traditional reports—printed or downloaded—hearing or reading public documentation or media sources, reading or watching the representation of research findings through text, visual work, performance, film and so on. Today's reader has discursive and material choices (should he or she want them and have access to them). Affects and intensities attest to the reader's immersion in materialities (Deleuze and Guattari, 1994), as well as in concepts, discourses and complex positionalities. The reader and the research text can be seen to be functioning within a specific set of relations and intensities, emerging from proliferating perspectives, modes and methods of communication and engagement, all with differing affective dynamics. Understood in this way, the project of research, beginning perhaps with a process guided by the movements of the researcher, ending with an encounter with the reader—is a relational one. Forms of affect in the research project exist not only in the site of research, not only in the encounter between researcher and participant, but also in the encounter between the representation of research and reader.

Premise #2: What We Can Know Depends on the Questions We Ask

"A question is really an ambiguous proposition; the answer is its determination," says Suzanne Langer (1990, p. 4) alluding to the provocations of philosopher of law, Felix Cohen. She goes on: "There can be only a certain number of alternatives that will complete its sense. In this way the intellectual treatment of any datum, and experience, any subject, is determined by the nature of our questions, and only carried out in the answers." This analysis of the functioning of questions is profoundly important when we think about the impacts, contributions or absences of any research, including those pertaining particularly to affect. Langer would argue that our primary contributions to our field lie in our formation of the problems we can pose, rather than the solutions to them. "Where did life go?" ask Leander and Ehret, of literacy research, in the conception of this volume. With this question, the contribution of this book is to point us to, and perhaps even take us to at times, an animate, living, breathing, becoming place where we might recognize our own lived experiences of literacy teaching and learning.

In contrast, consider the question: How can educators decrease the education attainment gap between high and low socio-economic status students? Arguably this is a core plight that has come to characterize contemporary educational research and policy in the UK. Embedded in that is the ambiguous proposition that the objective of education is to achieve academic attainment determined through standardized measures. The solutions therefore would logically revolve around either reducing the barriers to academic attainment for low-income populations or adding barriers to higher income students to cause them to fall into closer proximity to the poorer attainment standards of poorer students. Assuming the former is preferable, the research becomes a project in examining methods to help poor students achieve grades in standardized assessment that are equal to those of higher income students. Based on this example, our contributions to the field of education in the past ten years have been based in standardized attainment tracking and pedagogies to provide every student, regardless of economic and cultural background, with the best shot at being successful in that arena. The "push-and-pull of feelings that live in bodies" (Ehret & Leander, this volume, p. 00) exists as part of the experience of every student in our increasingly standardized classrooms. The affective dimension of teaching and learning however will not become better understood or better supported, until we find the language and the opening to ask the question of its nature. What if the question driving research, policy and legislation was: How can we increase the love of learning in each students' educational experience? Therein lies a very different ambiguous proposition, which paves the way for a very different set of inquiries, arguably one with more scope for recognizing affective relations and dynamics in learning. This question however is not the prevailing problem posed in our times in educational theory, practice or policy. How might our research landscape look if it were?

The implications of this premise—what we can know depends on the questions we ask—for the researcher are clear as we take up and mold research designs and frameworks to suit the type of knowledge we are looking for. If we are looking for movement or affect, our questions and subsequent methods need to be designed to prioritize, recognize and frame its presence in some way. Affect as a concept materializes in research through discourse; it can then be moved into a propositional role as part of a research question (where is the affect?), and thus this concept begins its relationship with data and knowledge made. It is worth, at this point, considering what the implications of this premise are for the reader.

As this chapter is substantially determined by the question "Where did life go?" (the working title to this edited volume), the directive power of that question recedes as the chapter encounters its reader, *you*. At this point, the research, in this case conceptual research, is substantially determined by the question or proposition that moved *you* toward this work in the first place. Central to the proposition of this chapter is the understanding of the reader as guided by pre-existing ambiguous propositions when encountering research. In the form of inquiry, curiosity, need or instruction, the reader is, like the researcher, already bounded by the position and proposition s/he brings to the encounter. I argue that the presence, indication or communication of affect, of movement and of life beyond the known and the representable in literacy education is determined as much by the scope of the proposition that the reader brings to the research, as it is by the questions or intentions of the researcher. The reading of the research therefore creates the reader and text relation, or assemblage (Deleuze & Guattari, 1987). This is not something that can be without intensities, affect, life, feeling or movement. The intensities of this encounter of reader and research do not depend so much upon the nature or extent of affect alluded to or acknowledged in the research, as they do upon the extent to which one (let's say the research representation) creates a rupture in the line of inquiry or expectation of the other (the reader). This new assemblage, reader and research, creates new impact and new coordinates.

Premise # 3: Research and Persuasion

Continuing to position the industry of research in relation to affect, I look here at one final aspect of emergence of the research in encounter with the reader. Persuasion, depending on the discourses at hand, may seem like a bit of a dirty word in ethical, critical, robust research. In research literature it is primarily associated with the field of psychology (with various theories and methods of persuasion in human engagement and research models), but here I take it up in the crudest sense of influence and impact. I propose that the process of research representation always involves some element of rhetorical persuasion, accomplished in different ways depending on the intended audience (see also Gilbert, 1976; 1977). Why is this relevant for the foundations of an inquiry into affect and literacy research? Because persuasion feeds on forces of affect; without affect, persuasion falls flat.

I use the term persuasion tentatively and not necessarily to indicate research as persuasion of viewpoints or of a certain version of events (although this may often be the case), but a persuasion of integrity, of competency and of clarity of argument. Without effective persuasion of these things, the impact of the research is diminished. How does this aspect of the research and reader relationship function? It functions through affective charges of personal, sociopolitical and cultural forces (Britzman, 2000; Ellsworth, 1997). In this way, research is an onto-epistemological practice of persuasion that requires the researcher to have an awareness of the tools of affect at his or her disposal in the representation of research. Discursive and material choices affect the reader who is in encounter with research, engaging in the emergence of new pathways of thought, new sensations and new impacts for this research. The choices therefore of medium, frame, structure, language, referencing, tone and so on are made to actively design and direct an intended type of affect. Of course this is an art more than a science, as the researcher cannot know the intensities to which his or her report will interact with on publication. Elizabeth Grosz positions art as "a system of dynamized and impacting forces rather than a system of unique images that function under the regime of signs" (2008, p. 3). I would argue that all forms of representation, including that of research, share to an extent this system of forces of affect. Seasoned researchers are in the position to publish for a reason, and, generally, knowledge claims are made with a well-honed craft, if not art, of engagement.

A sense of epistemological familiarity between the ideas conveyed in research and the reader will more likely serve to persuade the reader not only of the expressed ideas and outcomes of the research, but also of the validity and security of the reader's own positionality (as he or she recognizes him or herself in the encounter). Thinking with Deleuzian theory, that which is recognisable does little to disturb thought, rather it reconfirms and "recognises itself the more it recognises things" (Deleuze, 1994, p. 138). Relying on recognition depends on the assumption that the sensational encounters and conceptual tools of the past will be summoned to align with the experience of the present reading, causing the confirmation of a cohesive understanding of the world (Perry, 2010). Persuasion of a state that already *is* is a relatively manageable task. The research will more likely persuade the reader to engage with it, to apply it or build on it.

Other things "force us to think" (Deleuze, 1994, p. 139). When research emerges as less recognizable, from a very different epistemology to that of the reader, the encounter between researcher and reader will more likely emerge through the senses. Affective ruptures and unintended dissonance may characterize such an encounter, and the researcher may fail to persuade the reader of its validity due to its lack of proximity to the reader's perceived sense of being-in-the-world.

Persuasion feeds off material and discursive tools—the affective and persuasive charge for example of research presented through text, via an e-journal, is very different to that represented through movement or through a public pamphlet.

In the case of the conceptual research outlined in this chapter, my aim is that the reader is persuaded of the validity, and even, dare I say, the significance of my point of view. For this to emerge, I argue that you need to recognize yourself somehow in amongst the discursive–material object of this chapter. Both the editorial and physical context will play their roles in that, along with the onto-epistemological alignment or discord between you, the reader, and the ideas conveyed through this text.

Research and Affect

Putting the three premises, as described above, to the forefront of the research endeavor at once simplifies, bounds and liberates research in the living moments and movements of literacy. It *simplifies* it, as it renders research a process of answering questions (to which there can only be a certain number or type of answers), based on a series (a multitude) of individual, subjective decisions and steps toward an understood goal to persuade an audience of the validity of the knowledge claim. It *bounds* research as it assumes its contingency; research is bounded by the scope, capacities and positioning of the researcher. It also *liberates* research, as it doesn't have to pretend to be something that it is not. It is free to celebrate its own pride of place in the transparent construction, craft and communication of knowledges. Research is the result of a proposition made and the engagement with others and ideas, and in particular, it is the result of an encounter with a reader. The knowledge comes into being and moves into function with the colliding forces of represented research and reader.

The affective charge that research has on the reader is a powerful force, perhaps the crux of the entire research endeavor. Affect, says Leander and Rowe, is "the change that occurs when bodies come into contact" (2006, p. 433). To consider that in practice, in the context of this inquiry, we can assume, for example, affect occurring as researcher and research participant encounter one another. This might be via spending time together in a classroom, this might be on an online forum, it might be an exchange of information mediated by a third party. How do we encounter that change? In sensation. Building from Deleuze and Guattari (1987), a sensation implies the involvement of the bodily senses; it is an affect that is visceral, physical and results in embodied change. We can also assume affect occurring in the sensations of the researcher as he or she re-encounters data through analysis processes. But equally, we can assume the sensations of the participant as he or she moves on to his or her next encounter. Boundas explains, "Sensation is the affect, which is neither subjective nor objective; rather it is both at once: we become in sensation and at the same time something happens because of it" (2005, p. 131).

So, let's imagine now the reader coming into contact with the research, cognizant of content, form and all other contexts around that encounter. Through engagement with that research output, "we become in sensation and at the same time something happens because of it" (ibid). The reader is moved and always becoming in relation to the research regardless of the specific paradigm, question or mode of representation. The binding quality of these aspects of experience is the nature of interrelationality inherent in all of them: "no force can exist apart from its interrelationships with other forces" (Stagoll, 2005, p. 107). The priority of affective dimensions in literacy engagements will differ, the resonance of affect will emerge through various modalities, but the presence of affective forces will be consistent.

When we look at the incarnation of the research project, through to its delivery in terms of the researcher positions, the project's contexts, the webs of interrelations, the questions, the form of output and the reader, we can relate to, sense into and be affected by life at every turn. Affective intensities move, form and reform the industry in all its ugly and beautiful facets. In this highly striated space, researchers navigate the pressure and competitiveness of the research industry, the power and economic dynamics of politics and policy and their curiosity and passion for their subject. Seen in this way, the affective turn in the social sciences adds an exciting discursive challenge to an always already existing ontological state shared by all involved in the research industry from funder to reader. A Deleuzian-dancer-turned-performance ethnographer is no more alive or engaged in affective inquiry than a subcontracted RA from the center of statistics for the department of education who shall remain nameless and who will only refer to student participants by number. The questions asked, the methods used, the relationship with data generated is no more or less real, alive or affective in either case. The forces of affect, the scope of attention, the field of focus in the classroom is no more or less acute. And finally, the form and content of the research outputs, from two such very contrasting researchers, with such divergent and even conflicting methodologies, and two such different objectives, will have no more or less affect on the reader of the research. Affective forces will always be at play, their resonance appearing through differing sensations and to different effects.

Reading and Affect

To explore more tangibly the dynamics of affect in existing research, I turned to some contemporary literacy research that resonates with my own perspectives, epistemologically and methodologically, and some that challenges them. I read examples of traditional and non-traditional literacy research, looking for projects that seemed to attend to affective dimensions of learning, and projects that seemed to focus on standardized measures. I then did this with colleagues (at a research event in Sheffield Hallam University). I now extend this informal inquiry to the pages of this chapter. In inviting you to read and reflect on the sensations provoked by two research excerpts I am inviting you to occupy the space of both researcher and reader, explicitly and concurrently.

As a reader of this volume, you are most likely aware of the potential contexts of the research projects reflected in the following excerpts. We can assume they include employment terms, subjectivities, politics, resource limitations, objectives and the list can go on. Amidst that we know that the researcher will be moving in striated spaces, leaning on certain restrictions to afford opening spaces for inquiry and representation elsewhere. As a reader, we also know that we bring our own ambiguous propositions to this reading, our own positionality and so on. We have certain ideas about what counts as, or conveys, affective dimensions of learning and every moment we are being moved by forces of affect that include these very words.

As a researcher in this moment, I invite you to encounter these excerpts with as much attention as you can muster to the affective dimensions of the reading as you experience it. I am explicitly *not* asking for a critique of the methodologies, of the writing or of the findings, but rather an awareness of and reflection on the experience of encountering and being moved by the texts. What sensations emerge in you when you come into contact with these texts? How you carry out this invitation is up to you: You might simply read and think through with embodied awareness, you might vocalize or write out your responses. For the purposes of clarity, I will stay with you through the next few pages and propose moments to pause and consider your encounter with the research as presented. I will use the three premises laid out in the first half of the chapter to support my role in accompanying you.

The first excerpt is taken from a research report by A. Holliman, J. Hurry and S. Bodman (2016) in the *Journal of Research in Reading*. It is titled, "Children's Reading Profiles on Exiting the Reading Recovery Programme: Do They Predict Sustained Success?" The study addressed two major research questions:

1. What is the bivariate relationship between the standard Reading Recovery assessments (the Observation Survey and text reading level), phonological processing, reading comprehension and the reading, spelling and writing tasks at exit from the programme and at 3-month, 6-month and 12-month follow-up points, where available?

2. Can any of the variables measured at exit from the programme (Observation Survey, Text Reading Level, phonological processing, and reading comprehension) make a unique contribution (beyond the influences of the other predictors) to reading, spelling and writing at 3-month, 6-month and 12-month follow-up points, where available?

(p. 6)

At this point I remind myself of the impact of my own question (Where did life go?), as it comes into contact with the three questions above. I am surprised by the force of this, the coming into contact feels more like a crash than an encounter. As if after a crash, I struggle to orient myself again and find my way amidst the newly drastically rearranged pieces of the two vehicles that met with force. While I am slightly disoriented by this set of questions, I feel very much awake and alive and in a heightened emotive state—I wonder if this will quickly lead to disappointment, anger, discovery or something else, but I know that in this encounter I am being moved in some way. I invite you to consider what propositions or questions you bring to this chapter or this volume and how that interacts with the questions quoted above.

Later in this article, the authors outline their various findings at length. Below is one excerpt that considers the description of performance on individual measures (excerpts from pages 8–9). Although a substantial part of the excerpt is in the form of a table, I encourage you to pause and consider this table, in whatever way it is your practice or preference to do so. As the reader now and (I propose) the one that this research revolves around, the discourses that we are practiced at and comfortable with are not always presented back to us, and the tools of persuasion may take on various forms. As the reader, what does the following excerpt *do* to us?

Table 1 shows the mean and standard deviations for the Observation Survey subtests, Text Reading Level, phonological processing, reading comprehension and the reading, spelling and writing tasks at exit from the programme and at 3-month (3m), 6-month (6m) and 12-month (12 m) follow-up points, where available.

Measure	M	SD
Letter Identification, OS (Max = 54)	53	1.38
Duncan Word Test, OS (Max = 23)	22	1.52
Writing Vocabulary, OS (Max = NA)	42.32	13.7
Hearing and Recording Sounds, OS (Max = 37)	35.32	2.01
Text Reading Level (Max = 30)	17.51	1.7
Alliteration Test (Max = 10)	8.06	1.97
Non-Word Reading Test (Max = 20)	11.51	3.43
Rhyme Test (Max = 21)	14.07	5.29
Reading Comprehension (Max = 68.6)	40.92	24.7
BAS Word Reading Raw Score (Max = 90)	29.26	7.28
Spelling (Max = 30)	17.96	4.89
BAS Word Reading (3 m) Raw Score (Max = 90)	31.95	9.04
Spelling (3 m) (Max = 30)	18.04	4.08
BAS Word Reading (6 m) Raw Score (Max = 90)	38.07	10.07
Spelling (6 m) (Max = 30)	20.55	4.47
NC point score for Reading (12 m) (Max = 29)	14.78	1.42
NC point score for Writing (12 m) (Max = 29)	14.02	1.25

At this point we and the research are moved, slightly or significantly from the positions in which we began this encounter. If the movement has been significant for you, my interruption in your reading may prompt you to organize your feelings into emotions and statements of opinion. You might wish to distinguish yourself from this text, just as I attempt to persuade you that your encounter with it is the force affecting you, and so you cannot separate yourself from the research that you have just taken part in bringing to life.

The final excerpt from this research report is the most dense in terms of the practical activity of reading, but with your commitment to the process, may allow for the most sensational experience of engagement.

> On the phonological processing measures (Alliteration Test, Non-Word Reading Test, Rhyme Test) participants' raw scores were equivalent to mean standardised scores of 99, 106 and 107, respectively, which fall in the "average score" range. The mean word reading raw score of the sample at exit from the programme was 29.26 (SD = 7.28), which equates to a reading age equivalent of 7 years and 1 month (7 months ahead of their chronological age). At first follow-up 3 months later, the mean word reading raw score was 31.95 (SD = 9.04), which equates to a reading age equivalent of 7 years and 1 month (4 months ahead of their chronological age). At second follow-up 6 months later, the mean word reading raw score was 38.07 (SD = 10.07), which equates to a reading age equivalent of 7 years and 7 months (7 months ahead of their chronological age). A similar pattern of results was observed on the spelling measure where performance was higher at second follow-up (20.55) than it was at first follow-up (18.04), and this was higher than the mean score obtained at exit from the programme (17.96). At third follow-up 12 months later, for children attending English schools, they had reached an average of 2c in reading and 2c in spelling, which is within the expected Level 2 at the end of Key Stage 1, albeit at the lower end. Whilst these results should be treated with caution due to high attrition rates, they do suggest that children are maintaining their gains up to 12 months after the programme has been discontinued.

At this final opportunity to pause and take stock of movement and affect in this research as it is emerging with you as reader, I wonder to what extent you are persuaded by the reading recovery program and the evaluation of it here. If you are, I wonder what moved you to care, what moved you to believe and what you recognized within the text of your own onto-epistemology. If you are not becoming persuaded by the program, what are you becoming in encounter with your experience?

The excerpt that follows is a very different type of research representation that, I expect, will emerge very differently in your engagement with it. It is taken from a research report titled, "Listening to the Heartbeat of New York: Writings on the Wall," written by Joanne Robertson, and published in *Qualitative Inquiry*, in 2003. This report takes up 9/11 as a transformational literacy event and analyses the ways in which a group of graduate students navigate the event with language in the context of their daily lives. The very title makes some clear propositions about the scope of literacy that may be addressed in this work, and its potential to speak perhaps to the "surplus" that our editors refer to in the introduction—felt intensities that extend beyond the demographics, geography, culture or history of a city. Do these propositions move you? What becomes of them in encounter with your own questions (that might relate to "Where did life go?"). The excerpts below include very different discursive and material choices from the first example, but like the first, they are presented to you from the same industry of research with the same premises of production. Like the example above, the act of reading them begins the research-reader assemblage.

WAYS OF ACTING—SPACES TO RECLAIM TERRITORY

> Feelings of vulnerability and fear are freely acknowledged; however, sentiments of renewal, territorialism and optimism are equally reflected in the ways people posted their thoughts. "It's like they're tagging!" my student exclaims in class. We talk about issues of power and control and decide that the writings might mirror people's desire to reclaim lost territory. We talk about the permanence of the written word and its role as testament in a time of impermanence. We marvel at the ways in which people attempt to clothe the barren and sooty walls of New York with language that is fertile with images. One student brings in a picture taken by a firefighter beneath the ravaged Trade Towers (see Figure 10.1).

Here we might take our first pause together: What emerges in you with the reading of this account and what do you find in this encounter? A sense of story perhaps? Is it a story that you can easily piece together? Put images to? What forces might you recognize that help or hinder you in the movement in and through this encounter? Do you recognize the space depicted? Are you comfortable here? Are you moved? What have you created?

> We compare this still life to photographs we've seen of interior sections of the submerged *Titanic*. Time has stopped in this photo. We note the ways New Yorkers have etched more writing into the soot-covered storefront signage. These writings, including gang logos, are further testament to the ways New Yorkers' declared their "territorial rights."

> **The spirit of the World Trade Center is giving us the energy to rebuild this great city. Thank you!**

> The postings reflect both personal and shared ownership of ideals and emotions. It is a space where past and present intersect. These writings become the touchstone for defining the worldviews and literacy practices of New Yorkers. In this process, we redefine ourselves.

> **Tough Times Never LAST Tough People DO**

FIGURE 10.1 Reclaiming Territory

WAYS OF VISITING—SPACES THAT GIVE LIFE
TO LIVES THAT WERE LOST

Certain locations become grieving sites known as "walls of prayer," that is, where family members post flyers with pictures and descriptions of loved ones for rescue workers to review. As was the case with other writings, many were meticulously wrapped in plastic overlays to protect them from the elements. Firefighters, police officers and passersby visit and spend time reviewing these flyers every day.

Greg—You live in your children's eyes.

FIGURE 10.2 "Walls of Prayer"

At this point, you may notice that the visual elements of this research calls for other types of engagement with you, you may have noticed a shift in your relationship with the research as text moved to image, as type moved from normal to bold, from standard to capitalized, or from descriptive to performative script. Do you have tools to allow you to navigate this encounter with ease, do you recognize your own onto-epistemology in these choices? Are you persuaded of the validity, of the integrity, of the "truths" within this work? The final excerpt below brings the researcher into the foreground of this work, her intentions, propositions and claims for the work.

The photographs and accompanying messages are the most difficult for the class and me to process and understand. There are so many pictures of young people, faces beaming with vitality and optimism, beckoning to us from the walls. A reciprocal dialogue evolved; this is too close to home; this could be my son, my daughter, my husband, my father, my friend. For some of my students, this is indeed the case (see Figure 10.2).

Every time I have Irish money I'll think of you.

Denzin (1999) spoke of the way an ethnographer might "embed the self in stories of histories, of sacred places" (p. 510). My students help me to understand how I am moving "outward and backward" as Denzin wrote, experiencing, internalizing, and transforming my thoughts through introspection and conversations with my students and the texts of 9/11. I realize that my main purpose for writing is to give this piece life. For, it represents the transactions of multiple shared realities and has become an entity in its own right.

(pp. 138–140)

As I stated at the outset, this reading journey was not meant to enable us to evaluate methodology or critique writing style; but rather to notice our own impulses, movements, surpluses of affect that emerge in our encounters. Those dynamic intensities carry the research-reader assemblage forward toward the next encounter. You might have noticed the different sorts of affects and impulses at play in the encounter with these two very different pieces of research, and you will almost certainly have created two very different pieces of research with those encounters. One you might believe more than the other, one you might remember longer than the other, one might have confirmed your own cohesive understanding of the world, the other might have challenged it. What I would like to propose, however, is that forces of affect and intensity surge through research of all variation and paradigm, not least as it meets its audience.

Reflecting

Thinking back through the various phases of literacy research again, from conception to readership, the push and pull of feelings, the dynamized forces of affect, revolving around, in, through and with the research is constant. What is important to note is that the gritty, tangible reality; the messy, interrelational and affective aspects of all research encounters—whether they are summarized into tables and numbers or images and poetry—are commonly functioning in the industry of research. What is not commonly at play is the awareness or recognition of that, or the discourses to describe it.

In attending to affect in literacy research as it is conceptualized and produced in the industry of research, what comes to light is that affect, or the affective dimension of the learning encounter is neither innocent nor benign. In the onto-epistemological space of research production, the extent and nature of the affective dimensions included will be determined at least in part, by the personal, political and cultural proposition brought to the research. When discourses, materialities and practices are engaged to make affective dimensions explicit then the research begins to predict its future readership. The affects, sensations and the impulses caused by the two excerpts of research included above are not accidental, but contingent on the research industry context and the positionality of the reader. The readers likely to read any particular research do so due to an alignment, a conflict, a task set or a pragmatic need. In this way, the research, to an extent, determines the readers. With a paradigmatic alignment, conflict or pragmatic need comes an immediate and dynamic relationship with the research before the reading has even begun. With the act of each encounter research becomes something else again and again. I propose that multiple and emerging layers of purpose and person are present and alive in each piece of research, no matter how coded to smithereens or danced to abstraction it might be.

Of sociology, Fraser asks, "What would be the implications if the aim [. . .] was not only to theorize and explain experience but also, sometimes, to be an 'informed provocation' of experience?" (2012, p. 84). Of embodiment in literacy research and pedagogy, I have wondered, "perhaps the relative presence or absence of the body [. . .] is less about the text, or student, or research participant, and more about how the *representation* of that, which reminds you, the reader, the teacher, that you are a physical and emotional self, as well as an intellectual one" (Wager & Perry, 2015, p. 263). Literacy research, we might assume, imparts knowledge about literacy practices. Does affective literacy research tell the reader explicitly about the affective dimensions of literacy practices, or does it seek to produce certain affects or facilitate a certain experience of literacy in itself?

As a researcher deeply engaged in the arts and cultural production as spaces of literacy and research I conclude with a cautious look to the expanding landscape of arts-based, alternative, affect-focused methodologies. I propose that what we seek, as researchers and educators, is not to reinsert movement where it wasn't or to find or express affect where it wasn't; our literacy spaces and research sites are always moving and functioning in complex affective dynamics. Rather, I believe that we have a role to remind our readers and students of the force and inevitability of affect, and above all of our agency and role in the reading and experience of research.

References

Becker, H. *Art worlds*. (1984). Oakland, CA: University of California Press.

Boundas, C.V. (2005). Intensity. In A. Parr (Ed.), *The Deleuze dictionary* (pp. 131–132). New York, NY: Columbia University Press.

Britzman, D. (2000). "The question of belief:" Writing poststructural ethnography. In E. St. Pierre & W.S. Pillow (Eds.), *Working the ruins: Feminist poststructural theory and methods in education* (pp. 27–40). New York, NY: Routledge.

Deleuze, G. (1994). *Difference & repetition* (P. Patton, Trans.). New York, NY: Columbia University Press.

Deleuze, G. & Guattari, F. (1987). *A thousand plateaus: Capitalism and schizophrenia* (B. Massumi, Trans.). Minneapolis, MN: University of Minnesota Press.

Deleuze, G. & Guattari, F. (1994). *What is philosophy?* (H. Tomlinson & G. Burchell, Trans.). New York, NY: Columbia University Press.

Denzin, N.K. , Lincoln, Y.S. (Eds.). (2005). *The sage handbook of qualitative research* (3rd ed.). Thousand Oaks, CA: Sage.

Ellsworth, E. (1997). *Teaching positions: Difference, pedagogy and the power of address*. New York, NY: Teachers College Press.

Fabian, J. (1983). *Time and the other: How anthropology makes its object*. New York, NY: Columbia University Press.

Fraser, M.M. (2012). "Once upon a problem." In L. Back and N. Puwar (Eds.), *Live Methods* (pp. 84–107). Malden, MA: Blackwell Publishing.

Gilbert, G.N. (1976). The transformation of research findings into scientific knowledge. *Social Studies of Science, 6*, 281–306.

Gilbert, G.N. (1977). Referencing as persuasion. *Social Studies of Science, 7*, 113–122.

Grosz, E. (2008). *Chaos, territory, art: Deleuze and the framing of the earth*. New York, NY: Columbia University Press.

Holliman, A., Hurry, J., & Bodman, S. (2016). "Children's reading profiles on exiting the Reading Recovery Programme: Do they predict sustained success?" *Journal of Research in Reading, 39*(1), 1–18.

Hymes, D. (1974). *Reinventing Anthropology*. New York, NY: Vintage.

Langer, S. (1990). *Philosophy in a New Key* (3rd ed.). Cambridge, MA: Harvard University Press.

Leander, K. & Boldt, G. (2013). Rereading "A pedagogy of multiliteracies" bodies, texts, and emergence. *Journal of Literacy Research, 45*(1), 22–46.

Leander, K.M. & Rowe, D.W. (2006). Mapping literacy spaces in motion: A rhizomatic analysis of a classroom literacy performance. *Reading Research Quarterly, 41*(4), 428–460.

Mead, M. (2001). *Coming of age in Samoa* (Reprint ed.). New York, NY: HarperCollins. (Original work published 1928).

Perry, M. (2010). *Theatre as a place of learning: The forces and affects of devised theatre processes in education*. Unpublished dissertation, University of British Columbia, Vancouver, BC.

Robertson, J. (2003). 9/11 and its Aftermath. *Qualitative Inquiry, 9*(1), 129–152.

Said, E. (1989). Representing the colonized: Anthropology's interlocutors. *Critical Inquiry, 15*, 205–225.

Stagoll, C. (2005). Force. In A. Parr (Ed.), *The Deleuze dictionary* (pp. 106–108). New York, NY: Columbia University Press.

Wager A. & Perry M. (2015) "Resisting the script: An experiment in assuming embodiment in literacy education." In G. Enriquez, E. Johnson, S. Kontovourki, & C.A. Mallozzi (Eds.), *Literacies, learning, and the body: Putting theory and research into pedagogical practice* (pp. 252–267). New York, NY: Routledge.

11

TELLING STORIES OUT OF CLASS

Three Movements in a Reach for Affect

Cathy Burnett

Introduction

Grappling with affect offers much to an activist agenda through engaging with what matters as meanings get made and allowing the possibility that the potential to be otherwise is always immanent (Massumi, 2015). It sensitizes literacy educators and researchers to the feeling that drives those they work with and prompts us to imagine how we might work *with* feeling in generating more empowering and equitable literacy provision. Yet, as literacy researchers, we will always struggle to *know* feeling, and when we *feel* what we know, these feelings easily dissipate as we generate, analyze and share our data. As we do so, we fix, and embodied experience, ever ephemeral, slips away. Or at least, so it may seem. But, of course, research itself is a corporeal, affective process. Affect is not deleted through research, but inevitably generated by, through and with it. The challenge for researchers then lies not just in how to approach the unreachable aim of knowing affect, but how to work with the affective intensities that pulse through research as it unfolds. In this chapter, I reflect on aspects of moving "toward the unknown" (p. 00, Ehret and Leander, this volume) through three research stories—framed as three movements—that surface some of the complexities involved in trying to engage with the ephemeralities that so easily float away from research accounts of affect. The stories pay homage to my inevitable failure in this regard, but also raise questions about how affect plays into our work as researchers: How we catch hold of affect; how data move and move with us; how we address these feelings and movements in our encounters with data; and how we might work with the potentialities they generate as we operate at the intersection of research and practice.

Approaching Affect

In approaching affect, like others in this volume I draw on the concept of assemblage (after Deleuze & Guattari, 1987). Theories of assemblage have been used to explore how things of different orders coalesce to hold certain educational realities in place, how "economy and politics, policy, organizational arrangements, knowledge, subjectivity, pedagogy, everyday practices and feelings come together" (Youdell, 2011). Such work helps explain the persistence of certain realities and how they manifest in and are upheld through sociomaterial relations in local sites. In England, for example, testing arrangements, league tables, classroom routines, evidence-based practice, policy, resources and so on together sustain a reductivist literacy education (e.g., see Hamilton, 2012). My interest here however is on assemblage as a mobile, fluid, ongoing process, as an ongoing assembl*ing*:

> [A]ssemblage is a process of bundling, or assembling, or better of recursive self-assembling in which the elements put together are not fixed in shape, do not belong to a larger pre-given list but are constructed at least in part as they are entangled together.
>
> *(Law, 2004 p. 42)*

This focus on fluidity foregrounds affect. It evokes not just how, what and why things assemble, but how affective intensities are generated through assemblage, and what might be generated through such intensities. Engaging with affect in this way brings us into dialogue with the immanent "field of potential" which, as Massumi writes, "is not the elements in mixture. It is their becoming" (2002, p. 76). It alerts us not just to those commonly articulated forces that hold relationships and practices in place, but also to other ways of being and doing. Of course affect is slippery: "affect is unqualified. As such it is not ownable or recognizable and is thus resistant to critique" (Massumi, 2002, p. 28). With this slipperiness in mind, in this chapter I attempt to approach affect by sidling up to it, by telling a series of imperfect research stories that circle around a classroom episode. Through juxtaposing these stories and sharing my reflections on them, I hint at the affective intensities generated in educational settings as things—bodies and stuff and the relationships, histories, spaces, policies, discourses, etc. folded into them—coalesce in the moment and in the potentialities generated through these intensities. However, more pertinently, I raise questions about how affect plays through research and how this may be useful in signalling the potential for things to be otherwise.

Telling Stories

The three stories address a classroom "episode"[1] from a lunchtime Minecraft Club that I observed during an eight-month study of technology use in a class of 10 to 11 year olds in a primary school in England. At the invitation of their teacher, the children were building a community using *Minecraft Edu* which they subsequently named Bradborough (see Burnett & Bailey, 2014). I begin with a third-person narrative that describes how two girls sustained a shared space as they played in and around Minecraft. I focus on what I felt as a small act of kindness realized in part through the movements and rhythms of their on- and off-screen play. Next, I tell a personal narrative of trying to evoke the same episode during a symposium presentation, meshing my feelings as presenter with my felt responsibilities as researcher. In this, I attempt to portray how the episode assumed a life of its own as it re-emerged through my embodied performance in a seminar room, far from the classroom where it occurred. The third story tracks back to reflect on my feelings-movements during fieldwork as I framed this episode using video and translated it from an emergent, ephemeral process to an artefact, to *data*.

Each of these stories is knitted from reflections, memories, feelings and "chains of translations of inscriptions" (Lemke, 2007, p. 46). They are self-conscious narratives that, like all stories, involve choices about what to tell and how to tell it (Clough, 2002). I present them therefore not as objective accounts of what happened (or even descriptions or evocations of assemblages), but as a series of iterative reassemblings of myself-data-reader/audience, that are as significant for what escapes them as for what they manage to narrate. The stories are interspersed with reflections on what it means to extract this small episode from the knot of practices that constrained and constructed it, to pull it free, render it data and tangle it up with others.

By offering these stories in three movements, I do not want to imply a progressively deepening understanding, but more a series of unfoldings that each hint at different ways of feeling or knowing. Together the stories and their accompanying reflections are intended to hint at how this episode may play into and be enacted through multiple assemblages that are generated through or generative of affect. They are offered as tangential retracings that sometimes converge or reflect, and sometimes unsettle each other. By considering how these three stories fold into and interrupt one another as they stack together (Burnett & Merchant, 2014), I explore different ways in which bodies, movements and affect do or do not dance across each.

First Movement

On the Edge

Fran and Sophie were sitting next to each other in class, playing in Bradborough on separate laptops. Sophie was working on a squid aquarium she had begun making during a previous session, while Fran was looking for pigs to ride. She had ridden pigs before, but on this occasion couldn't find any until Sophie came to her rescue and generated some new ones especially for her. Here is my story of what happened.

Fran is leaning forward, her eyes fixed to the screen, fingers pressed on the keys so that her avatar flies high and fast over Bradborough, the skyscraper far below. She's looking for pigs. Sophie is also facing her screen, fingers on keyboard. Her avatar's on the ground at the bottom of the skyscraper, where what look like pink rectangular blocks are appearing rapidly in front of her. She points at her screen and calls, "Fran."

Fran is still flying so Sophie reaches across and points at Fran's screen, indicating a pink block just by the skyscraper. Fran leans forward even further to look, fingers still on keyboard. She recognizes the pink blocks for what they are in Minecraft *and squeals, "Pigs!" Fran rapidly moves her avatar next to the pigs and as she does so, Sophie lifts her hands up together in parallel indicating the screen (like a magician's reveal gesture), then leans back in her chair, first looking at her screen and then turning to Fran and wagging her finger repeatedly, "Which you don't know . . . is that I spawned them."*

Fran doesn't appear to be listening. She is intent on moving her avatar closer to the pigs and her eyes are fixed on the screen. When she arrives she is still staring at the screen—"Pigs . . . yes!" She gets her avatar to jump onto a pig and starts riding. Sophie, meanwhile, turns to me, cupping her hand over her mouth to shield it from Sophie: "What she don't know is I just spawned them." Indeed Sophie is still spawning pigs—four pink blocks rapidly appear on the screen in front of her—about one per second. She shakes her head from side to side as the pigs appear.

Fran leans back and clenches both fists in triumph—"I'm on top of a pig." Sophie turns to Fran again, and repeats, "What you don't know is that I spawned them." This time, Fran seems to hear. She turns to Sophie, then looks back at her screen and starts typing in the chat screen—"Hallelujah." She points at her screen and, when Sophie doesn't look, reaches across her friend and points at the chat screen appearing on Sophie's laptop, indicating what she just wrote. Fran smiles, then looks back at her screen and shakes her head, rapidly chanting, "Pig, pig, pig, pig, pig, pig, pig, pig," continuing to ride her pig.

Sophie turns back to her screen, reads the comment and starts typing. Her words appear on the chat screen in front of her, but I don't catch them this time. I do though, see her reach across Fran and point across at what she has just written, which is now appearing on Fran's screen. Fran sees it and starts typing a new entry into the chat screen.

This rather unremarkable story focuses on a few quiet moments from the eruption of ebullient play that was Minecraft Club. Elsewhere children were building skyscrapers, staging musicals, creating traps, chasing one another and setting buildings on fire, whilst shouting across the classroom, rushing over to look at one another's screens or singing and dancing as they played. While I have many stories to tell of this on/off-screen virtual play, I am still entranced by this particular episode. When I recall it, I do not just visualize it, I feel it. And yet, as I write this chapter, I realize this all happened several years ago now. I am interested therefore in why this particular story stays with me, why it moves me and what is happening to it as *it moves with me.*

The story I tried to tell is not just one of building Bradborough, but of building a friendship through being together. In telling it, I tried to open out this tiny moment, to slow things down and muse on what was going on, to track how bodies and things played into feeling. I hoped my story might add in some small way to arguments for attending to the sensitivities and possibilities imminent in being together, as a route a humanizing literacy provision that works for social justice (e.g., Comber, 2016; Vasudevan, 2011). The story tells I hope of how a friendship may be tentatively mooted through a small act of kindness and consolidated and maintained through interlacing on/off-screen actions. In it, Fran and Sophie mostly sustained a separateness in their play: Fran riding, Sophie building. When they shared what they did they didn't point at their own screens, inviting the other into their play, but reached across to indicate it on the other's. Even so, their proximal on/off-screen play seemed to construct and sustain a sense of togetherness. Rhythmic repetition of words, deictic gestures and on-screen actions ("Pig, pig, pig . . ." pointing, spawning pigs, etc.) provided the backbeat for their play, perhaps binding them together. The laptop seemed to participate in this too, its screen sometimes a wall to demarcate their private space, sometimes a window on Bradborough. In my story, through foregrounding these aspects of what I observed, I tried to convey what I felt to be the affective dimension of this episode and, in doing so, illustrate how the generative emergent dimension of their play seemed partly driven by being together.

Of course we cannot know the affective intensities generated for Fran and Sophie by being together as they played in/around/through Bradborough. And yet I felt this feeling of togetherness to be important because of the way seemed both generated *by* their play and generative *of* it, even as they played separately. Togetherness of course is complex, occurring not just in the moment but across multiple time-spaces and a mesh of practices (Burnett, 2015). Through my fieldwork, I had, for example traced one possible history of Fran and Sophie's togetherness across lessons. While Fran seemed readily accepted within multiple friendship groups, Sophie's belonging seemed more contingent. I had watched Sophie sometimes working closely with others and sometimes alone or apparently distressed by others' behavior towards her. Sometimes, what I saw as her kindness was acknowledged by apparently more popular girls, like Fran, but sometimes she seemed upset when others didn't see it. Sometimes she was at the heart of group activities, welcomed perhaps for her willingness to help and her technological expertise; but sometimes she was left out, on the edge. On this day, sitting next to Fran, Sophie interrupted her own play to spawn the pigs. If their play was partly about togetherness, then it may not just be the game that was important, or even just the proximity of bodies, but the fragile complex feeling of friendship. But, again, all this is conjecture.

I have written about the Fran-and-Sophie-episode before (Burnett & Bailey, 2014), presenting it as a transcript that juxtaposes Fran and Sophie's on/off-screen actions side by side, an attempt at a kind of split-screen rendering. While the transcript perhaps foregrounds how actions, words and movements bounce on and off-screen and between the pair, it is rather imperfect as reading it requires lots of to-ing and fro-ing across columns to get a sense of what happened and it all starts to feel rather technical. This story was a second attempt to represent the episode, written to be read in conference presentations, to give a better sense of how things emerged. However the even rhythm of my narrative, constructed to meet certain prosodic conventions and to fall out easily in the telling, somehow misses the rhythm and cadence of Fran and Sophie's play, and the linear organisation fudges its rhizomic nature. While I wrote the story to open things out, its form inevitably closes things down. However much I had intended to capture messiness and ephemerality, my story can't escape the relentless ordering of language. It tells of fixities—"an episode," "the girls," "the laptops," "the squid aquarium"—failing to evoke the multiple ways in which each of these human and nonhuman participants morphed and interfaced with each other and with other happenings and emergences. I am also struck by *my* absence from the narrative. I perhaps unintentionally imply the "benign, detached and seemingly objective gloss" of the "ethnographic present" (Jones et al., 2010, p. 484).

Yet, through writing this episode, and rereading it now, I do feel my relationship with what happened. As I make a case for the affective intensities generated through the assembling of Fran, Sophie, their screens, Bradborough, etc., I also feel how this story resonates with me and how this resonance—of feeling *for* these two girls—plays through my telling. In telling it, I have extracted it from the complex mesh of practices that was Minecraft Club on this particular day, and it has assembled with other feelings, not just those generated by my memories of being in this classroom, but others wrought through my experiences as researcher, teacher, friend, colleague, etc. I feel for how this episode sits with others I observed in this class, but also for how it sits with my life. As such, I feel *for* Sophie, and yet my feelings of solidarity seem to escape my narrative. When I reread my story with all this in mind, it feels thin.

Second Movement

Out Front

The dimensions of the room are strange. Wide enough for rows of 50ish chairs I guess, but only about ten rows deep. There is a lectern. I hate lecterns. It is planted in the middle third of the room, while the other two thirds—each side—are obstructed by two hefty pillars. There are multiple screens displaying the speaker's PowerPoint behind the lectern—the one the speaker naturally turns to and indicates, and others facing the other two thirds of the room. The easiest thing to do is to talk to the middle third and leave the others to sort themselves out. When it comes to my turn to present, the symposium organizers ask me to use a hand-held mike instead of the one at the lectern, to move freely around and address all sections of the room. Nervous and keen to please, I dutifully take the mike and hold it awkwardly in front of me. A problem, as I always wave my arms around when I talk, marking out the rhythms. For me, talking and moving are inseparable. With the heavy mike in hand, I'm encumbered. It slows me down.

I do try to share my presentation with all. It's tricky though: if I directly face the leftest third, I turn my back on the rightest, so I try to parcel up my presentation into equalish segments, walking out to the neglected margins on the left, then dancing back to the middle third, and then turning to the other marginalized group on the right. I find this frustrating: With each turn toward one section of the audience, I turn away from another, breaking the web of shared engagement I am trying to weave. As I do this, I feel myself slowing, as the walking and turning means I pause more. I feel the presentation running away from me. I have rehearsed and timed it to the second, to fit politely into my 30-minute slot, but with all the pacing, presenting, turning and re-establishing, time is escaping. I hear a bell ring to signal "5 minutes to go," and I know I don't have long. It is at that point in my talk that I reach the part when I tell the Fran-and-Sophie-story.

I want to give them time, these two quiet girls, playing quietly in a hectic class. So I remain stationary for their story: I want stillness. I do my best to make a case for them, for Sophie in particular. I pull myself to my full height as I narrate, embodying a confidence I lack in myself but have in them. I hold my paper clumsily in one hand, the hefty mike in the other.

I have read this story a few times now in presentations, I'm not sure why I read it rather than tell it. Somehow, through reading, I shift to a different register, one that's comfortable to me, reminiscent of reading stories as a teacher, using my voice in ways I used then to try and draw my audience in. I speed through the contextual parts, but slow as I get to the bits I really want them to hear, pausing slightly before certain moments ("Pigs!"), and looking up to make eye contact, to try to bring my delight in Fran and Sophie's play to my eyes and the timbre of my voice. I settle into a rhythm and lilt that feels right. Sometimes I use gesture to bring bits of the episode into the room. Like Sophie, I reach across an imaginary screen to point at Fran's. Like Fran, I squeal, "Pigs, pigs, pigs." Like Sophie, I cup my hand around my mouth to signal the aside not meant for Fran's ears. And I signal my delight in Sophie's tiny act of pig-generating kindness with a wide smile. I know it has "worked," for me at least, when some people in the audience laugh or smile or—the ulti-mate signal of academic alliance—nod.

I have no idea what the audience for this symposium made of, or with, the Fran-and-Sophie-story. There was no time for questions, and afterward, the peo-ple who talked to me were fascinated with the baroque ebullience of Minecraft Club, not these two quiet girls. They were more interested in the teacher's inspired work in enabling this activity and what it might offer to schools (see Bailey, 2017), than in my thoughts and feelings about this episode and how it might speak to literacy education. So afterwards I felt I had let Fran and Sophie down. I had failed somehow to celebrate their friendship, to make enough of Sophie's generosity. And, in doing so, I had failed to move the audience to feel the potentialities generated through being together in literacy classrooms.

There is of course nothing new in noting that people make sense of what others present in diverse ways; it has long been recognized for example that the meanings of novels are made between reader and text (Rosenblatt, 1933). Work in performance studies, however, highlights the embodied dimension of such reworkings: the "perceptual multistability" (Fischer-Lichte, 2008) generated as audiences make meanings not just in response to what the performer wishes to portray, but in relation to unintended meanings conjured as text is mediated by *that* performer in *that* place on *that* day: as Fensham writes:

> For surely the material body plunders the symbolic body and the symbolic body presses the material body into existence. The spectator and the theatrical bodies, with their different methods of being present, rub against one another in the shadows.
>
> *(2009, p. 17)*

A story becomes something else when performed, as it assembles with the people, the furniture, the objects that are co-present. The Fran-and-Sophie-story was realized, if realized at all, in relation with what else was happening in that room. My clumsy handling of microphone and paper, my awkward pacing between parts of the room, for example, will all have tugged at my story. Co-presence (Urry, 2002) involves not just people but things. Just as, in story 1, the laptop helped enclose the Fran-and-Sophie-Minecraft-space, in story 2, the microphone, paper, furniture and room all assembled with symposium delegates to generate what was felt.

So again: being together matters. My story tells of how I tried to bring a version of Fran and Sophie into the room (through my voice, posture, gestures). But it also tells how I, like many teachers and performers, tried to bring the room together (through eye contact, pausing, pacing). Some of my presentation—the parcelling up of the room, for example—felt *wrong*, but some of it felt *right*. At times I felt very much *with* my audience while, at others, I felt definitely *out front*. Gumperz (2004) urges us to temper our consideration of discursive "meaning effects," with attention to "presence," in particular, "that specific serenity [. . .] the feeling of being in sync with the things in the world" (p. 117). Of course traditions of presentation and storytelling are culturally located and what feels right will itself be discursive. My presentational style holds traces of my previous lives as teacher and performer, as well as academic, and the audience will have brought to the room their own experiences of attending and responding to presentations. But in-sync-ness is hard to pin down, hinting, as it does, at a rhythm and confluence that is tough to describe. We do feel it though, when it happens, and feel it when it does not. I have stubbornly ignored feedback that I speak too fast and move too much when I present, because speaking fast and moving feels right to me: I like the energy it produces, the sense of momentum. Sometimes this seems to work with an audience and I feel a reciprocity in smiles, laughter, nodding, stillness. Sometimes it is at odds with the rhythm of the room as my embodied performance clashes with what I imagine are audience expectations and falls flat on its face.

In this story, my co-presence with other people and things in the room mattered as much or more than Fran and Sophie's. My story of *Fran and Sophie's* being together in that classroom converged with *my* being together with others in the symposium room. *Our* data, our stories, aren't held safely to be handed over glossed securely with analysis and commentary; they are unstable and lively. Again, insights from performance studies help articulate what happened as the story came to life in that place with those people:

> The pivotal point of the process is no longer the work of art, detached from and independent of its creator and recipient, which arises as an object from the activities of the creator-subject and entrusted to the perception and interpretation of the recipient and subject. Instead we are dealing with an event, set in motion and terminated by the actors of all the subjects involved- actors and spectators.
>
> *(Fischer-Lichte, 2008, p. 22)*

The Fran-and-Sophie-episode morphed as it assembled within a new set of "brain-body-world entanglements" (Blackman, 2012, p. 1). Captured as narrative, the episode got made again in conversation with another place, and with other people and things. Perhaps I might better engage with the feeling generated through this episode by going back in.

Third Movement

Back In

I look back at the original video footage to try and jolt myself from the story I've crafted. Used now to reliving this episode (if it is an episode) through my story, I feel it differently when I go back in. Going back in, I notice some of what my story filters out.

I feel my clumsy presence in the hot, noisy classroom, the clutter of furniture hemming me in. The video is shot from a high angle so I must have been standing behind the girls, towering over them and squished between tables and chairs.

I wonder why I chose to film this pair at this time. My methodology had involved following participants across lessons: Sometimes things (iPads, laptops, etc.) and sometimes individuals. While Sophie was one of the children I was following, the unpredictability of classroom life and the physical difficulties of manoeuvring in the cramped classroom meant that I could not always follow who or what I wanted, so this footage would have been unplanned; it was of the moment. Perhaps I was attracted to this pair on this day as they were relatively static, easier to look at than some of the apparently erratic play that ranged between multiple locations on and off screen. Perhaps I filmed them because they were easy to access; I was physically able to position myself close enough for the microphone to pick up what they said and far enough away to frame what they did. Or perhaps my interest was shaped by other kinds of relationships with what was happening. As Ahmed (2010) writes, "orientations matter;" we "face some things more than others" (p. 245). Perhaps Fran and Sophie's rather modest play felt (to me, the ex-teacher always hidden in my researcher body) like the sort of thing that "ought" to be documented. The affordance of the video frame (what I could fit in the picture) perhaps conspired with my teacher frame (what seemed worth looking at) as I focused on the two girls.

Looking back at the footage I get a sense of how this orientation must have intensified as I translated the video to narrative. While Fran and Sophie are in the foreground, in the background and on the sound track I see/hear/feel the noise and energy of other children's play, the rubble of classroom stuff, and the teacher walking round, leaning in every now and again to look at a screen. None of this features in my narrative, which focuses tightly on Fran and Sophie to the exclusion of other activities caught in the frame.

Reviewing the video footage I wonder what would happen if I could, like Matthew Hall, capture interactions across a classroom in the form of musical notation (Smith, Hall & Sousanis, 2015). Hall explores how students working in a making/designing workshop were sensitized to the rhythms and harmonies of others' interactions, and how these were significant to their engagement in composing multimodal texts, even when working individually. What might a similar analysis suggest about how Fran and Sophie were attuned not just to each other but to the rest of the class? How did the volume, pace, regularity, pitch and tone of Fran and Sophie's play chime with the volume, pace, regularity, pitch and tone of everything else that was happening? I'm reminded of those sudden silences that sometimes fall in primary classrooms, when the chatter fades for some reason, perhaps a shared sensing that something has shifted, like a herd of deer turning at the snap of a twig. Often such silences are followed by a moment of shared realisation, exchanged glances, perhaps laughter, before the noise rises again. Individual activity so often has an ear to the other.

The video revives a sense of immediacy, evoking an apparent portal to Fran and Sophie in the classroom on that day that takes me back in to some of the rhythms that escaped my narrative. But it also, as Lemke argues (2007, p. 44), prompts me to focus on "brief timescales to the neglect of long timescales" and "magnify small details and minor events." Through video, I framed Fran and Sophie's emergent play; I put it into pictures. I turned their experience into something to be looked at and, transduced to a narrative written to be read, I designated it an "episode."

Recent analyses of classroom literacy practices have done much to expand our thinking about rhythmic dimensions of being together: Hollett and Ehret's (2016) exploration of the "civic rhythms" generated as young people worked together in a digital media learning lab in a public library, for example, and Leander and Hollett's (2016) exploration of diverse ways in which rhythm plays through learning across settings. Such work chimes with much of what I tried to convey in the Fran and Sophie story, in the generative rhythms of pig creation and of playing together, for example, or in the resonance of Fran and Sophie's play with the rhythm of other activities in the moment or over longer time-scales. However, rhythm plays out too through research processes. How might the rhythms of on/off-screen Minecraft play have marked out the beat of my filming, for example, or inflected what I did and didn't record? How might the process of generating the representation have followed or disrupted the rhythm of the represented event?

The rhythm of writing, for example, perhaps shaped how the episode fell out as a story. When I watch the video I am struck by the speed of what happens: the "episode" takes only 32 seconds. Writing it, however, has slowed things down, and reading it takes over two minutes. My story has an even, measured rhythm that's at odds with the high pitched voices, rapid responses and intense energy that characterize the video footage. Is it too much to read a subplot into this story, one of the calm and quiet that settles around my desk in my home office, where I wrote my story, drawing on notes and memory: The writing-reading rhythms of prose drummed out on my keyboard, the rhythm of my typing playing out in the rhythm of the sentences that coalesce as the story?

I notice that in reflecting on the footage I have drifted from my purpose. I went back in to engage more with my feelings for the episode, my solidarity for Sophie. Again I have been seduced by what I can see and what I might be able to track and measure (the rhythm, the speed). While I started this movement with an impulse to examine my felt connection to this story, the multimodal vibrancy of the video footage distracted me. Distanced from what happened, I am not only unable to feel what they felt, but have lost what I felt too. Going back in via video troubled my story, but it also chucked me out again.

Reassembling Movements of Meanings

In telling these stories and reflecting on how and why this episode moved me, I have hinted at how *it* moved: From that classroom to video footage, a transcript, a story, a symposium presentation, a chapter. The first story extracts me from the episode and positions me as (almost) neutral observer. The second foregrounds how my embodied representation of the episode was produced partly in concert with what and who were co-present in the conference room. The reflections in the third play with an imagined re-entry into the world of the study, a sensitization to other ways of knowing or feeling what happened. And, of course, there will be other movements. As you read this, for example, you may be curled up on a sofa or hunched on a train—if your "reading nooks" (Rainbird & Rowsell, 2011) are similar to mine—reading straight through or drifting off to more engaging thoughts or tasks, interrupted by the rhythms of your life. We may work hard to embed data within an argument or to fix it in time and space, but as data variously assemble with other thoughts, feelings, practices and so on, they shift.

My stories account for feeling in different ways. In Movements 1 and 2, feeling is at times explained in terms of emotional commitment, as "qualified" intensities rather than "unqualified" affect (Massumi, 2002, p. 28): In my empathy with Sophie, for example, and my attempted championing of what I describe as her kindness. Elsewhere, particularly in Movement 3, I reflect on the rhythmic and embodied relations that exceed emotion. Together, I hope, these movements generate an inside/outside quality, that prompt both *reading of* and *feeling with* representation, a duality that reflects the "unboundedness" which Law and Ruppert (2016) identify in baroque artwork (Burnett and Merchant, 2016). Unboundedness operates

> by pleating insides and outsides together. Think of audiences and actors. On the one hand they are still separate, the outside and in, but on the other hand they are not separate at all. We are in the world of the Mobius strip. The inside becomes the outside, and the outside becomes the inside. Or they are both at the same time.
>
> *(Law & Ruppert, 2016, p. 13)*

I was of course *part of* the assemblages conjured through and with my narratives, but so too were the other people, things, spaces and places in whose presence the episode was given life. If I look across these three movements, the Fran-and-Sophie-episode assembled: Between Fran, Sophie and their screens in their play; between me, my camera and the class as I videoed; between me and the others (people and stuff) in the conference room. And, folded into these assemblings, were multiple other histories, intentions, memories and ways of doing/being. As Ingold (2007) has it, "After all, what is a thing, or indeed a person, if not a tying together of the lines—the paths of growth and movement—of all the many constituents gathered there?" (p. 5). The Fran-and-Sophie-episode may become *data*, to be lifted and taken, but it then always assembles again, with other people and things. At the symposium, my feeling *for* Fran and Sophie was meshed with my feeling *with* the people and things in that room. My felt responsibility to Fran and Sophie was inflected by my felt responsibility for my audience; my *account of affective intensities* was intensified or derailed by *affective intensities in the moment*. Pink (2009) argues that ethnographers should work at being "emplaced," opening up to what it is like to be in a place, to sense and feel what participants sense and feel. Perhaps we also need to be alert to how emplacement seeps into our tellings as we seek to represent our life in the field and as our stories get taken up by others. Sophie's rhythmic spawning of Minecraft pigs may well have been inflected by the rhythms of friendship, but becomes something else when mediated through the rhythms of an emplaced narrative, again through an embodied storytelling, and again as it resonates with the rhythms of readers' lives.

Concluding Thoughts: Where Next?

My stories of pig riding, aquarium building, researcher insecurities and an unsatisfactory research presentation seem rather trivial, self-indulgent even, given the inequitable, often terrifying times in which we live. Yet I would argue that telling stories of such moments does matter because of the apparent paradox that it is through such apparently inconsequential moments that power structures play out, *and* because such stories foreground the humanity and improvisation that mean that other realities are always possible. Acknowledging affect in research focuses us on the relations *between* people and things and what emerges moment to moment. As such, it pushes us to engage with what next, with what might be. This has implications, however, for what we do with research.

If data aren't stable but move, if researchers live through and with what they study, and if research does not just investigate life but *is* life, then research cannot be a process of arriving at and disseminating fixed understandings. It needs to be approached as a process of *moving with* practice and playing its own part in generating potentiality. As Massumi argues, engaging with affect

> is all about the openness of situations and how you live that openness. And you have to remember that the way we live it is always entirely embodied, and that is never entirely personal—it's never all contained in our emotions and conscious thought.
>
> *(2015, p. 6)*

This perspective requires research activity that works to open out rather than close down; that exposes rather than smooths the gaps in between what we can know. Maybe this chapter's three movements generate such openness and come closest to hinting at affect as they assemble *together* and, in so doing—by disrupting one another—evoke the feeling that each inevitably misses.

Acknowledging such indeterminacy and instability would seem to offer much to an activist agenda. If research *always* interfaces with or disrupts what happens moment to moment—if it always works to construct the reality it seeks to represent (Law, 2004)—then there is potential in sensitizing ourselves to how research does and *might* work to interface with or disrupt educational practices in ways that are empowering. This involves being alert to what research becomes and what it generates as it comes into relation with other people and things, from fieldwork through to dissemination. Rather than thinking with research, what might we gain by acknowledging how we feel with it too? And by finding ways of working with the potentiality that emerges as data, people and things come into relation? How, for example, might we share data in ways that close the gap between researchers and practitioners and disrupt the structures and academic hierarchies that work to sustain research as reified practice? Rather than reaching for meaning, maybe we need to liberate data to work into the stories, perceptions, feelings and ideas of others. Stacking stories may be one way of approaching this, as may be co-produced and arts-based research (e.g., Burnett & Merchant, 2019; Pahl, 2016; Stirling & Yamada Rice, 2015). How might we combine such lively engagements with practice with the ethical engagement that Massumi (2015) argues should always go hand in hand with the politics of affect? The unsatisfactory representations *of life* generated through research may be brought differently *to life* as they are animated differently through different assemblages: As Law and Ruppert (2016) write, "knowing is a matter of moving" (p. 15). Perhaps it is through sensitizing ourselves to this ongoing assembling that other potentialities can be realized.

An Aftershock

There is another twist to the tale of my symposium presentation. When I finished and sat down, I felt the knee length cardigan I had been wearing ruck up in the small of my back. As I went to smooth it, I felt some tension and a horrible thought occurred. Had it been tucked in my trousers all through my presentation? Did it catch there when I went to the bathroom beforehand? Did I tell the Fran-and-Sophie story with a cardigan bulging from my waistband? My stomach lurches: Costume malfunctions just don't work with academic gravitas. Afterwards, I tell no-one and the cardigan-stuffed-in-trousers-moment doesn't feature in my stories of the event. I love a self-effacing story; I think they help hold people together, but I just can't bear to make it more real through talking about it. As I think myself back into that room, though, I can't help feeling the bulging cardigan stuffed in the back of my trousers and I think it might have happened. If it did, what on earth did this Fran-Sophie-room-presentation-microphone-cardigan-stuck-in-waistband assemblage mean for how and what my story became?

Note

1 I use the term "episode" here, while acknowledging that the term is problematic. References to literacy "episodes" and "events" can imply a boundedness in time and place that can elide the complex multiplicities that inflect literacies (Burnett & Merchant 2014). "Episode" is used here to refer to my account of a segment of ongoing action I perceived during fieldwork. I make no assumption, as the chapter explores, that the boundaries I place round this episode were significant to anyone other than myself.

References

Ahmed, S. (2010). Orientations matter. In D. Coole & S. Frost. (Eds.), *New materialisms: Ontology, agency and politics.* Durham, NC: Duke University Press.

Bailey, C. (2017). *Investigating the lived experience of children engaged in collaborative virtual world play.* (Unpublished doctoral thesis). Sheffield Hallam University, Sheffield, UK.

Blackman, L. (2012). *Immaterial bodies: Affect, embodiment, mediation.* London, UK: Sage.

Burnett, C. (2015). Being together in classrooms at the interface of the physical and virtual: implications for collaboration in on/off screen sites. *Learning, Media and Technology.* Retrieved from: Online First: DOI:10.1080/17439884.2015.1050036

Burnett, C. & Bailey, C. (2014). Conceptualising collaboration in hybrid sites: playing *Minecraft* together and apart in a primary classroom. In C. Burnett, J. Davies, G. Merchant & J. Rowsell (Eds.), *New literacies around the globe: Policy and pedagogy.* Abingdon, UK: Routledge.

Burnett, C. & Merchant, G. (2014). Points of View: reconceptualising literacies through an exploration of adult and child interactions in a virtual world. *Journal of Research in Reading, 37*(1), 36–50.

Burnett, C. & Merchant, G. (2016). Boxes of poison: Baroque technique as antidote to simple views of literacy. *Journal of Literacy Research, 48*(3), 258–279.

Burnett, C. & Merchant, G. (2019). Stacking Stories as Method: Research in Early Years Settings. In N. Kucirkova, J. Rowsell, and G. Falloon (Eds.). *The Handbook of Children's Learning and Technology* (pp.143–154). New York, NY: Routledge.

Clough, P. (2002). *Narratives and fictions in educational research.* Buckingham, UK: Open University Press.

Comber, B. (2016). *Literacy, place and pedagogies of possibility.* New York, NY: Routledge.

Deleuze, G. & Guattari, F. (1987). *A thousand plateaus: Capitalism and schizophrenia.* London, UK: Continuum.

Fensham, T. (2009). *To Watch Theatre: Essays on genre and corporeality.* Brussels, Belgium: Peter Lang.

Fischer-Lichte, E. (2008). *The transformative power of performance: A new aesthetics.* London, UK: Routledge.

Gumperz, H.U. (2004). *Production of presence: What meaning cannot convey.* Stanford, CA: Stanford University Press.

Hamilton, M. (2012). *Literacy and the Politics of Representation.* New York, NY: Routledge.

Hollett, T. & Ehret, C. (2016). Civic rhythms in an informal, media-rich learning program. *Learning, Media and Technology.* Retrieved from: http://www.tandfonline.com/doi/full/10.1080/17439884.2016.1182926

Ingold, T. (2007). *Lines: A brief history.* London, UK: Routledge.

Jones, L., Holmes, R., Macrae, C. & Maclure, M. (2010). Documenting classroom life: How can I write about what I am seeing? *Qualitative Research, 10*(4), 479–491.

Law, J. (2004). *After method: Mess in social science research.* London, UK: Routledge.

Law, J. & Ruppert, R. (2016). *Modes of knowing: Resources from the Baroque.* Manchester, UK: Mattering Press.

Leander, K. & Hollett, T. (2016). The embodied rhythms of learning: From learning across settings to learners crossing settings. *International Journal of Educational Research.* Retrieved from: http://www.sciencedirect.com/science/article/pii/S088303551530433X

Lemke, J. (2007). Video epistemology in-and-outside the box: Traversing attentional spaces. In R. Goldman, R. Pea, B. Barron & S.J. Derry (Eds.), *Video research in the learning sciences.* Mahwah, NJ: Erlbaum.

Massumi, B. (2002). *Movement, affect, sensation: Parables for the virtual.* Durham, NC: Duke University Press.

Massumi, B. (2015). *The politics of affect.* London, UK: Polity.

Pahl, K. (2016). The university as the "imagined other:" Making sense of community co-produced literacy research. *Collaborative Anthropologies, 8*(1/2), 129–148.

Pink, S. (2009). *Doing sensory ethnography*. London, UK: Sage.

Rainbird, S. & Rowsell, J. (2011). Literacy nooks: Geosemiotics and domains of literacy in home spaces. *Journal of Early Childhood Literacy, 11*(2), 214–232.

Rosenblatt, L. (1933). *Literature as Exploration*. New York, NY: Noble and Noble.

Smith, A., Hall, M. & Sousanis, N. (2015). Envisioning possibilities: visualising as enquiry in literacy studies. *Literacy, 49*(1), 3–11.

Stirling, E. & Yamada-Rice, D. (2015). *Visual methods with children and young people: Academics and visual industries in dialogue*. London, UK: Palgrave.

Urry, J. (2002). Mobility and proximity. *Sociology, 36*(2), 225–274.

Vasudevan, L. (2011). An invitation to unknowing. *Teachers College Record, 113*(6), 1154–1174.

Youdell, D. (2011). *School Trouble*. London, UK: Routledge.

AFTERWORD

Michalinos Zembylas

After reading these chapters, it might seem crudely commonsensical to repeat their main point, that literacy is affective and that literacy education would benefit from turning to recent scholarship on the "affective turn." Rather than reiterating these contributions and their compelling affective power, in this afterword I will take a different direction. In particular, I will emphasize a theme the chapters point out but which deserves further attention in future research and scholarship, because it is associated with the critical and transformative power of literacy—namely, how affective literacy creates important openings of ethical and political potential in educators' efforts to make productive interventions in pedagogical spaces that address issues of inequity, oppression and coloniality. Insofar as *critical affective literacy* becomes a viable pedagogical tool of addressing human vulnerability, educators are enabled to raise new questions and enact new possibilities about how attending to and through affects can work to extend rather than diminish the ethical and political field in which educators and students move.

The chapter authors, in order to demonstrate the affective power of literacy, challenge analytic categories that have pertained in literacy research by decades of scholarship practice. The introduction to this volume nicely illustrates these scholarship traditions, tracing the recent attempts in literacy research—which follow a similar trajectory to other subject-matter areas in education and beyond—to theorize affect from a nonrepresentational theoretical perspective in contrast to constructivist and sociocultural emotional categories that have prevailed so far. I will not rehearse those insights here, except to highlight the groundbreaking significance of the intervention that these authors make, namely that, through ontologizing affects as relations, practices and performances, the field of the ethical and the political in which educators and students might move in literacy education is considerably enriched with new possibilities. My aim here, of course, is not to engage in a comprehensive discussion of all the possibilities that a nonrepresentational theorizing of affects might open for literacy research and pedagogical practice, but rather to elaborate on two major contributions that can be identified regarding ethics and politics in education (see also, Zembylas, 2017). In particular, I will discuss these contributions in terms of their ethical and political salience to offer ontologies of affect in literacy research and education more generally, namely, affects that can have transformative and political consequences. While doing so, I will also mention a few possibilities for future research that come to my mind.

First, a nonrepresentational theorizing of affect highlights that the ethical and the political are always implicated in and emergent from the diverse sensibilities of embodiment, that is, the ways in which bodies come together in space (Barnett, 2008; McCormack, 2003; Thrift, 2008). The chapters in this volume, by providing nonrepresentational accounts of literacies, not only show lives as embodied and relational becomings of reading and writing, but also inspire more readers and writers in education to think of ways to move and be moved, beyond traditional paradigms, beyond the doxa of literacy studies and education. A critical and transformative orientation to literacy research requires a radical rethinking of the nature of literacy, as the introduction points out. But such an orientation can inspire much more, as it can open up what McCormack (2005) has termed "an ethics of enactment" (p. 142)—namely, the ways in which various kinds of bodily performances take place and enhance our capacities to enact new forms of living together and engaging in transformative action and responsibility. Various chapters in this collection show these powerful possibilities not only by illustrating the transformative potentials of certain pedagogical interventions (e.g., interrogating the production and circulation of affect and emotion in everyday politics) but also by offering evocative accounts that highlight the performativity of affects and emotions to engage in action for social justice.

A major issue, then, in future research in literacy studies and education is how to turn these possibilities into spaces for ethical encounters and political engagement that have the potential to bring change—e.g., how these encounters in pedagogical spaces may become the locus of conviviality and solidarity. This implies, for example, pursuing the recognition by some authors of this volume that affective capacities of the body are signified unequally within social spaces of being and feeling (Tolia-Kelly, 2006). For educators and researchers in literacy studies this means that they need to systematically trace how power operates through affect and how affective life in schools and beyond is imbued with power relations. Hence, a nonrepresentational theorizing of affect helps literacy researchers raise new and admittedly challenging questions regarding the intersection of affect, politics, social justice and literacy learning.

Second, a nonrepresentational theorizing of affect contributes to the effort to open up the ethical and the political to the relational-material entanglements of more than human worlds. Several chapters show these entanglements by considering the relationships between teachers, students, objects, practices and how these relationships between the human and the nonhuman agents change completely the way we do research. But more importantly, the significance of this move is not merely to extend the methodological landscape or the ethical entanglements of care and responsibility to include nonhuman agents. Rather, this move energizes ethics and politics "by admitting that the corporeal finitude of the human is emergent from a connective multiplicity of non-human and in-human forces and processes that exceed this corporeality" (McCormack, 2003, p. 489).

For example, a nonrepresentational theorizing of affect in literacy research allows the development of an ethics and politics of materiality in education in which all things can be treated *as if* they were relevant and interrelated aspects (Fendler, 2014). In relation to pedagogical practice, this would imply the inclusion of material conditions *as if* they mattered to our pedagogies—from collegial relationships, feelings about particular educational policies, histories of personal animosities and affections, the setup of the classroom room, the absences and departures of people from our school, to the materials used in teaching—for instance, the feeling of written pages, artifacts and drawings, as shown in several chapters.

For future research, this would mean, for example, recognizing the potential for a new politics of care and conviviality performed through "on-the-ground" and "in-the-moment" action (Nayak, 2010) in everyday school life and beyond. Recognizing how everyday relational ontologies in schools instill certain affective modalities and inhibit or inspire the creation of particular affective relations could be the starting point of designing pedagogical practices in literacy education that actively promote friendship, solidarity and care for the "other" (Zembylas, 2011; 2015; 2017). This task would appear to be particularly urgent in contemporary neoliberal times in which collectivities are important in increasing people's capacities to act. Conceptualized in this way, and if we are to pursue this kind of ethics and politics, then attending to affect in literacy studies and education opens up a series of questions about how literacy may be used to create, sustain and extend events and relationalities that are enfolded into the collective. How do collective affects such as solidarity and care for those who suffer become part of pedagogical practices in literacy education? How do collective affects forge and restrain what is thinkable and doable in everyday life, setting limits to struggles against social injustice and inequality? Finally, how do *capacities of affect and being affected* emerge in literacy classrooms and how can they be redirected to change normative encounters and relations? These questions reorder our sense of how deeply embedded harm, inequality and injustice are in fabric of everyday life (Thrift, 2008), including schools. These questions also challenge our understandings of just what manifestations effective ethical and political agency might take in literacy studies and education in the wake of this acknowledgement.

Despite the ethical and political promise emerging from the ideas outlined in the chapters, there are two important risks that need to be acknowledged in the process of attending to the mobilization of affect in literacy studies and education. First, it is important to highlight that pursuing a critical and productive mobilization of affect (e.g., critical affective literacy)—namely, one with the potential to open up new affective encounters especially with those deemed as "others"— entails considerably ethical and political responsibility for educators. The risk for educators is to underestimate or overestimate the fact that while solidarity and care may be ontologically and materially performed in schools through literacy practices, they are performed in particular social and political conditions. Local and global narratives still have much to say about the nature of events, encounters and collectives (Thrift, 2008). We need to ask then: How and why are certain affect categories deployed for certain ends in particular settings? Why not some alternative affect? What makes some literacy practices more productive than others? What does this mean in practice?

Second, the task of ethical and political responsibility for educators comes with another risk. Thrift's (2008) account of the ethics and politics of affect highlights that affect can be "engineered" and deployed instrumentally for the pursuit of expanded commodification. Similarly, the risk of affect as a medium of manipulation of students lurks above any effort claiming to undertake a strategic use of affects and emotions in schooling (Zembylas, 2013a, 2013b). It is important, as educators, to constantly interrogate our pedagogies of affects and emotions and whether they might (unwittingly) contribute to sustain hegemonic norms of relational encounters with others by ignoring the affective potentiality of these encounters or by simply attempting to manipulate the affective atmosphere in the classroom.

One of the most challenging aspects of this risk is to end up instilling a "cheap sentimental" approach—for example, the reading of sad and sentimental stories of horrendous suffering which move us to pity, patting ourselves on the back and then resuming our ordinary life (Zembylas, 2013a; 2017). There is considerable skepticism about the potential for sad and sentimental stories to impel privileged individuals—who may be distant spectators to suffering and human rights violations—to establish meaningful empathetic connections with others. To echo Berlant's (2000) acute critique of sentimental narrative or sentimental liberalism, injustice and oppression cannot be reduced to feeling bad about others' pain. Suffering, which is in part an effect of socio-economic relations of violence and poverty, is problematically assumed to be alleviated by empathetic identification with others through reading or writing about others' sufferings, yet there is no assurance that the feelings evoked will not be those of pity, a feeling which does not lead to any action. Pity refers to a type of affective relationship between the spectator and a sufferer, which shows empathy and tender-heartedness towards the spectacle of human pain, but it is not necessarily accompanied by action to alleviate the structural conditions and effects of suffering (Boltanski, 1999). The object of pity exists primarily within an imaginary realm that sentimentalizes the other. As Woodward argues:

> [T]he experience of being moved by these sentimental scenes of suffering, whose ostensible purpose is to awaken us to redress injustice, works instead to return us to a private world far removed from the public sphere. Hence, in a crippling contradiction [. . .] the result of such empathetic identification is not the impulse to action but rather a "passive" posture. [. . .] The genre of the sentimental narrative itself is morally bankrupt.
>
> *(2004, p. 71)*

This critique highlights the trappings of reading about stories that might eventually lead to voyeurism and passivity—trappings that evoke superficial feelings of sympathy and pity for the sufferers rather than compassionate action which can make a difference in sufferers' lives (Zembylas, 2013a).

To go *beyond* a sentimental literacy education, the first step needed for educators and students is their ability to trace the process of sentimentalization of narratives of suffering and how this process can end up being fixed into self-centered accounts of others' suffering in our globalized world. The emerging testimonial culture of personalized stories of suffering makes the pedagogical challenges of educators and learners even greater, because as Brown (1995) has shown, the fetishization and sentimentalization of narratives of suffering tend to turn all political claims into claims of emotional injury, thus depoliticizing the histories that have produced suffering and rendering action to alleviate the structural conditions and effects of suffering impossible. What is needed, therefore, is a pedagogical orientation that is more balanced—one which can offer critical affective literacy, inspired by the fertile ground of sentimentality, yet one that is not restricted to a superficial engagement with stories of injustice, oppression and coloniality. A literacy pedagogy that does not apprehend these limitations is less likely to acknowledge emotion and affect as a crucial aspect of a renewed ethics and politics in our encounters with others.

In conclusion, I want to emphasize once again the value of the works brought together here for the larger field of literacy studies and education, particularly in promoting critical affective literacy. As I have recently argued (Zembylas, 2017), a critical account of the ethics and politics of affect in educational theory and practice sensitize us to become aware of the multiple ways in which affective experiences can readily become powerful naturalizing forces that erase the prospects of ethical and political action. The chapters in this collection are in the forefront of suggesting new approaches in literacy studies and education that demand an openness to the uncertain affective potentiality of encounters with "others"—both human and nonhuman—from which new ways of "becoming" might emerge.

References

Barnett, C. (2008). Political affects in public space: Normative blind-spots in non-representational ontologies. *Transactions of the Institute of British Geographers, 33*(2), 186–200.

Berlant, L. (2000). The subject of true feeling: Pain, privacy, and politics. In S. Ahmed, J. Kilby, C. Lury, M. McNeil & B. Skeggs (Eds.), *Transformations: Thinking through feminism* (pp. 33–47). London, UK: Routledge.

Boltanski, L. (1999). *Distant suffering: Morality, media and politics.* Cambridge, UK: Cambridge University Press.

Brown, W. (1995). *States of injury: Power and freedom in late modernity.* Princeton, NJ: Princeton University Press.

Fendler, L. (2014). The ethics of materiality: Some insights from non-representational theory for educational research. In P. Smeyers & M. Depaepe (Eds.), *Materialities in educational research* (pp. 115–132). Dordrecht, Netherlands: Springer.

McCormack, D. (2003). An event of geographical ethics in spaces of affect. *Transactions of the Institute of British Geographers, 28*(4), 488–507.

McCormack, D. (2005). Diagramming practice and performance. *Environment and Planning D: Society and Space, 23*(1), 119–147.

Nayak, A. (2010). Race, affect, and emotion: Young people, racism, and graffiti in the postcolonial English suburbs. *Environment and Planning A, 42*(10), 2370–2392.

Thrift, N. (2008) *Non-representational theory: Space/politics/affect.* London, UK: Routledge.

Tolia-Kelly, D. (2006). Affect—an ethnocentric encounter? Exploring the "universalist" imperative of emotional/affectual geographies. *Area, 38*(2), 213–217.

Woodward, K. (2004). Calculating compassion. In L. Berlant (Ed.), *Compassion: The culture and politics of an emotion* (pp. 59–86). New York, NY: Routledge.

Zembylas, M. (2011). Investigating the emotional geographies of exclusion in a multicultural school. *Emotion, Space and Society, 4,* 151–159.

Zembylas, M. (2013a). The "crisis of pity" and the radicalization of solidarity: Towards critical pedagogies of compassion. *Educational Studies: A Journal of the American Educational Studies Association, 49,* 504–521.

Zembylas, M. (2013b). Critical pedagogy and emotion: Working through troubled knowledge in posttraumatic societies. *Critical Studies in Education, 54,* 176–189.

Zembylas, M. (2015). Rethinking race and racism as technologies of affect: Theorizing the implications for antiracist politics and practice in education. *Race Ethnicity and Education, 18*(2), 145–162.

Zembylas, M. (2017). The contribution of non-representational theories in education: Some affective, ethical and political implications. *Studies in Philosophy and Education, 36*(4), 393–407.

A SHORT NOTE CONCERNING THE INDEX

An index, with its categories and subcategories, systems of reference, implied definitions and hierarchy, is in most ways contrary to the point of this volume. Posed in contrast to a structural and definitional approach, authors in the volume have attempted to engage readers in experiences that feel and move in connective, emergent ways. The chapters are not intended to "contain" ideas; our hope is rather that they engage, as connective bodies, in moving other bodies. So, with that vision, what to do with an index? Here's an image: What if the index were a collection of loose threads, hanging at the edges of the volume, imagined as a tapestry? What if you picked a loose thread and pulled on it, feeling the other threads it unraveled? What if the square referenced volume fell apart and twisted up into something new, as you pulled and pulled?

INDEX